By These Hands

"I'm one that enjoys hard work. I always have."

"I feel this way that, as long as the good Lord gives me my health I would like to keep working."

"A lot of the people on the floor come to work so that they can have the health-care insurance for their children."

"One of the problems we face is there always seems to be someone new—different."

"And it's a little scary. You go in there, you're different from everyone else—you're in a wheelchair. . . . They don't know how to communicate with you."

"They say, 'You got a white man's job.' They ask me, How long do I think I'm going to be able to keep that job?"

"We were always together. You'd stop after work—as a crew you'd stop after work—and have a few beers or whatever."

"They're the best people in the world. They make me real proud."

"We're kind of dreamers but we try to make our dreams come true."

By These Hands

PORTRAITS FROM THE FACTORY FLOOR

David L. Parker

Selected by Ted Hartwell

With an introduction by Peter Rachleff

To Tom,
Best wishes
David Parker
11-8-02

MINNESOTA HISTORICAL SOCIETY PRESS

For information, write to the Minnesota Historical Society Press, 345 Kellogg Blvd. W., St. Paul, MN 55102-1906.

www.mnhs.org/mhspress

Manufactured in Hong Kong

10 9 8 7 6 5 4 3 2 1

International Standard Book Number
ISBN 0-87351-442-4 (paper)

This publication is printed on a coated paper manufactured on an acid-free base to ensure its long life.

Library of Congress Cataloging-in-Publication Data

Parker, David L. (David Lewis), 1951–
By these hands : portraits from the factory floor / David L. Parker ; selected by Ted Hartwell ; with an introduction by Peter Rachleff.
p. cm.
ISBN 0-87351-442-4 (pbk. : alk. paper)
1. Portrait photography—Minnesota.
2. Working class—Minnesota—Portraits.
3. Working class—Minnesota—Interviews.
I. Parker, David L.
II. Title.

TR681.W65 P374 2002
779'.9305562'09776–dc21
2002075735

For my father, who worked hard all of his life and died before he got to retire. He wanted to do other things but was never sure what. So he kept working.

For my mother, who knows what she wants and continues to work. She could retire but understands the value of work.

PREFACE

The Genius of Work

DAVID PARKER

This book is a tribute to the women and men who process the foods we eat, manufacture the cars we drive, and produce the goods that make our lives comfortable. After photographing hundreds of workers in dozens of factories, now more than ever, I believe in the collective genius of the American worker. I can only hope that my work reflects their ingenuity and dedication.

A decision was made at the start of this project not to include service workers. This decision was made primarily to narrow the scope of the task I set for myself. It was also made because most people know about the types of jobs that go into producing services. Most of us have stayed at a hotel and seen the rooms cleaned, eaten at a fast food restaurant, had a car repaired, visited a relative in a hospital, received care in a clinic, or used any of the hundreds of services provided by these workers. This is not to say, however, we have a good understanding of the hardship that comes from working a minimum or low wage job. In the end the definition was simple: a person had to make something. She had to do more than repair a product or provide a service.

The intent of this book is to provide a glimpse of industrial workers and the factories in which they work. However, of the two, it is more about the workers than the places in which they work. It is also about how workers interact with each other and their environment. The culture of work is reflected in the jobs women and men do. Factories are still divided by race, gender, and at times age. Many workers struggle to meet their basic needs; they also work hard and do their best for their employers.

Emma Olsen is a seventy-three-year-old line worker at Rosemount Engineering. She divorced when she was young and raised her children as a single mother. Half remembering her own time as a mother and half thinking about her co-workers, she reminisces, "It's hard when they have children because of the expense of someone taking care of their kids." Considering what is bought for an hour's work or even a day's labor, she notes, "I mean, it's tough. And it's tough when you have children. Kids need clothes, they need medication, they need their shots, they need this and that. And then they start wanting things. Well you can only say 'no' so long, you know, they have to have some things."

The loyalty workers show toward their employers is reflected in their long-term employment and the relationships that are formed within the workplace. Mark Froemke, a labor leader, went to work at American Crystal Sugar in East Grand Forks when he was twenty-three. "I came here to pay some debts. And the place grabbed me. I met my wife here. I was married to her for eighteen years before she died of breast cancer." And describing the relationship between his employer and the community, Mark says:

> *They live in the Red River Valley. Their children go to the same schools as our children go to, we go to the same churches, many of the workers at our factories, their uncles and nieces, and cousins, and brothers-in-law of the farmers who own these factories, and so the farmers have a great interest in also supplying jobs and having their community survive.*
>
> *And for us as workers, union workers, as farmers, as Crystal Sugar management, we have a unique opportunity to come together. I am not saying that we don't have differences on other issues, but where we can agree let's agree, and where we disagree, let's talk about that later. But on issues on which we can agree, about saving jobs, about saving our jobs, saving farmers, our farmers, saving our communities, that means management, farmers, and us. These are our communities. If we can do that and deal with each other very honestly, openly and put our cards on the table and don't try to get an upper hand, we can do tremendous things, because we all come from the same community.*
>
> *With all this globalization it's the trend to go to the bottom line. And we are following that trend. We don't want government subsidies, what we do want is a fair playing field. And until that day of a fair playing field, yes, we do need a sugar bill to help us; we do need the government to intervene if necessary to protect domestic industries. Just the same as the steel industry or the auto. But for us and the farmers, they know they have to compete globally. But should the total emphasis be on destroying jobs, destroying community, destroying farms so you can buy your loaf of bread for a penny cheaper?*

While an industry is often an integral part of a larger community, work frequently forms its own community. Mark Froemke met his wife at work; Emma Olsen continues to find companionship at work, "Yes, I work pretty much by myself now. And yet my working table, everybody comes to it because I always have candy. And I get to see everybody. And they are all pretty joyful and pretty cheerful. And we enjoy each other's company. You'd think that being older we don't have any part of being a kid in us yet. But you would be surprised at some of these big technicians and them. When they come in they'd come to my place and they'd look around the corner to see if I'm there so they can steal the candy. It's still the kid in them. And it's pretty nice. They're pretty wonderful and I get a big enjoyment out of that."

However, the industrial community is changing. Along with a shift away from social involvement in the United States in general, there has also been a shift away from forming communities in some workplaces. Robert Oswald, a long-time employee of Potlatch, reflected on this change, "We were always together. You'd stop after work—as a crew you'd stop after work and have a few beers or whatever. It wasn't just by yourself. Or if you had car trouble out in the parking lot at eleven o'clock at night there'd be people pulling up finding out what's wrong. They'd be in there, tearing into the engine if they had to, to get you going so you could go home that night.

"Now it's changed. It's not like that anymore. It's just kind of 'on your own'—they jump in their car, and they're gone. There's a few that if you see their hood up you may stop and ask or something, but normally, they just go. In the old days, we used to sit and wait even until the whole crew got out more or less, make sure their car started when it was real cold. Not anymore, it's just when you get out you're gone—put your time in and gone. And so the camaraderie and getting together with the crew, the stopping after work, going snowmobiling or going hunting or anything like that—you don't see that like you used to."

In the end I was only able to visit a small number of Minnesota's factories and interview a handful of workers. I tried to assure that this work represented a range of industries throughout the state and a cross-section of workers; however, there are many thousands of places I never saw in the three-year period during which I took these photographs. Peter Rachleff and I spent many hours discussing which industries to include and deciding if I had missed a critical aspect of the changing work environment or the changing demographic structure of Minnesota. There is always another place to visit.

INTRODUCTION

To See the Invisible

PETER RACHLEFF

Commodities of all kinds proliferate in our daily lives, from TV sets and cars to sneakers and t-shirts, but how they got made and who made them is a mystery. They seem to have blossomed fully formed on the shelves of department and specialty stores, and they dominate TV commercials as talking, thinking, walking, dancing, and singing objects, objects of need and desire, able to address consumers' basic needs and grant their wishes for freedom, sex appeal, and perennial youth. But the work that makes these commodities remains invisible, unmentioned, unrepresented, and unnamed.

Industrial work has long been invisible in our society. Shielded by laws protecting private property, reams of insurance regulations, and a mythology of danger, it is often hidden behind barbed wire, mesh fences, flanks of security guards and dogs, thick walls, and darkened windows. School trips to the local factory have disappeared as public education budgets have shrunk. Popular TV shows and movies rarely offer stories about women or men working, unless they're doctors, lawyers, or police officers. We never see people performing industrial labor.

As work has been rendered invisible, so, too, have workers. "We are starved for images of ourselves," wrote Stan Weir in 1980, "for identity and for aids to communicate the condition of our lives and the good in them. But the millions who do the so-called 'unskilled,' 'semi-skilled,' 'craft,' and even 'professional' jobs in American workplaces are seldom, if ever, represented fairly in the popular literature and media of the nation."

Weir, who worked as a longshoreman for two decades, wrote this passage as the rationale for his lifelong project, "Singlejack Books," a small publishing house that produced work narratives and poems, written by workers for workers. The very format of the books, sized to fit in the pocket of a pair of overalls or a work-shirt, expressed this goal. Sadly, "Singlejack" languished after producing fewer than ten wonderful volumes (my favorite was Steve Turner's *Night Shift in a Pickle Factory*), having failed to reach its ultimate goal: to make "the question of work and how it could be made more fulfilling by the people who actually do it . . . an issue of public discussion in America."

The absence of public discussion about work flows all too logically from its invisibility and that of the women and men who do it. "The proper study of the blue collar worker is the workplace," insisted former steelworker Charles Spencer in his 1977 memoir and call to arms, *Blue Collar: An Internal Examination of the Workplace*. "No matter what other institutions are searched for prints or clues, all trails lead back to the workplace itself."

By These Hands offers us just such a trail, into the industrial workplaces of turn of the twenty-first century Minnesota. Recent census data in Minnesota shows that the number of industrial workers in this state has held steady for the past thirty years. *By These Hands* offers compelling visual evidence that industrial labor remains a vital force in our region and a significant source of jobs and labor culture in communities across the state. David Parker's lens opens up a world that has typically been closed to us, and we can begin to generate and participate in that public discussion called for by Stan Weir, Charles Spencer, Studs Terkel, and others. A collection of stunning photographs like this can get such a discussion going in our own Minnesota communities.

But we also need analytical tools, frameworks, and historical grounding. Fortunately, there are wonderful resources for our discussions about work, waiting in libraries and bookstores. There are useful theories, some as old as the industrial revolution itself, and there is new scholarship, especially in the fields of labor history and industrial sociology, which can be called into service. Scholars in both disciplines have made the workplace a center of their investigations, and they have much to offer us as we look at David Parker's beautiful and unusual images.

Work and the workplace are rife with contradictions within a capitalist economy. Work produces not only commodities but also profits, and, let the profits decline, the demand for the work will dry up, even if there is a social need for the commodities it produced. The workplace is a site not only of empowerment (the feeling of accomplishment, of making something in the world) but also of alienation (the inability to control the work process) and exploitation (wages and benefits that are incommensurate with productivity and output). Work is an experience of cooperation and conflict with other workers and with management. These features have characterized work ever since men and women have had to go to work for other men and women, whatever the actual nature of their tasks.

Labor historians have constructed a useful narrative of the evolution of work since the onset of the industrial revolution. Their studies suggest that the artisan, the quintessential citizen of the era of the American Revolution, practiced a craft that gave him not only economic independence but also a social identity and a political role to play. Out of this lifestyle and community standing emerged an ideology of "independence" that infused not only daily life but the very political definition of the new nation.

For decades (1820s–1890s), these artisans and their descendants resisted the industrial revolution's transformation of their work. Although being independent no longer meant being one's own boss, it still expressed limits to being bossed around. Independence could still mean the right to work harder in the morning and easier in the afternoon, or to work without constant observation, or the latitude to make some choices about the ordering of tasks.

Within each workplace, now as well as then, a moving "frontier of control," an invisible line, demarcates the division between management's authority and the autonomy of workers. While this line might be invisible to outside observers, every worker and manager within that workplace knows exactly where it is—and tries to move it in her or his favor.

The struggle over workplace authority begun by the industrial revolution reached a qualitatively new stage at the beginning of the twentieth century with the conceptualization of "scientific management" by industrial engineer Frederick Winslow Taylor. Popularly known as "Taylorism," this new system radically transformed much industrial work into a monotonous routine, with the assembly line emerging as its most thorough manifestation. This process was dramatically depicted by Upton Sinclair in his 1936 novel *The Flivver King,* whose protagonist's job devolved from affixing tires to new vehicles in the 1890s to, by the 1920s, simply tightening the lug nuts on the left front wheel of vehicle after vehicle, brought to him by an endless, perpetually moving, assembly line.

During the first thirty years of the twentieth century, millions of immigrants from southern, central, and eastern Europe found employment in these transformed or wholly new industries—auto manufacture, tire building, coal mining, meat-packing, steel manufacture, machinery manufacture, and electrical appliances—most of which were located in the growing industrial cities of the North and Midwest. Beginning with World War I, they were joined by a million and a half African Americans who left their rural homes in the South for the factories and mines of the urban North. Women as well as men from these groups found employment in many of these reorganized workplaces.

No sooner had these workers become adjusted to the new regimens of industrial labor than the Great Depression of the 1930s shook and transformed their world, from factory shutdowns and massive unemployment to profound shifts in the government's role in the economy. But nothing was more important for work, workers, and workplaces than the emergence of a new labor movement based in these mass production industries. The new industrial unions did not just demand higher wages and benefits. They fought for workplace power, to limit the authority of foremen, to govern layoffs and callbacks by seniority rather than favoritism, to negotiate work rules and job descriptions, and to resolve workplace disputes through a grievance procedure. While barely two million workers belonged to unions at the beginning of the Depression, ten million carried union cards by 1939, and fourteen million by the end of World War II.

Though it had certainly changed, the language of independence had not disappeared. It was expressed with a variety of accents and dialects, while its meaning became refracted through the experiences of different groups and their interactions with each other, from sharing lunches (burritos, heroes, gyros, pasties, and the like) to sharing stories about their own people's struggles for independence from the Austro-Hungarian and Ottoman Empires to Poland, Ukraine, southern Italy, and the cotton fields of the American South. With the emergence of industrial unions and detailed collective bargaining contracts, independence became more of a social than an individual concept. Work rules, job descriptions, seniority provisions, and the grievance procedure—together known as "the contract"—became industrial workers' new "Magna Carta." These guidelines, structures, and practices defined the contours of workers' freedom and independence, even as workers punched time clocks, responded to bells and whistles, and obeyed foremen's orders. Some observers and scholars even ennobled this new system with the term "industrial democracy."

But these changes proved as evanescent as all the others had in their own times. Post-World War II America experienced a set of interrelated revolutions as both the workplace and the workforce again changed profoundly. From the 1960s to the present, the "information revolution," "deindustrialization," economic "globalization," and a new influx of immigration would reshape workplaces throughout urban and rural America. These are the workplaces David Parker makes visible in *By These Hands*.

An information revolution swept through the economy in the second half of the twentieth century, with computers changing everything from cash registers to punch presses and creating entirely new industries. Whole sectors of industrial work long thought too complex (e.g., machine tool work in specialized small batch production) began to experience a new Taylorization. In industries where workers had once had tactile contact with raw materials and semi-finished products, glass windows, computer screens, and electronic images now mediated their very physical space and redesigned their physical motions. New manufacturing industries emerged (e.g., computer chips) whose "clean rooms" required workers to wear heavy protective suits and breathing apparatuses. Instead of robots replacing workers, workers were being asked to dress and work like robots.

In the same era, a wave of deindustrialization engulfed America's manufacturing core. Plant closings, downsizings, and corporate reorganizations transformed the steel belt into a rust belt. Although they did not disappear, millions of manufacturing jobs did relocate, first from North to South and, then, as capital's mobility expanded and economic globalization widened, to Mexico and beyond. Millions of workers were displaced. The security that industrial workers of the 1940s and 1950s had come to associate with their jobs disappeared for many, not just those who lost their jobs but also those who feared that they might lose them—and not just the wages but also the health care and pension benefits that had come with them.

The combination of technological and organizational changes with industrial capital's new mobility was especially deleterious to those industrial workers who continued to toil in factories, mills, foundries, packing plants, and mines. As their work became less skilled and more Taylorized, they discovered that their employers could replace them more easily and that their unions' power to negotiate wages, benefits, and work rules was rapidly undercut. Thrown into competition with an increasing pool of workers who could do their jobs not only in the U.S. (including millions of new immigrants arriving from Central America, Asia, and Africa) but also in countries where employers had even freer hands than in the U.S. to require long work days, pay low wages and no benefits, and dump their wastes into the surrounding environment, their job security and compensation deteriorated with stunning speed.

By the early 1990s, Harvard economics professor Juliet Shor could report in her book, The Overworked American, that the average industrial worker was putting in a whole month's more work per year than s/he had twenty years before and taking home twenty percent less real pay. Industrial workers also found themselves prone to newly identified "repetitive motion injuries," like carpal tunnel syndrome and back strain, and other nagging maladies from insomnia to migraine headaches. By the end of the twentieth century, work, particularly industrial work, had become harder and more "alienated."

In an important and related change, new workers were entering American industrial workplaces at unprecedented levels. By the early 1990s, as many as one million new immigrants, with and without documents, were arriving annually, seeking jobs that paid more than they had been able to earn at home, which, in most cases, had not been much. Scholars, journalists, and union organizers noted that from meat-packing to garment manufacturing, from the workforce to the working conditions and the wages, the turn of the twenty-first century was looking eerily like the turn of the twentieth century.

David Parker's photographs in *By These Hands* speak to us of both constancy and change. They remind us that the new incorporates and preserves the old, even as it transcends it. From a foundry in which the very fires of hell seem to blast to an air-conditioned computer control room in which the workers seem casual and comfortable, we witness a performance, a ritual, an exercise centuries old, the expenditure of human energy through machines onto raw materials. Although this process changes from the brute force of hammers, tongs, and anvils to the sophisticated precision of computer-numerically-controlled (CNC) machines, its core remains the same. Work remains a hidden but vital part of our lives. The issues faced by workers in 2002 are much the same as those faced in 1902.

Despite the sameness of the basic process, its setting, its tools, and its actors remain as foreign and unfamiliar as life on another planet. This universe has been invisible for so long, we're not sure what we're seeing even when we get a look at it. *By These Hands* reveals the setting in which work takes place, the tools with which it is performed, the faces of the men and women who do it, the exertions of their bodies, the gear they often wear that protects their bodies and obscures their faces, and the corners and break rooms in which they find respite. But these images are not simple documents to be glanced at, nodded at, and filed away. If they are to be used to see the invisible, we must take our time with each image, look at it and into it, awaken our imaginations, and, above all, talk to each other about it. Through our conversations and by our hands, we can render work visible again.

By These Hands

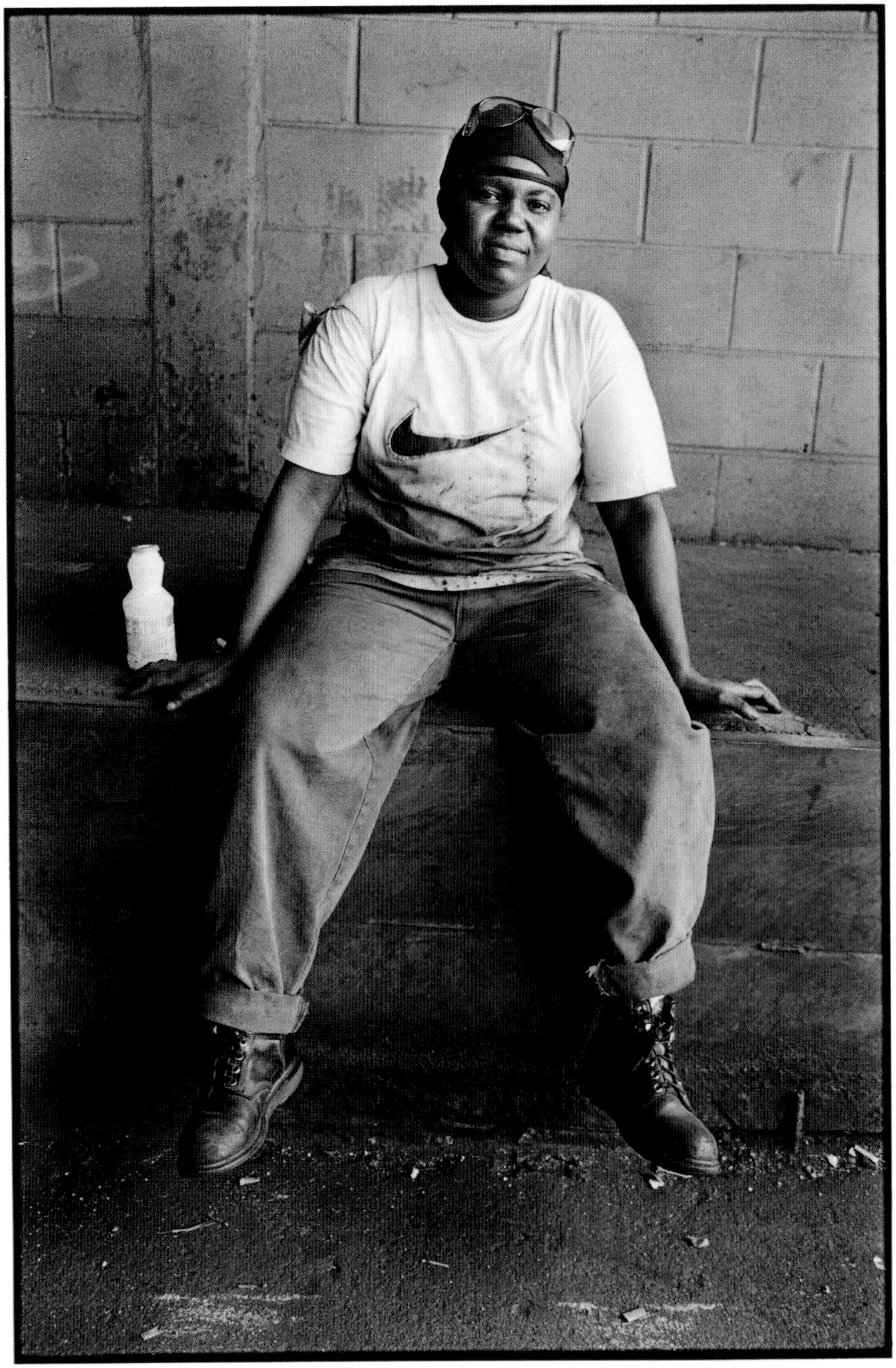

Rest break on hot day
Acme Foundry

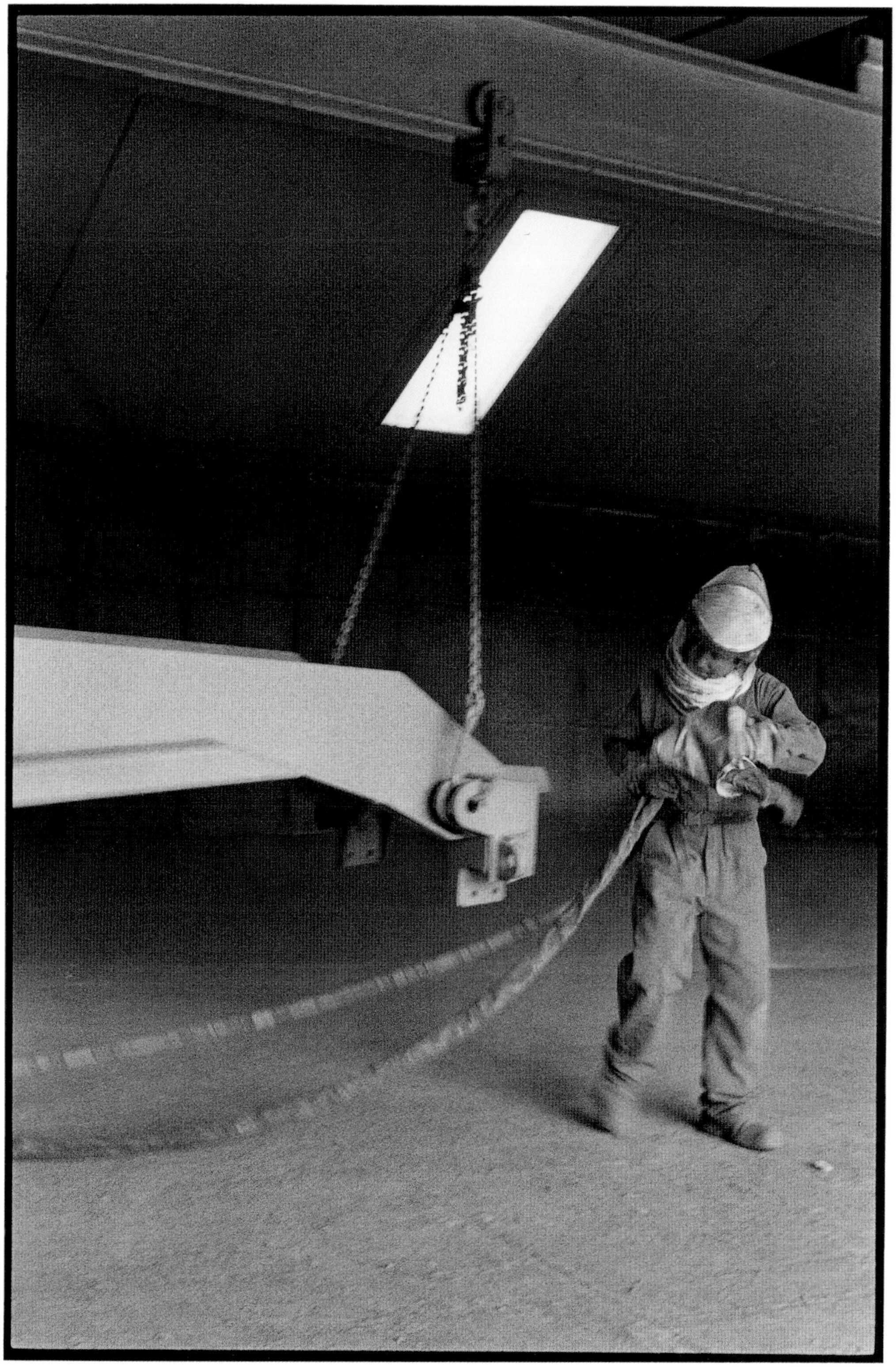

Spray painter
Lull International

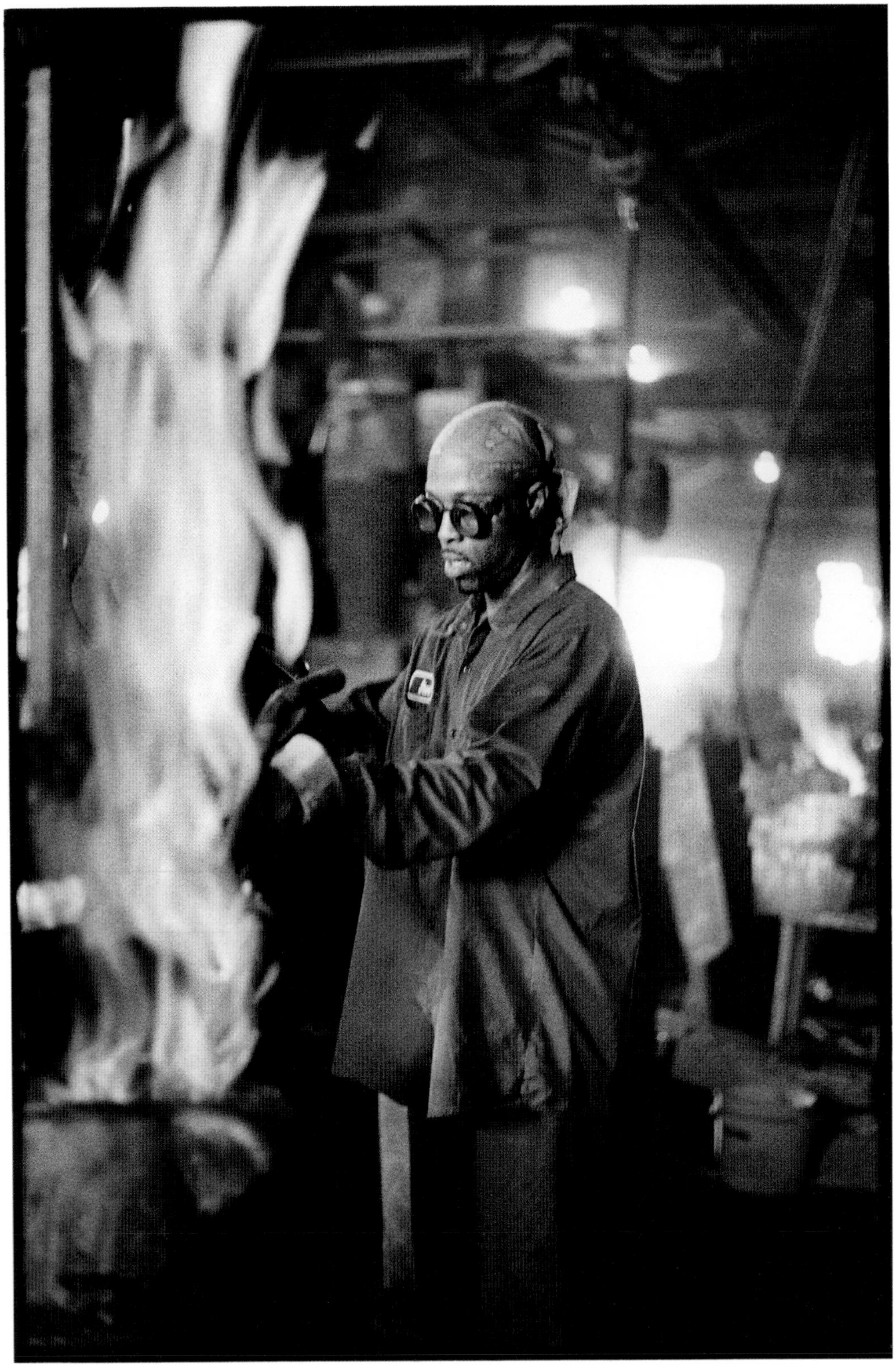

Pouring molten steel
Acme Foundry

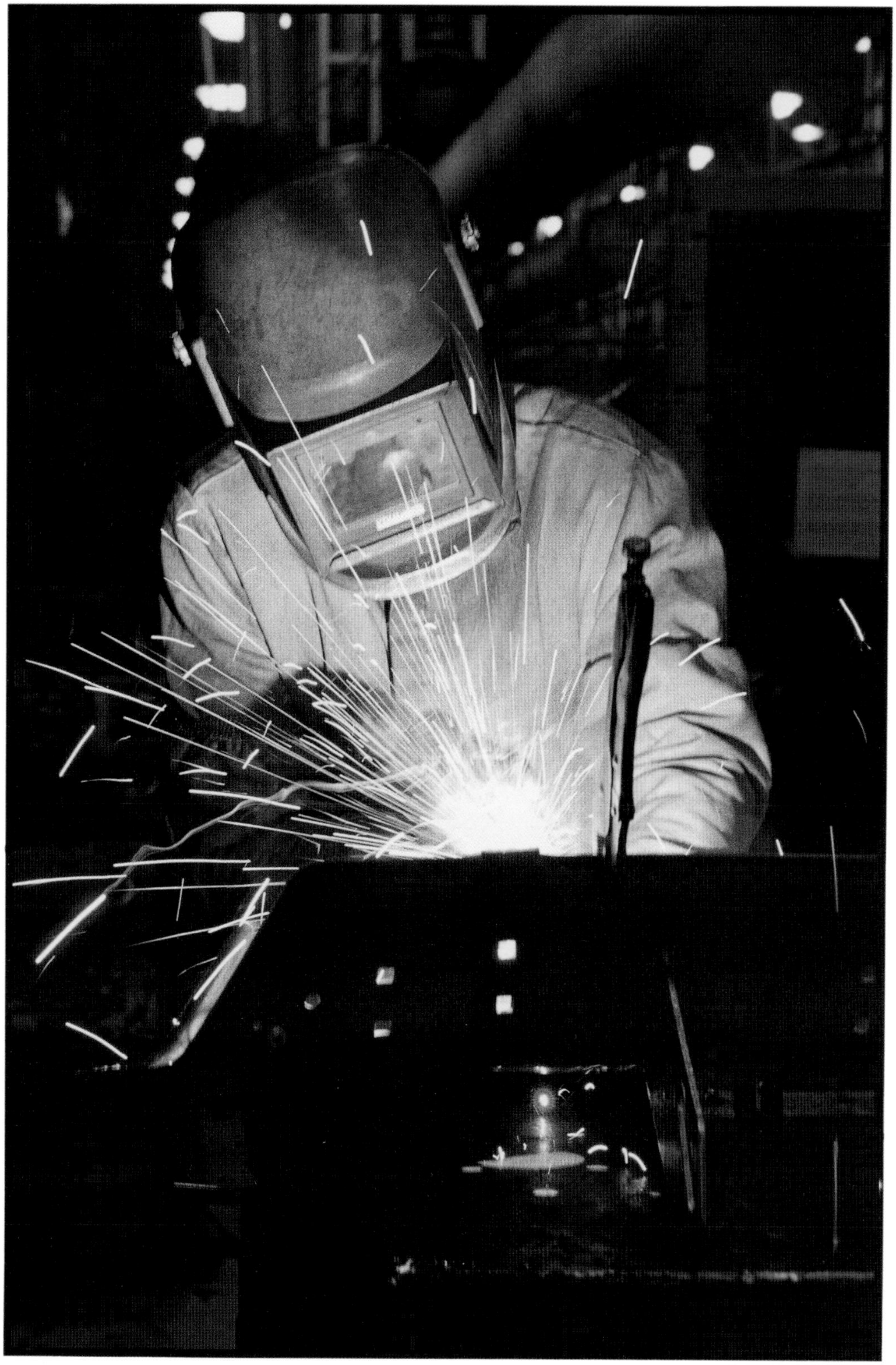

Welder

Toro

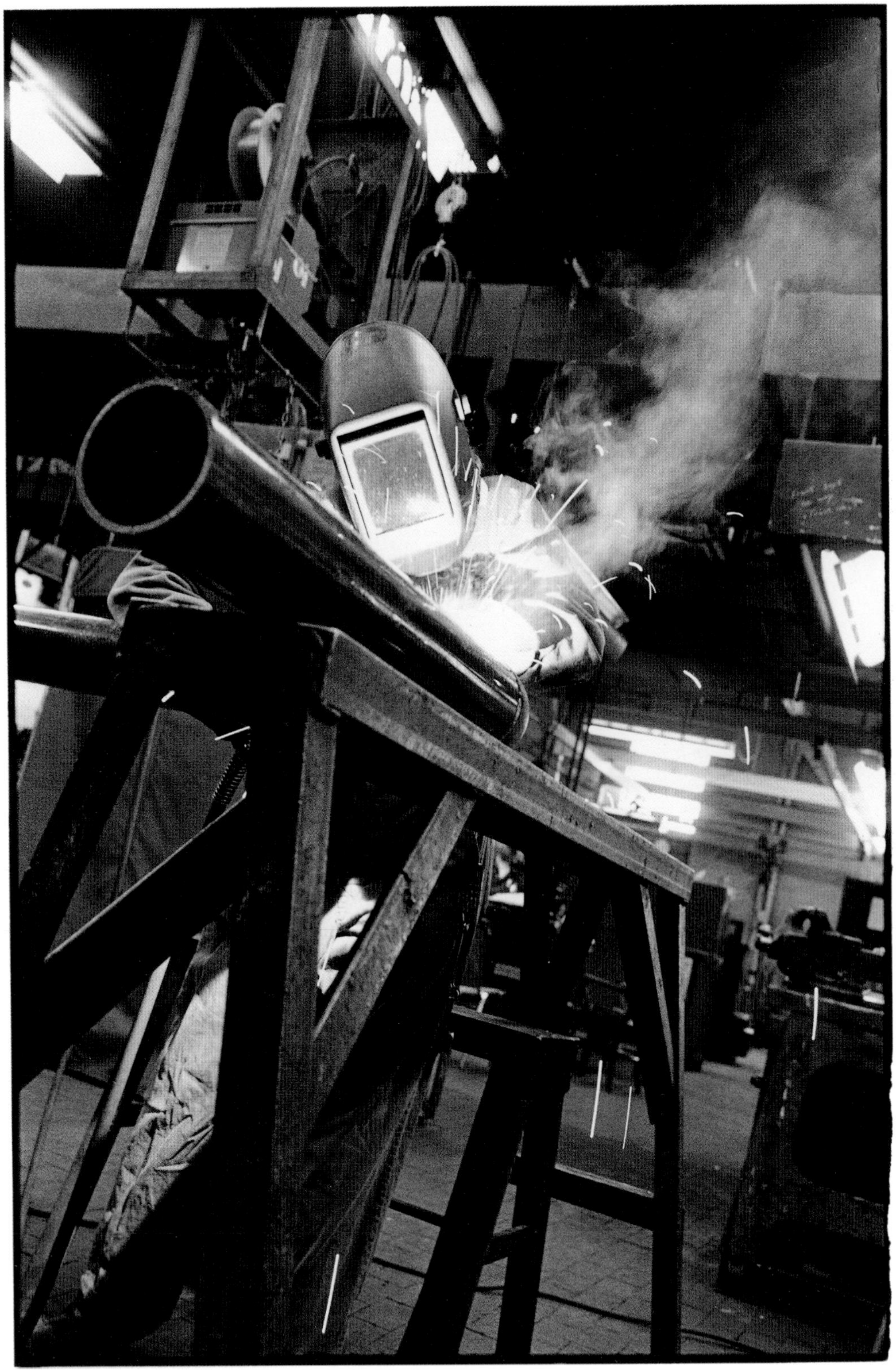

Welder
Ford Motor Company

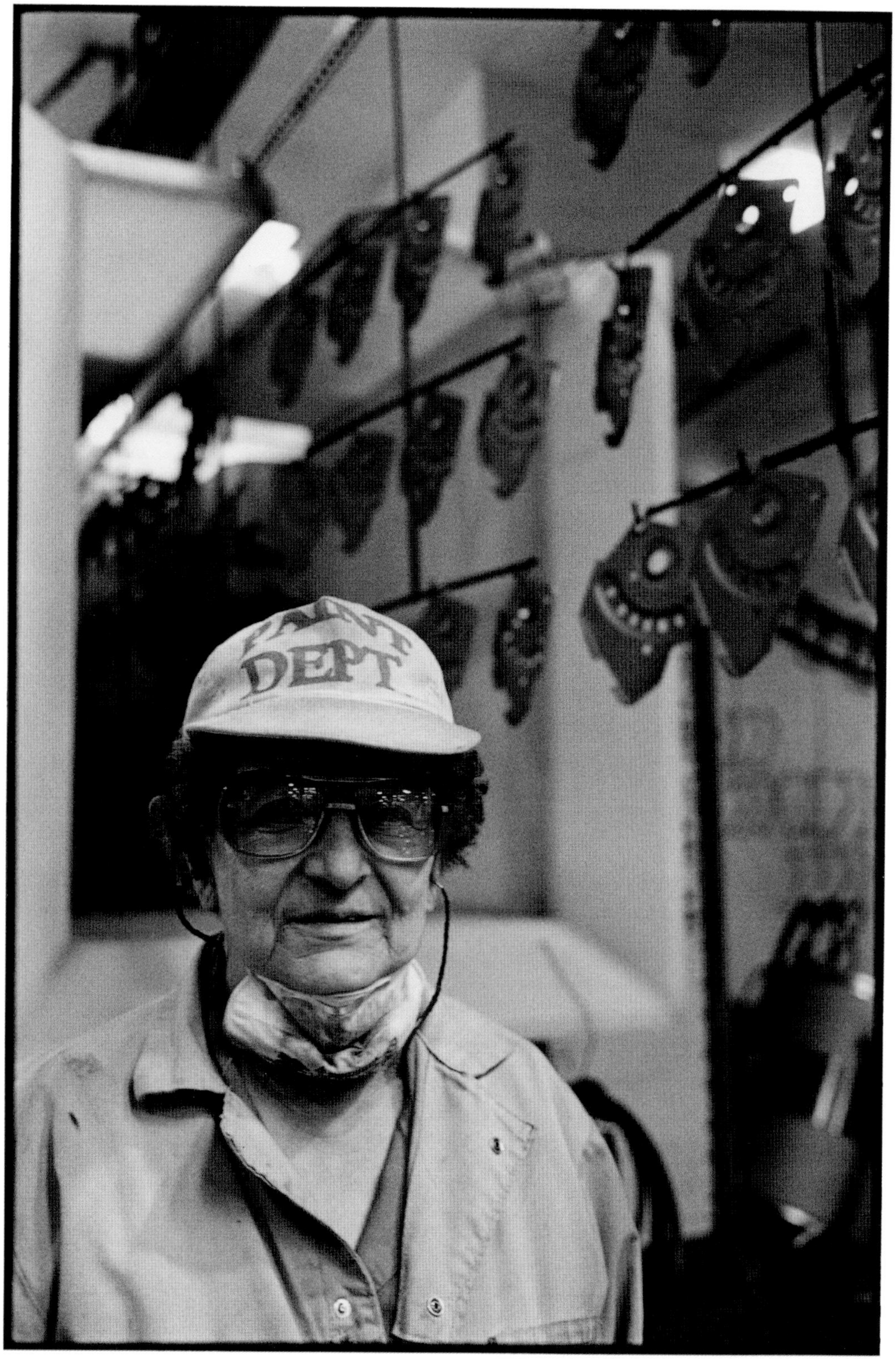

Spray paint operator
Toro

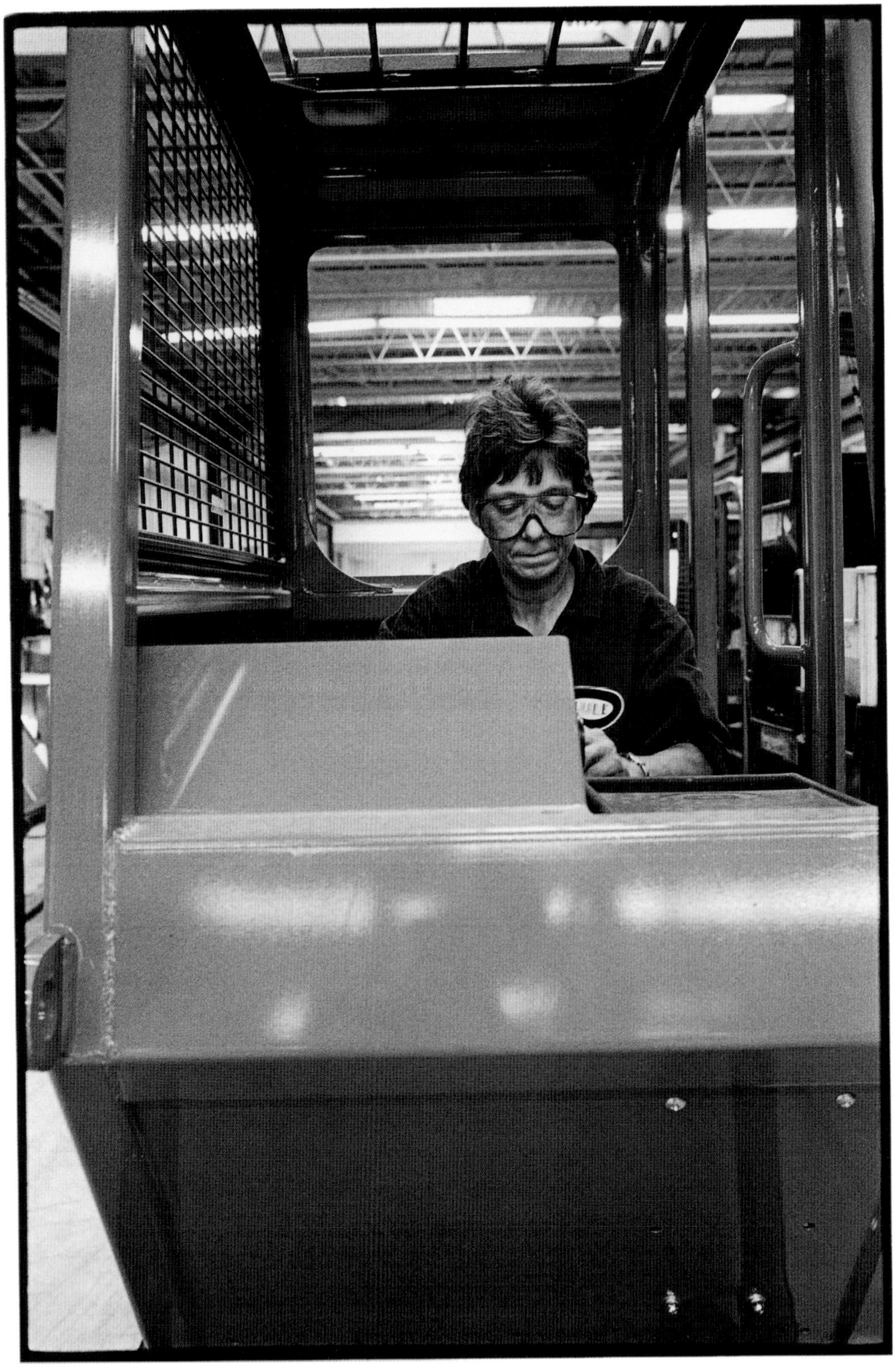

Assembly worker
Lull International

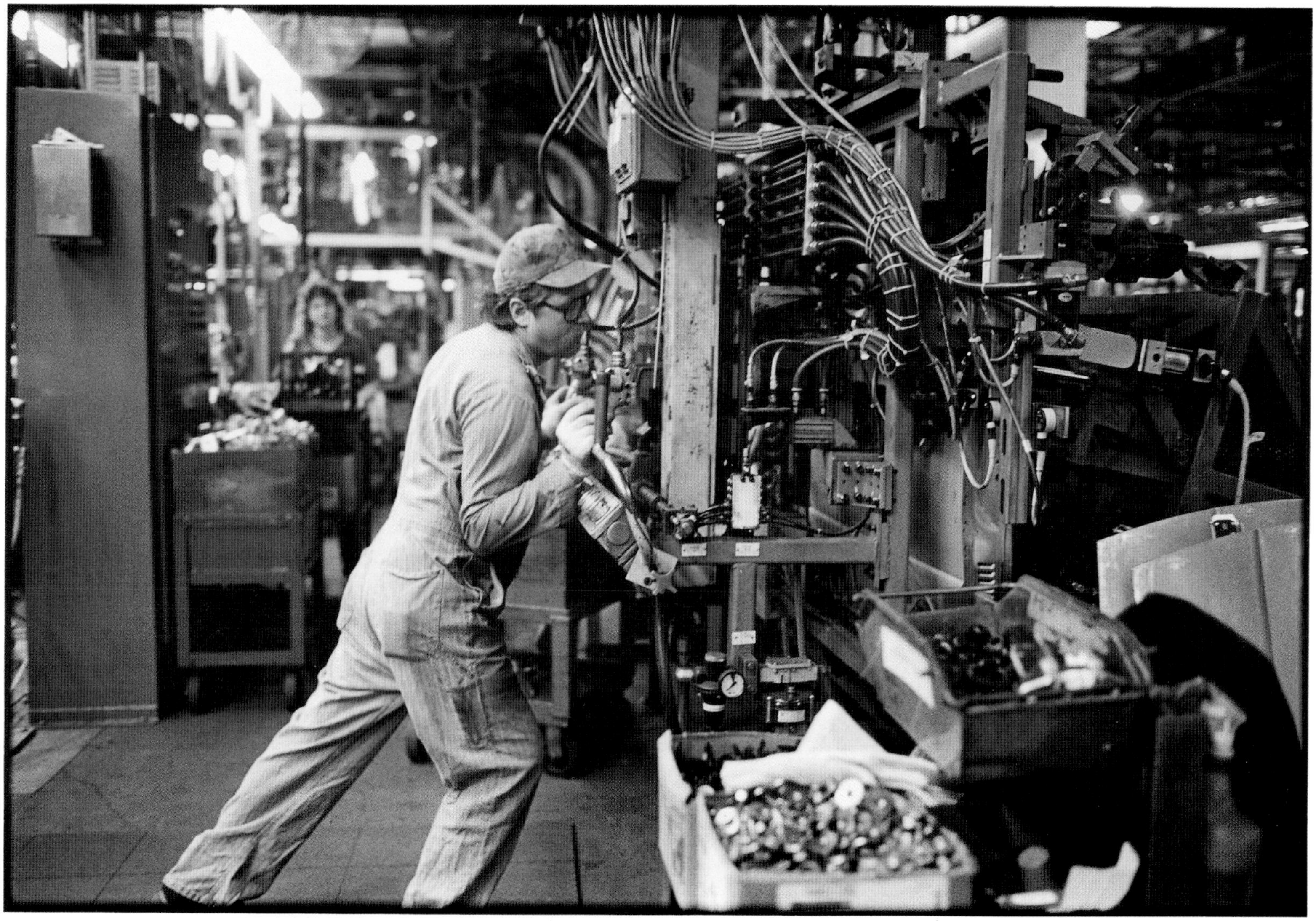

Assembly worker
Ford Motor Company

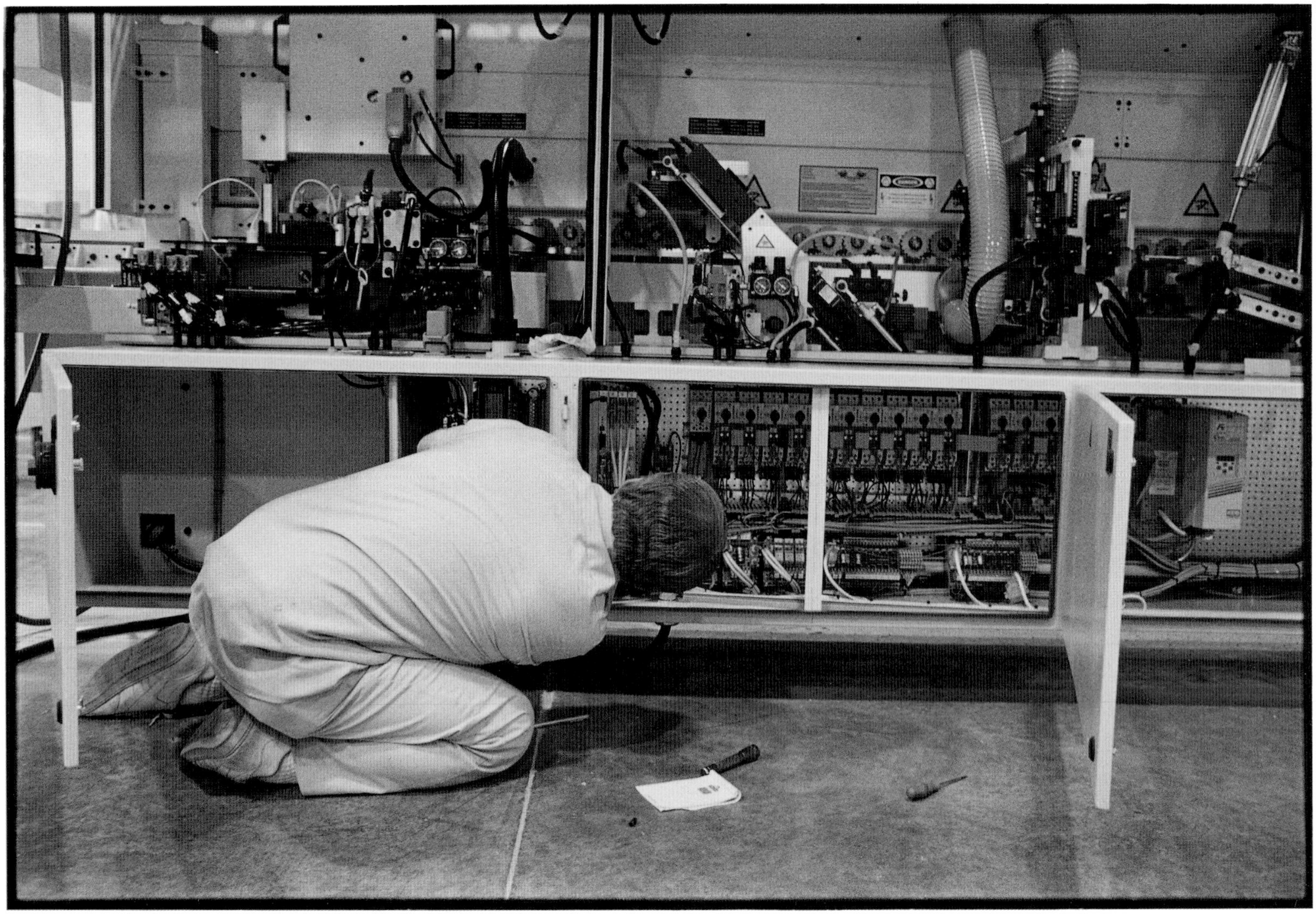

CNC repair
Siewert Cabinet

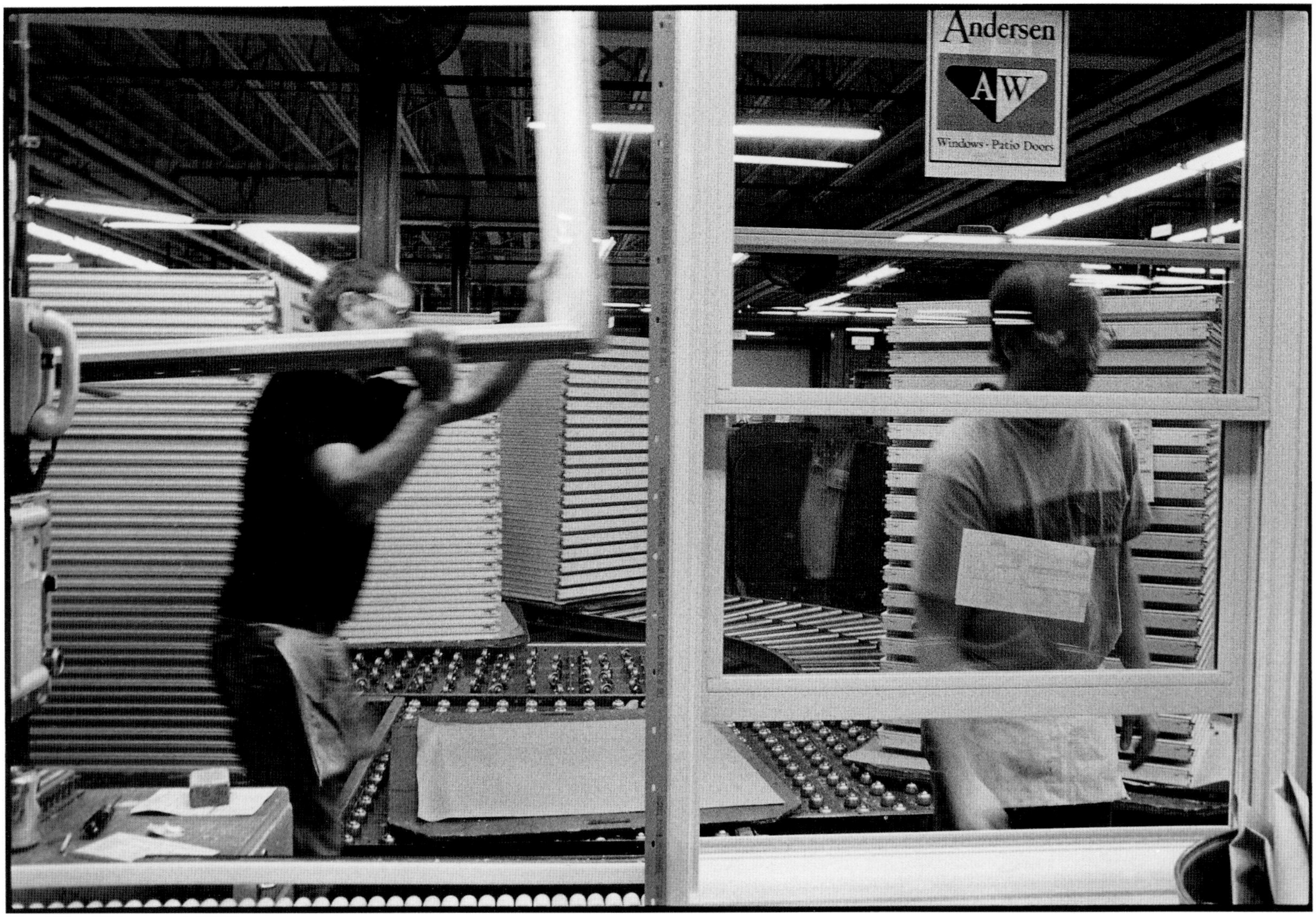

Window assembly
Andersen Window

"I'm one that enjoys hard work. I always have. My daddy thought I was kinda strange because I could find joy in something that most people would be complaining about. But if you've got to do it, I mean, it's the only way you're gonna make it."

CLARENCE (SONNY) DOBBINS
SMITH FOUNDRY

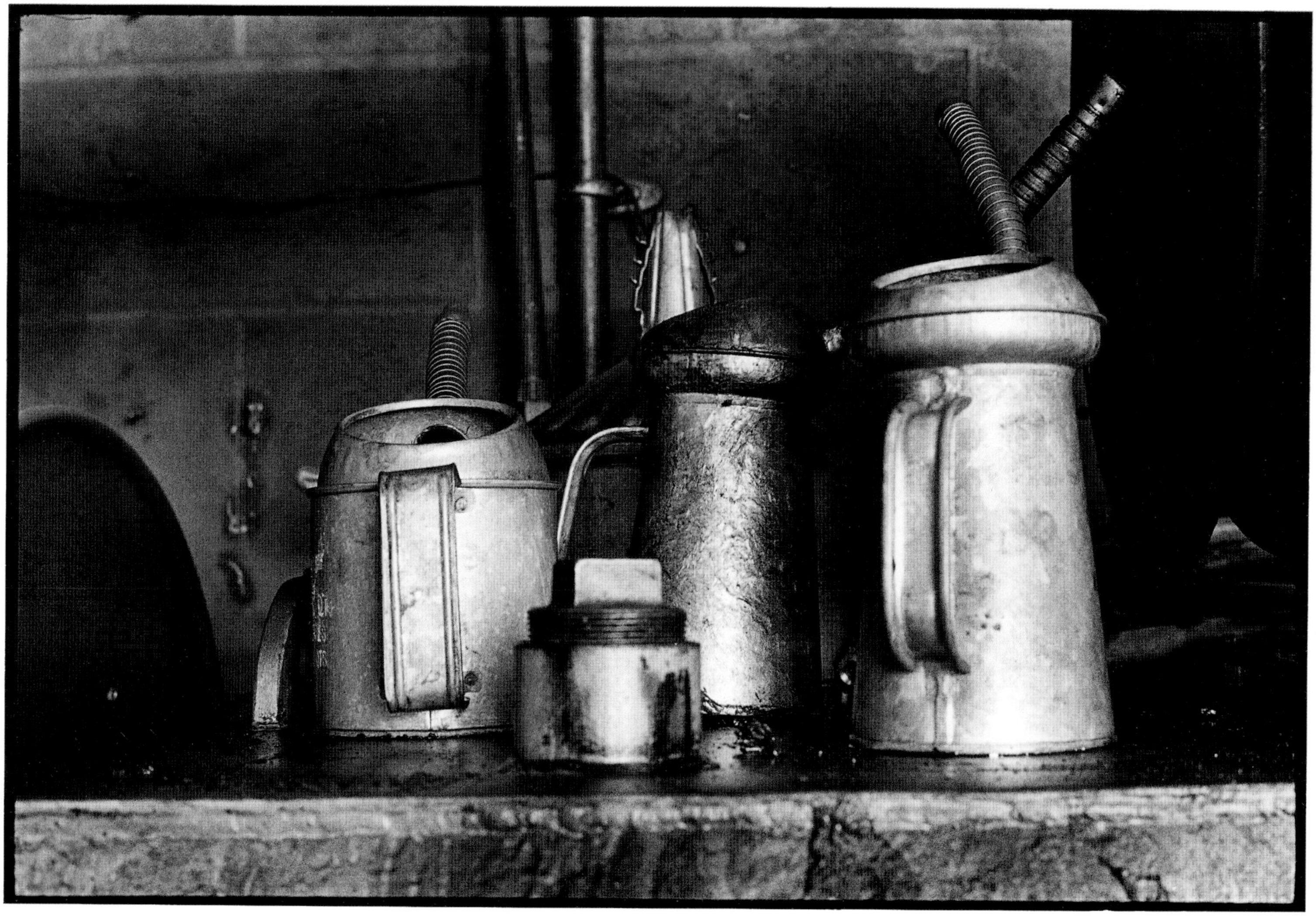

Oil cans
Ispat Inland Mining

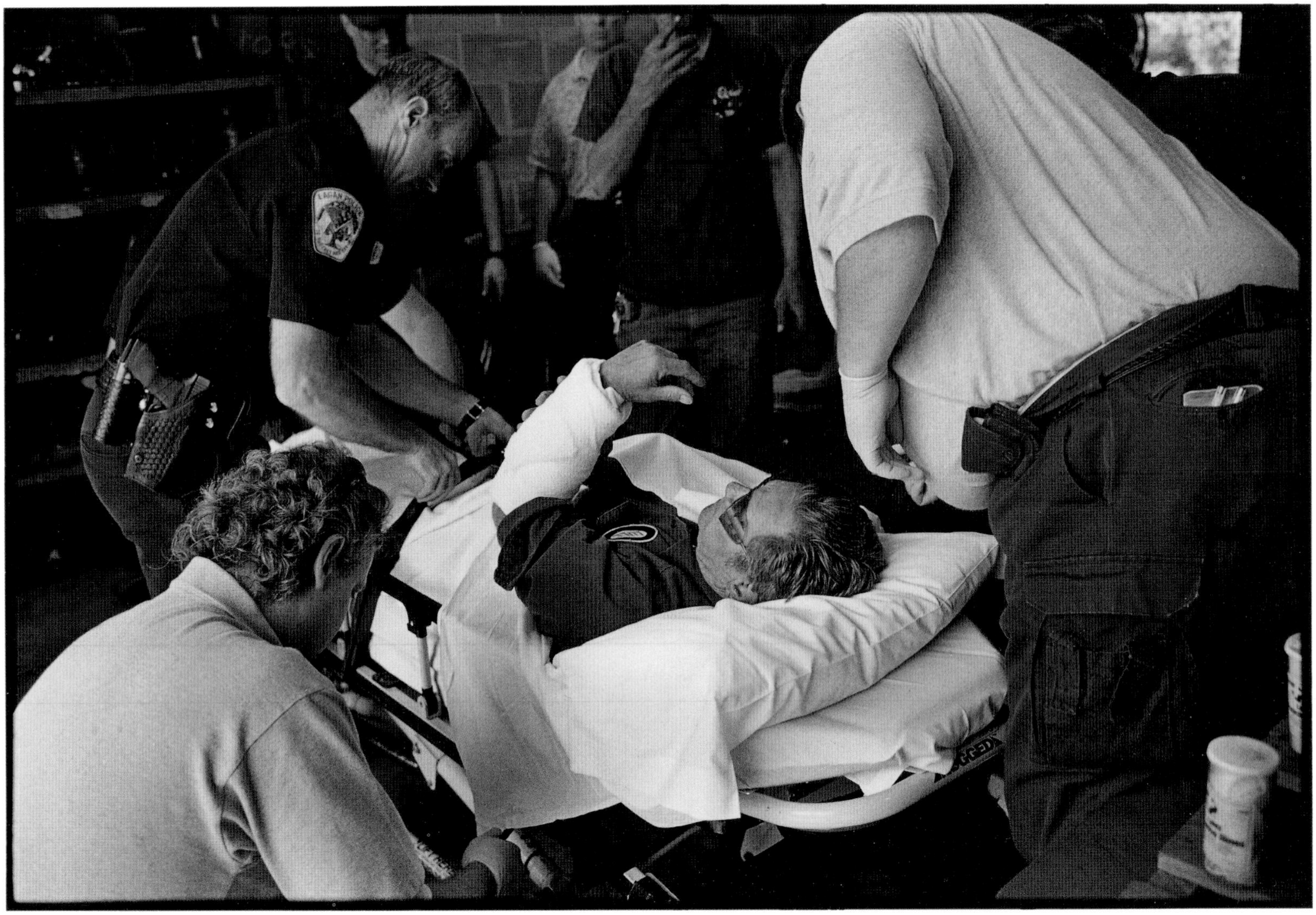

Injured worker
Lull International

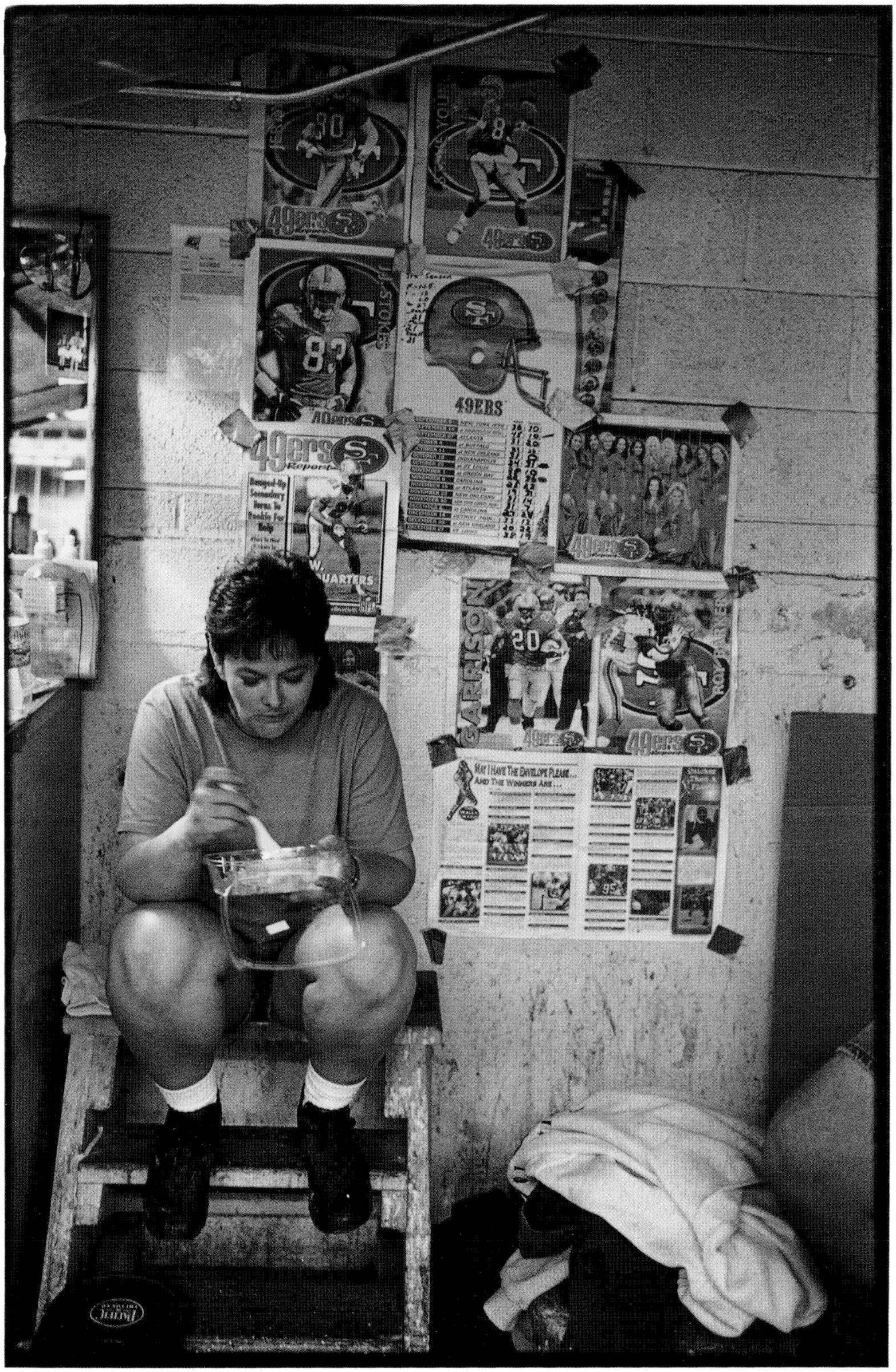

Lunch break

Andersen Window

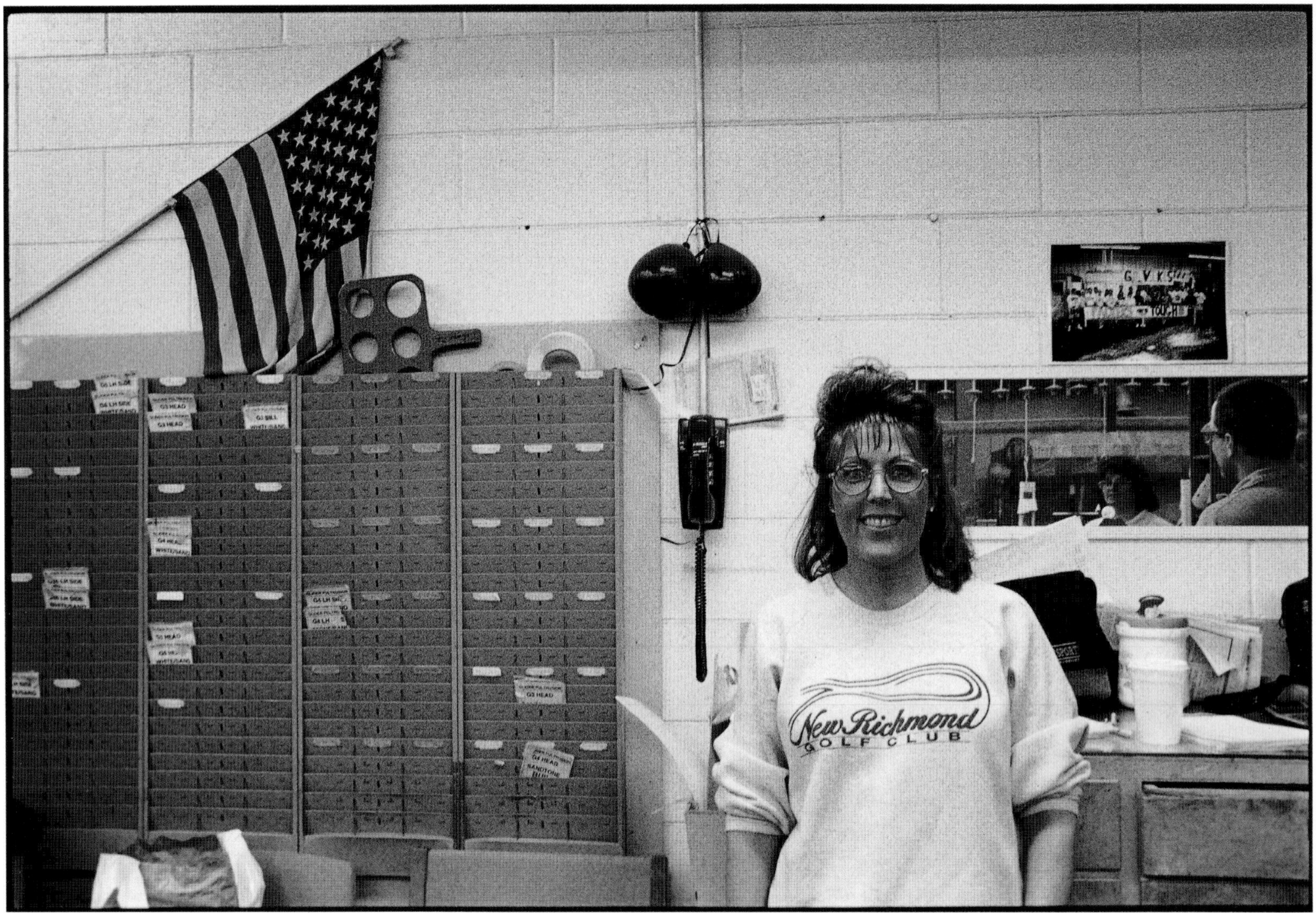

Rest break

Andersen Window

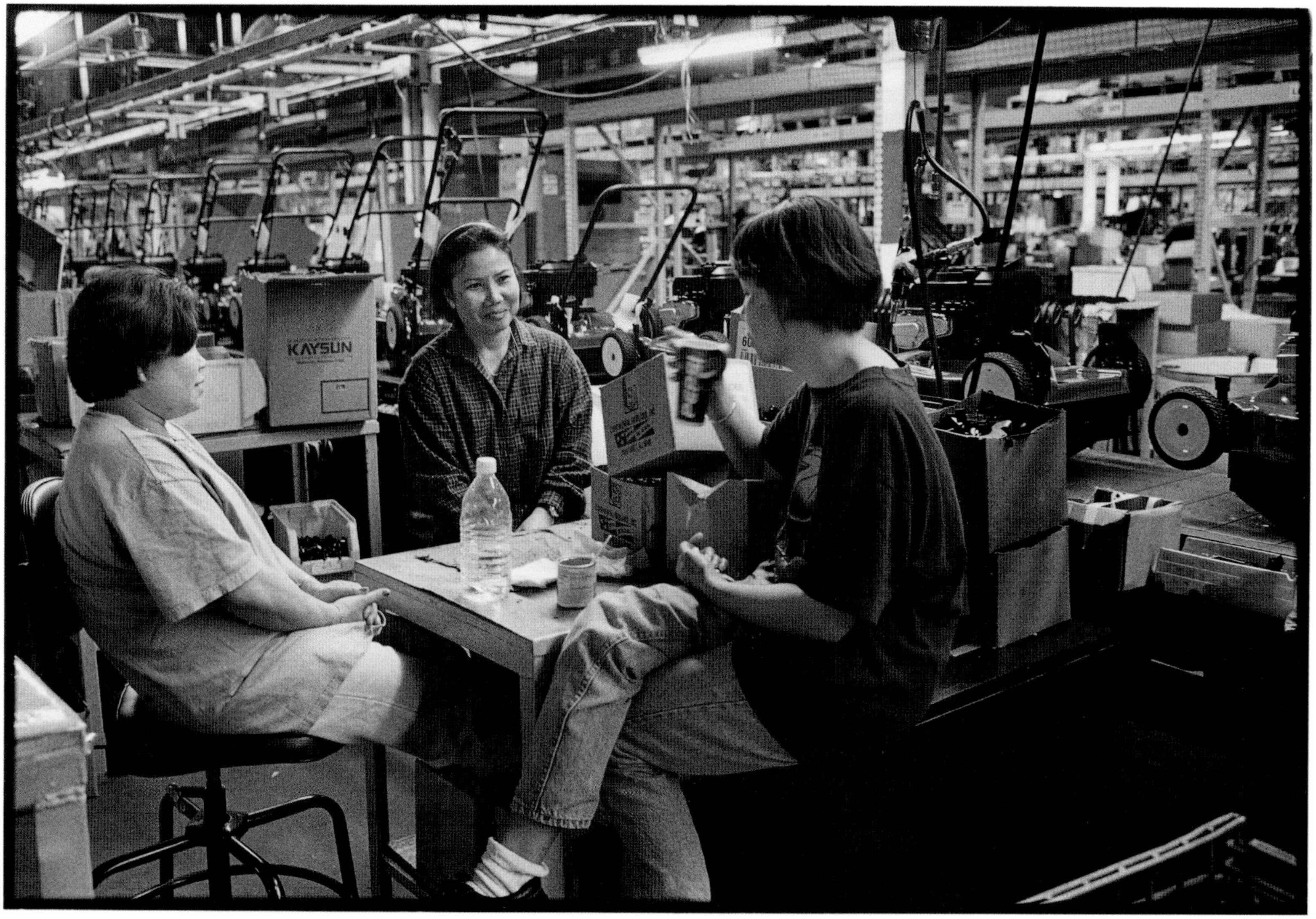

Lunch break
Toro

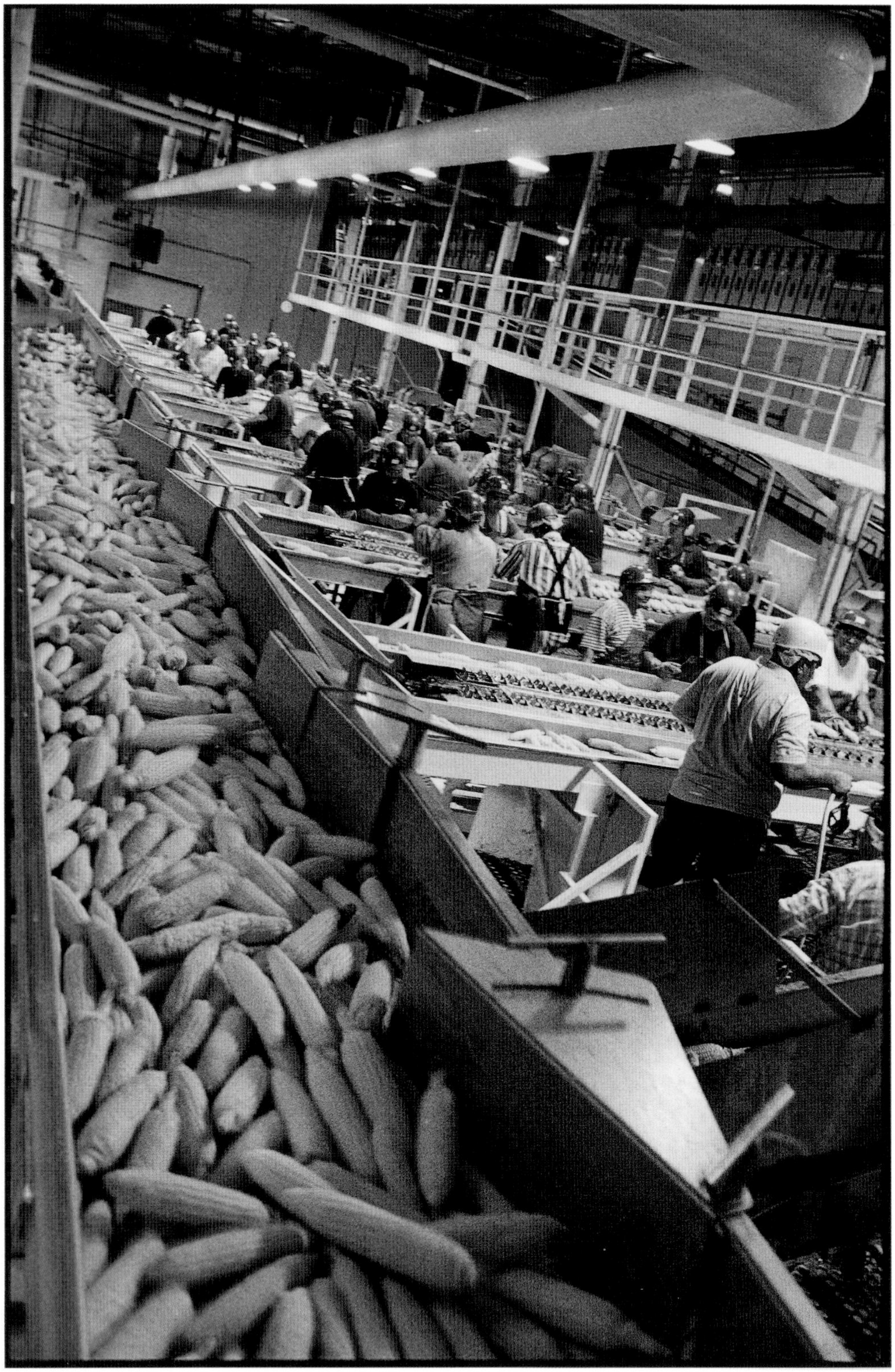

Corn processing
Agrilink

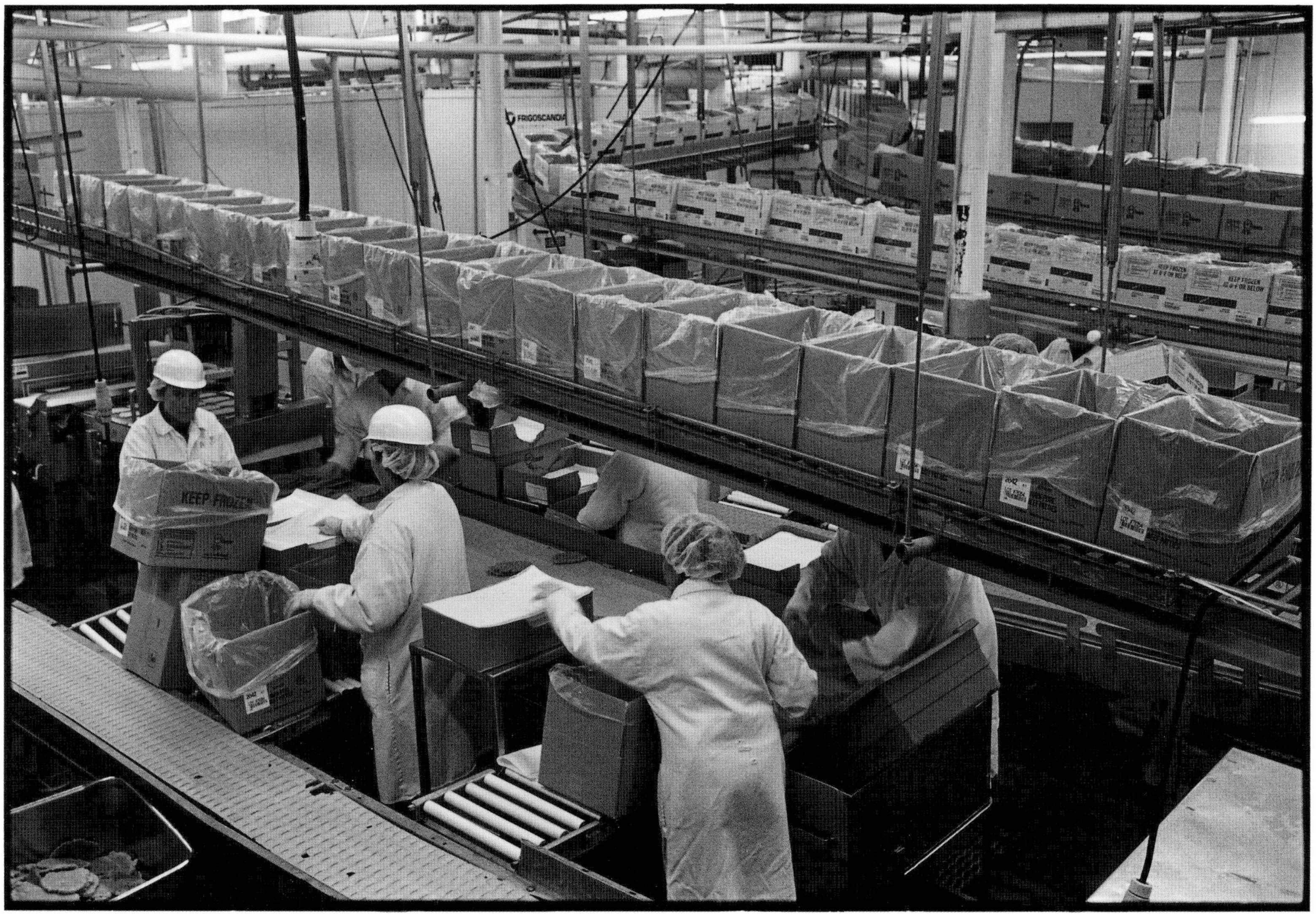

Boxing hamburgers
GFI America

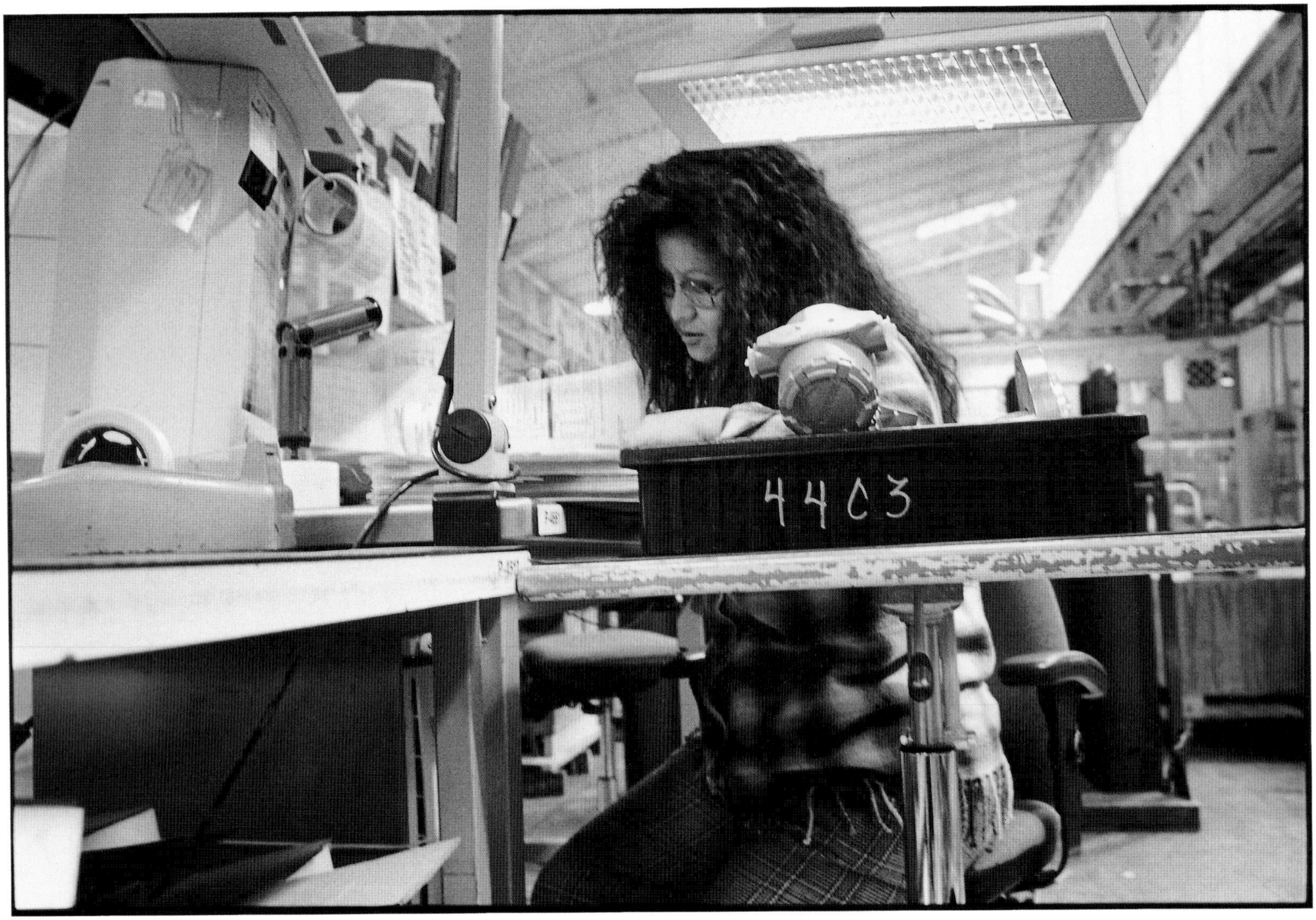

Parts assembly
Rosemount Engineering

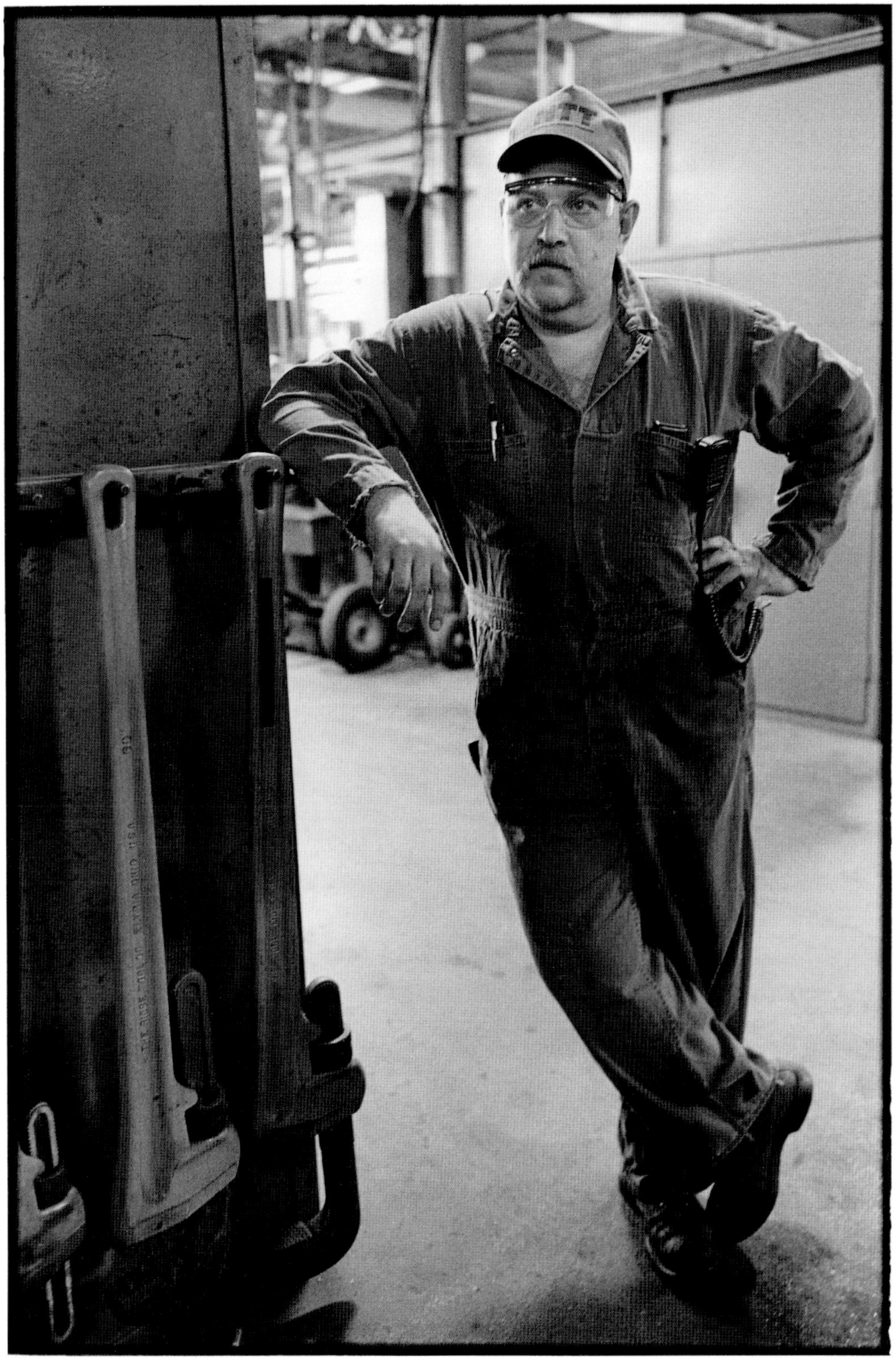

Repair worker
Ford Motor Company

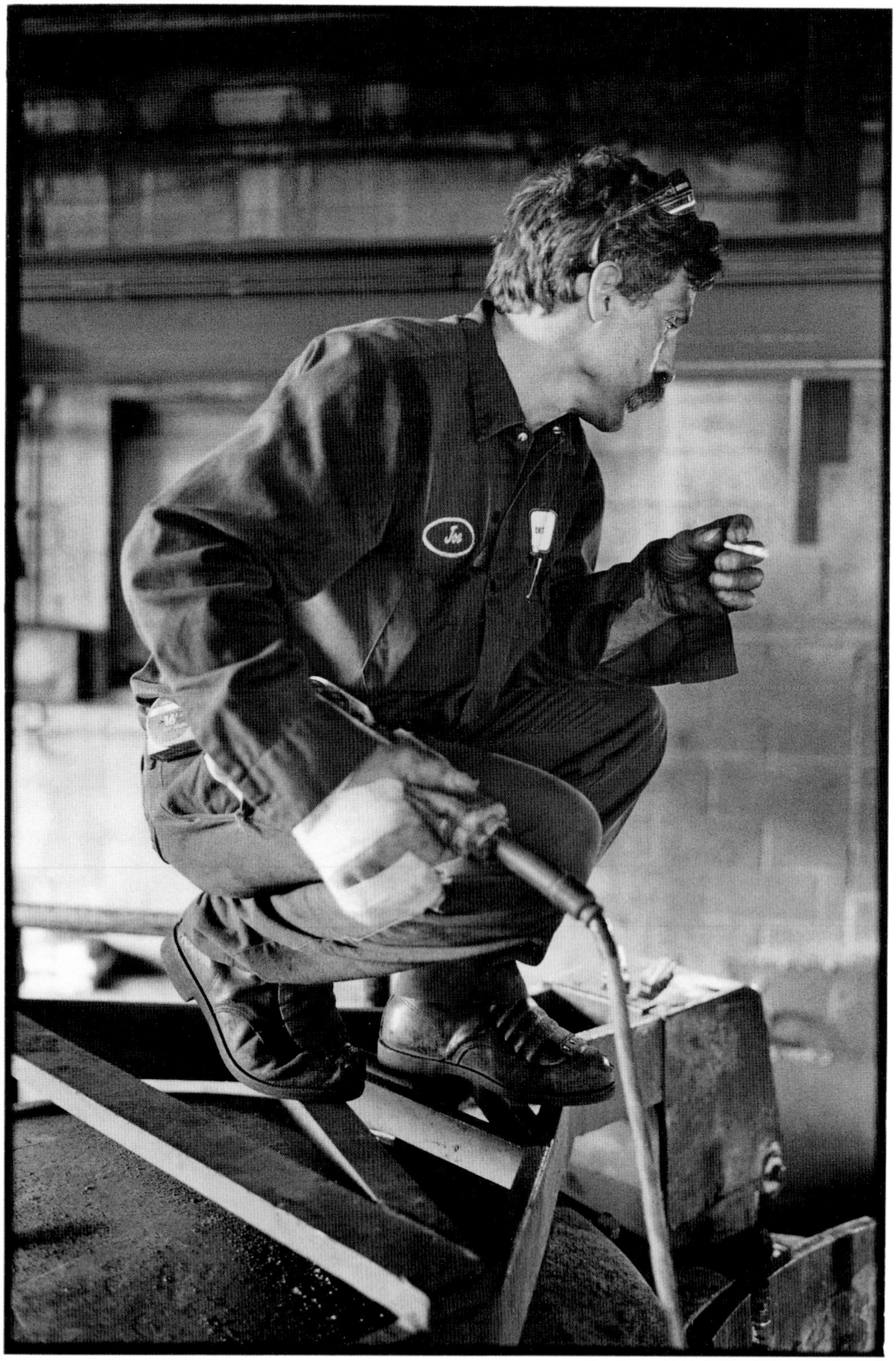

Laborer

Smith Foundry

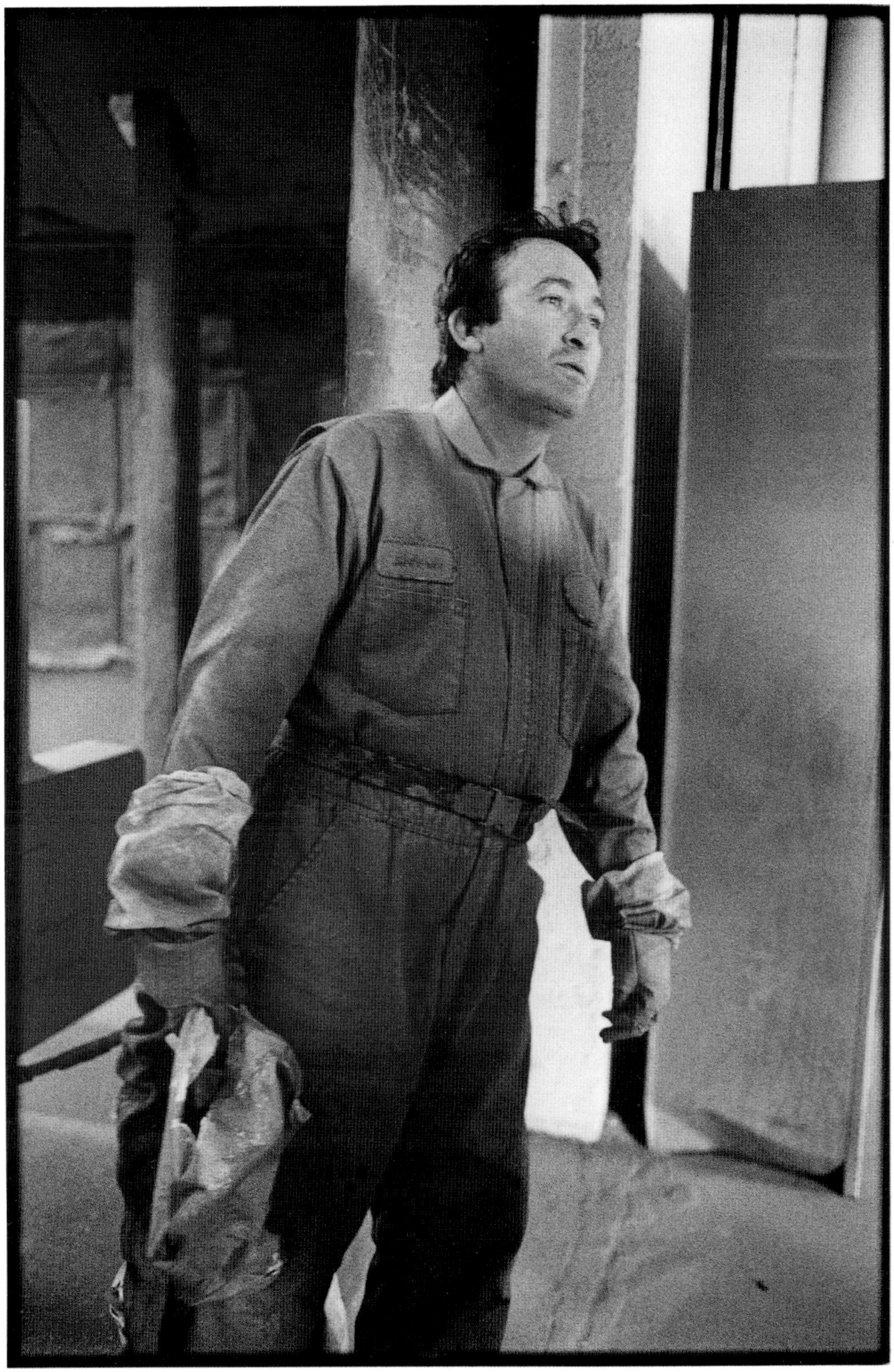

Welder
Lull International

"I feel this way that, as long as the good Lord gives me my health, I would like to keep working. I want to be out among people. And where else can you be among people? Go to a shopping center? No."

EMMA OLSEN
ROSEMOUNT ENGINEERING

"I don't foresee myself retiring—just coming home to play golf, which I don't do, or fishing, which I don't do. I do go hunting but that's once a year. I just don't see retirement for me."

MARK FROEMKE
AMERICAN CRYSTAL SUGAR

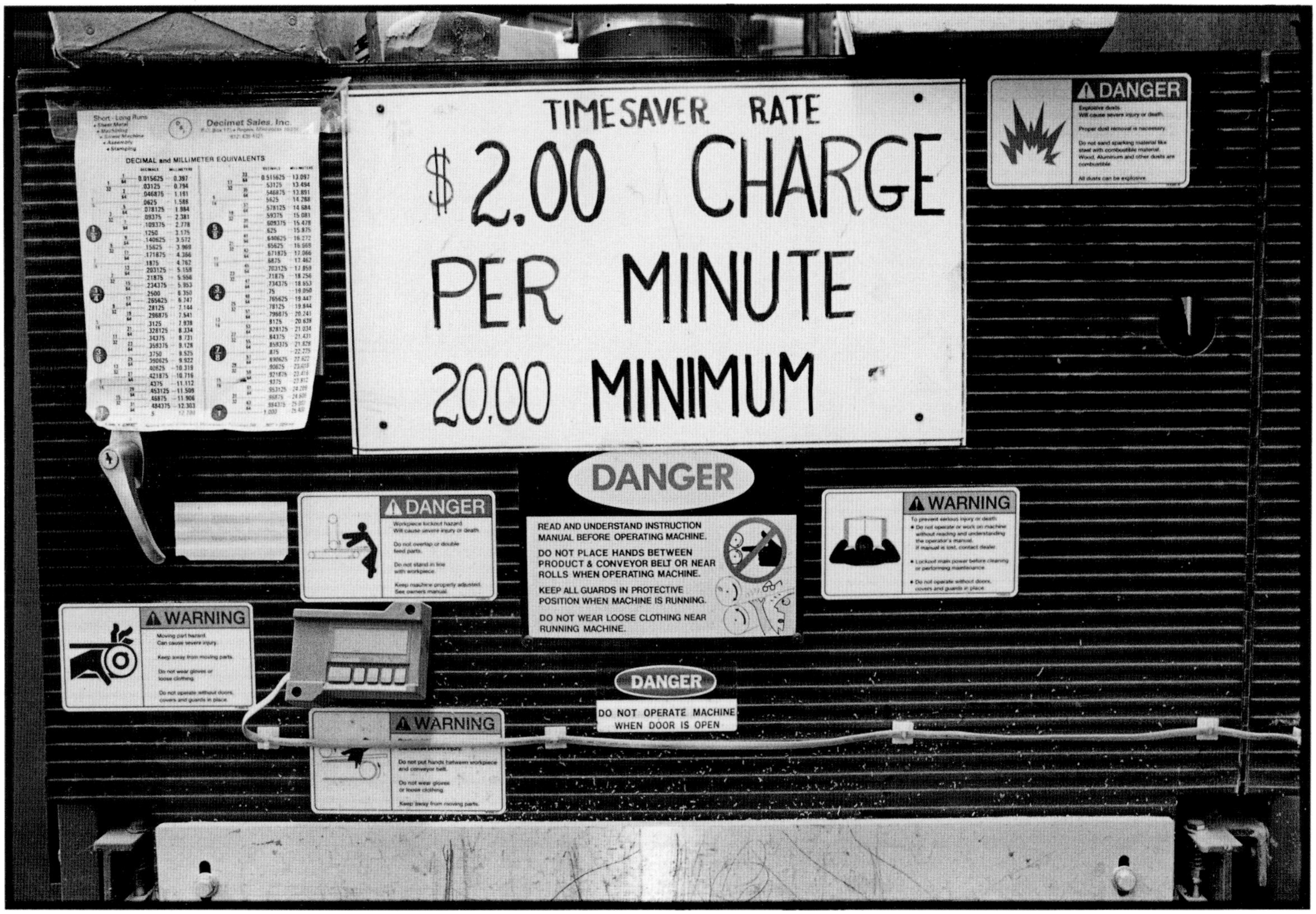

Signs
Siewert Cabinet

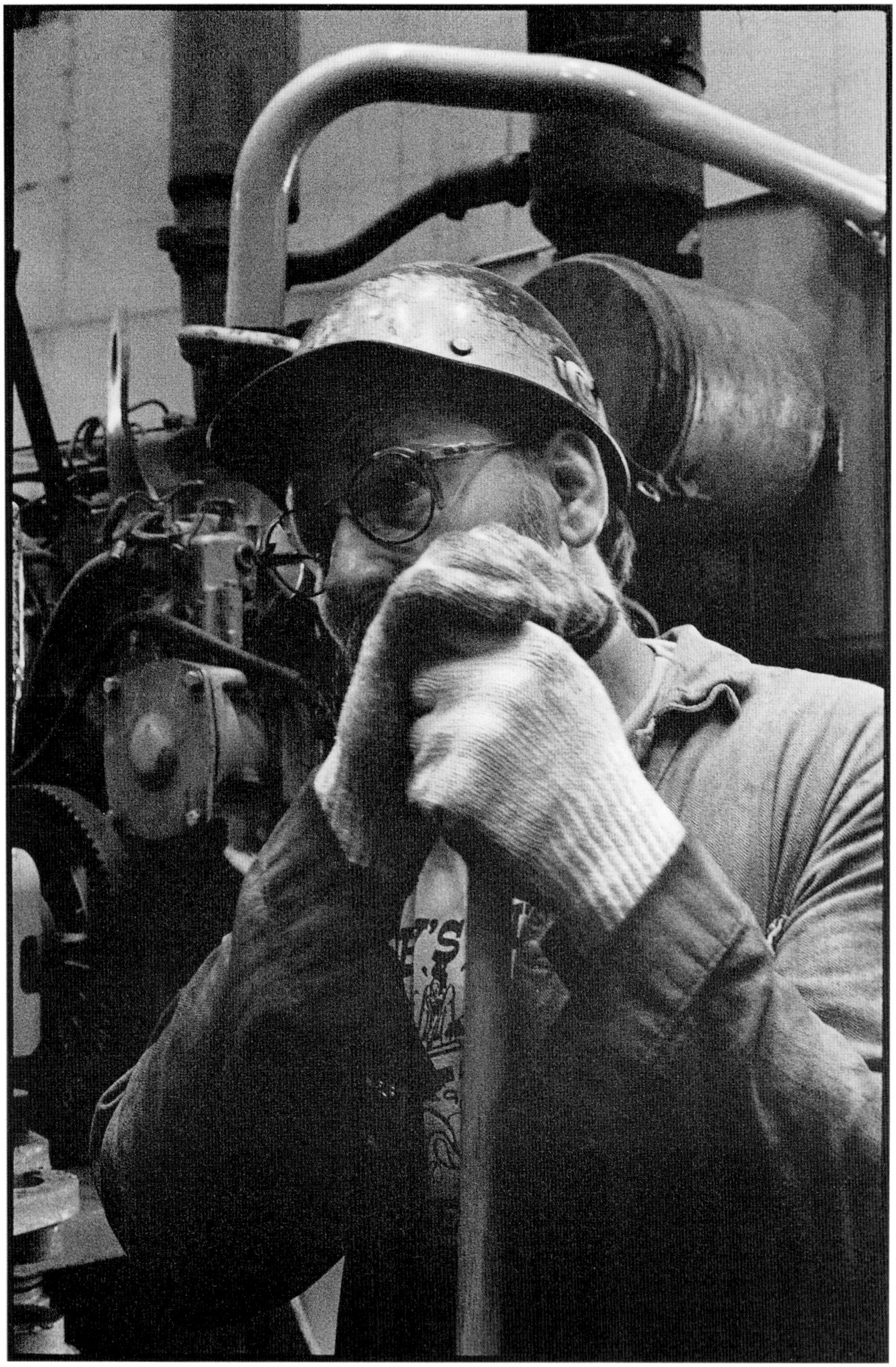

Laborer
Ispat Inland Mining

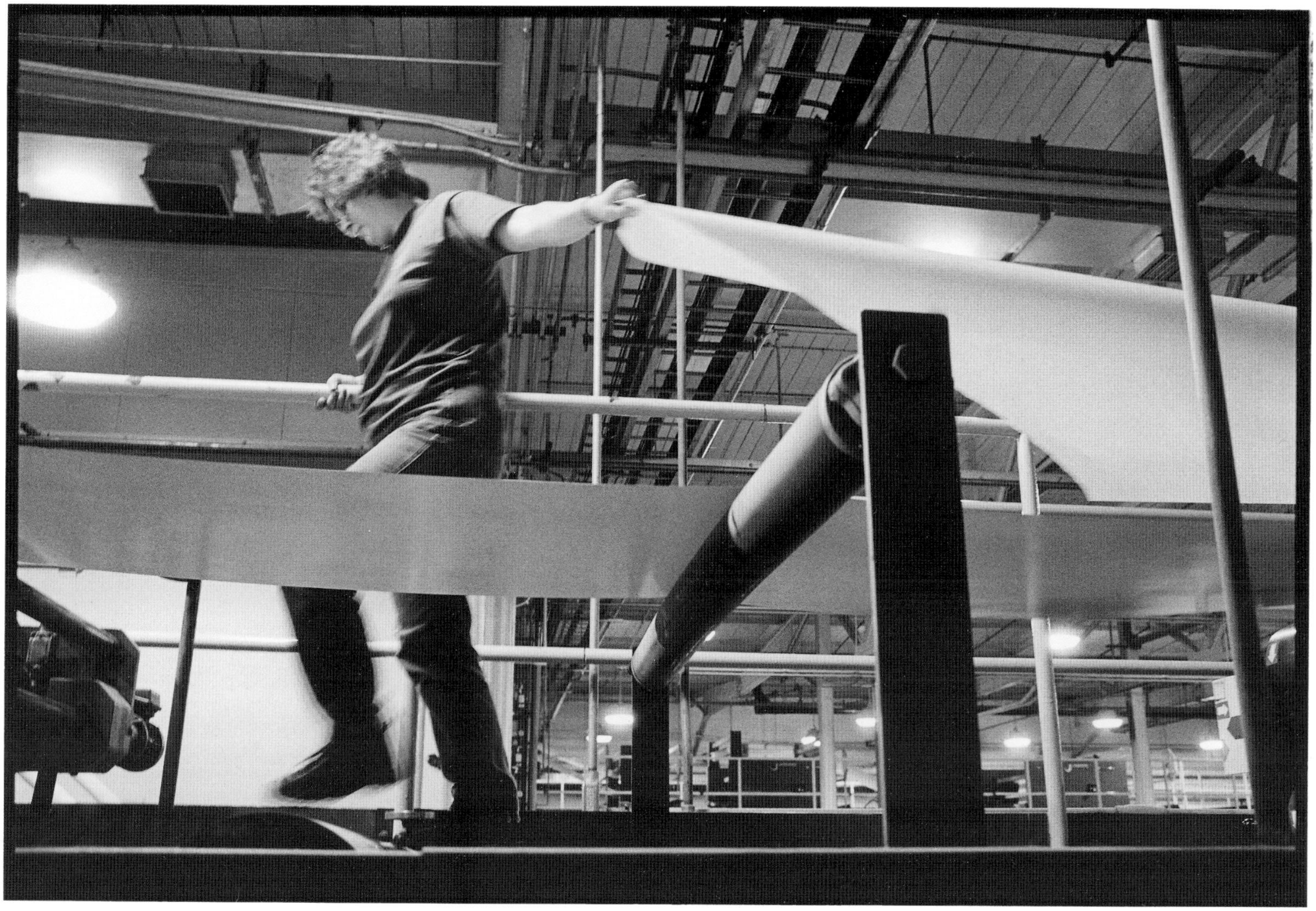

Machine operator
Potlatch

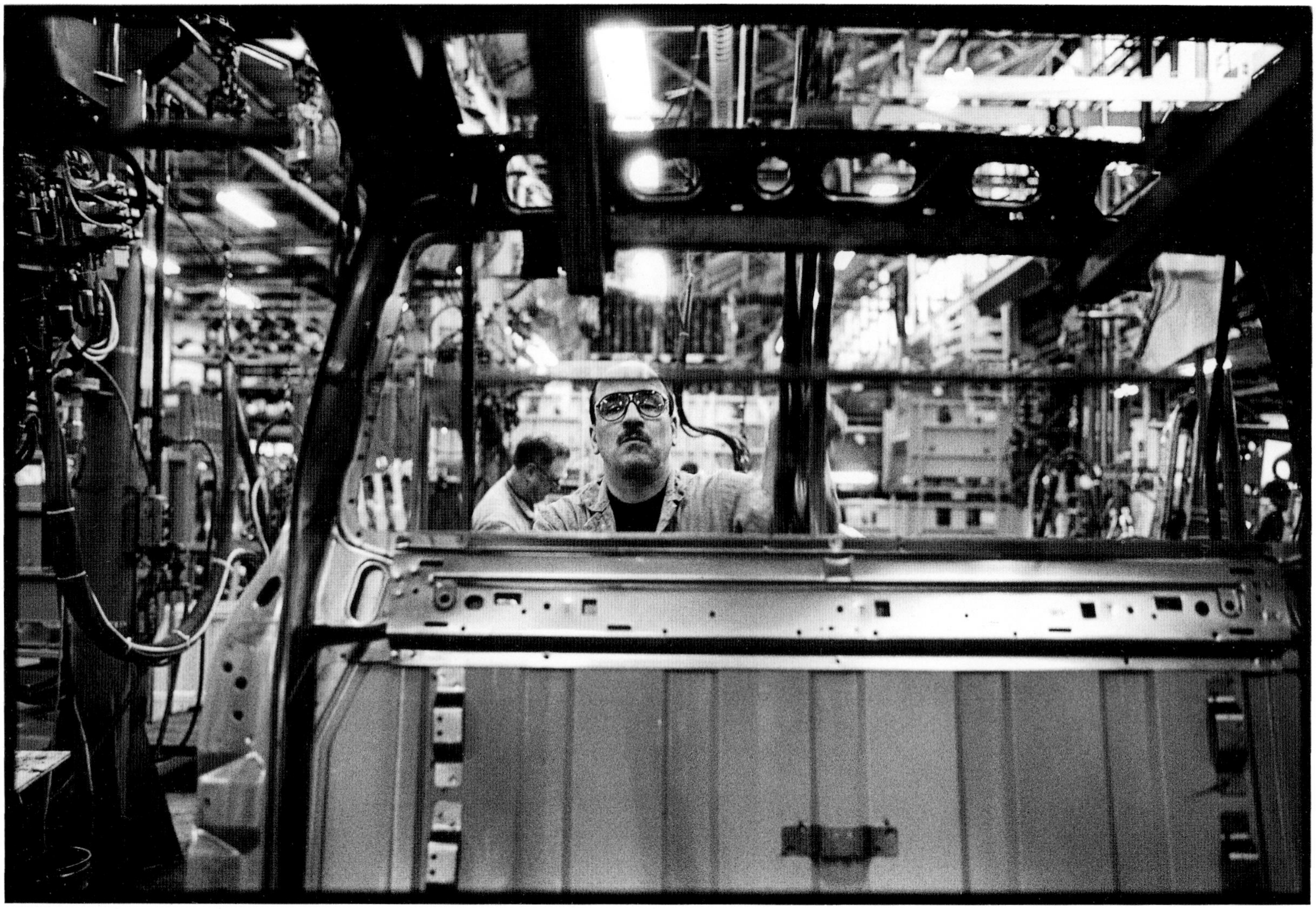

Assembly worker
Ford Motor Company

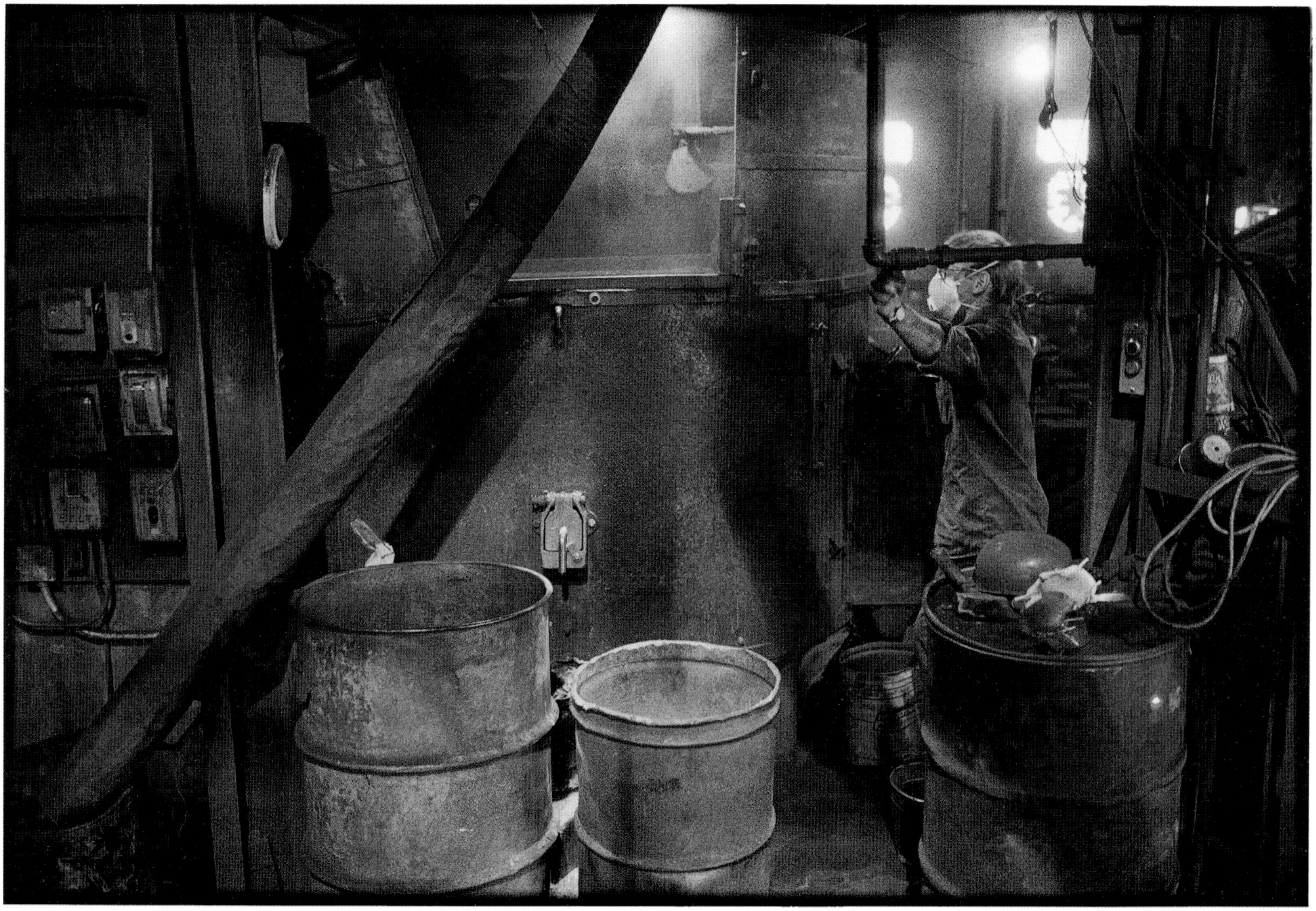

Shakeout
Acme Foundry

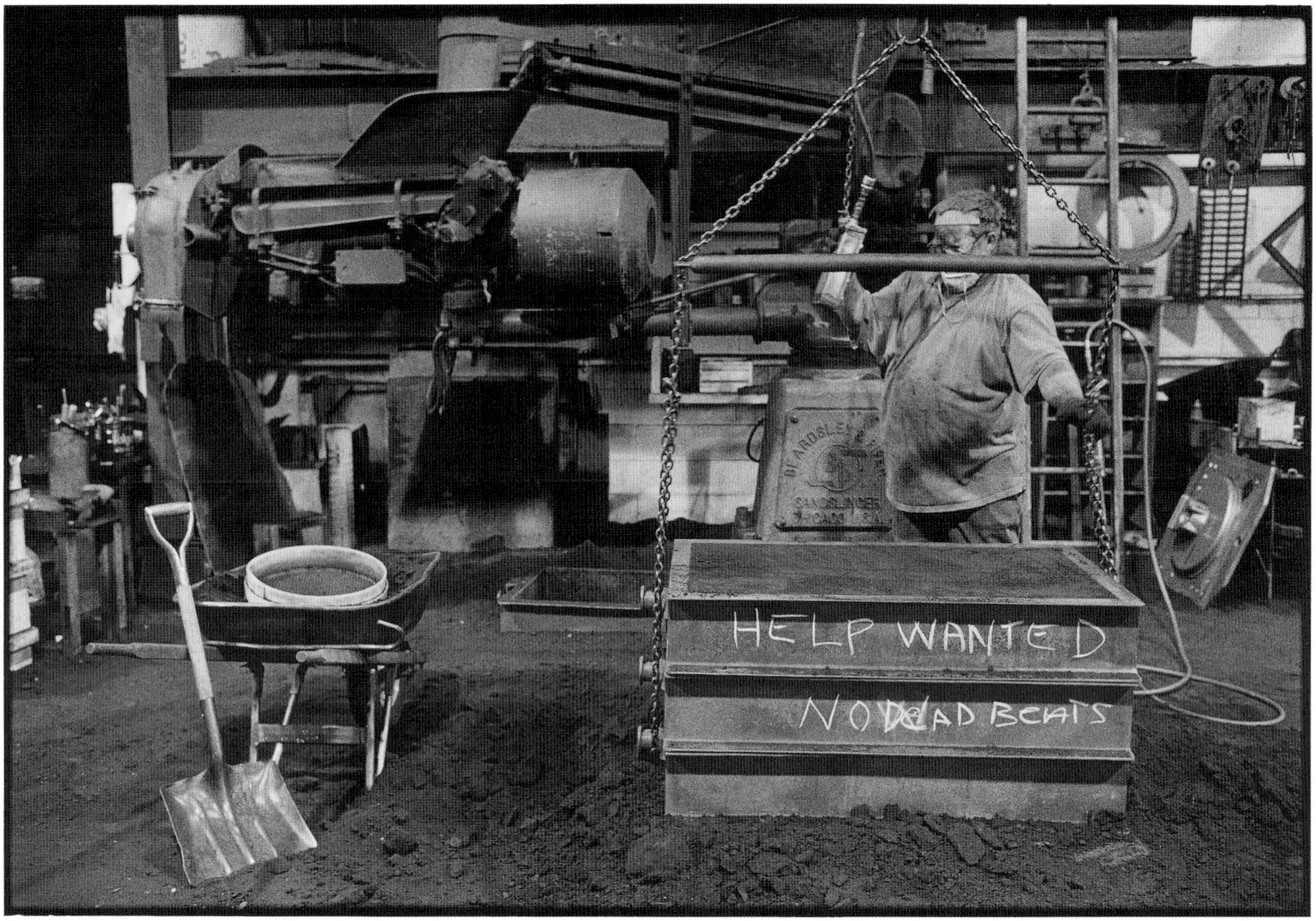

Making molds
Acme Foundry

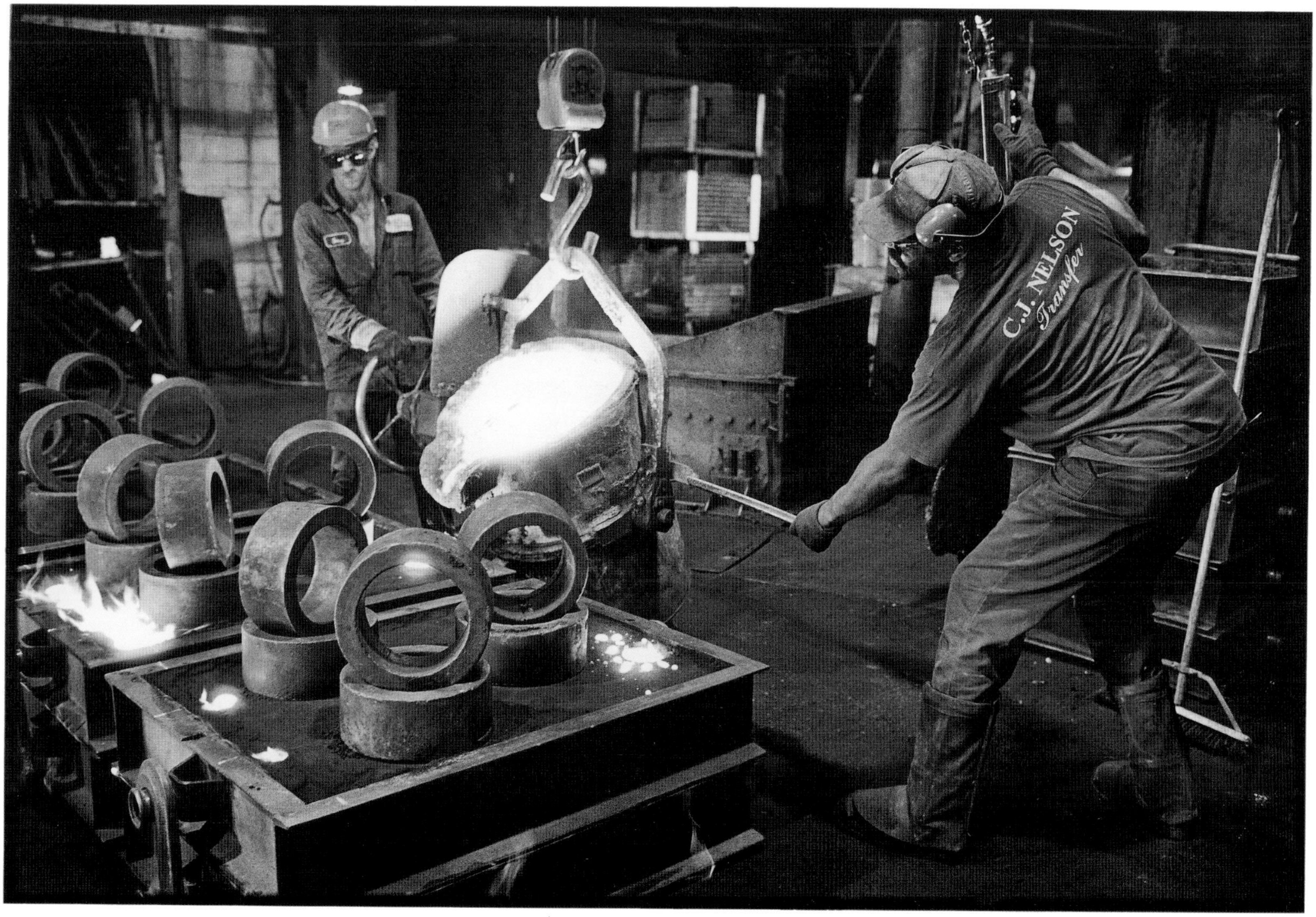

Pouring molten steel
Acme Foundry

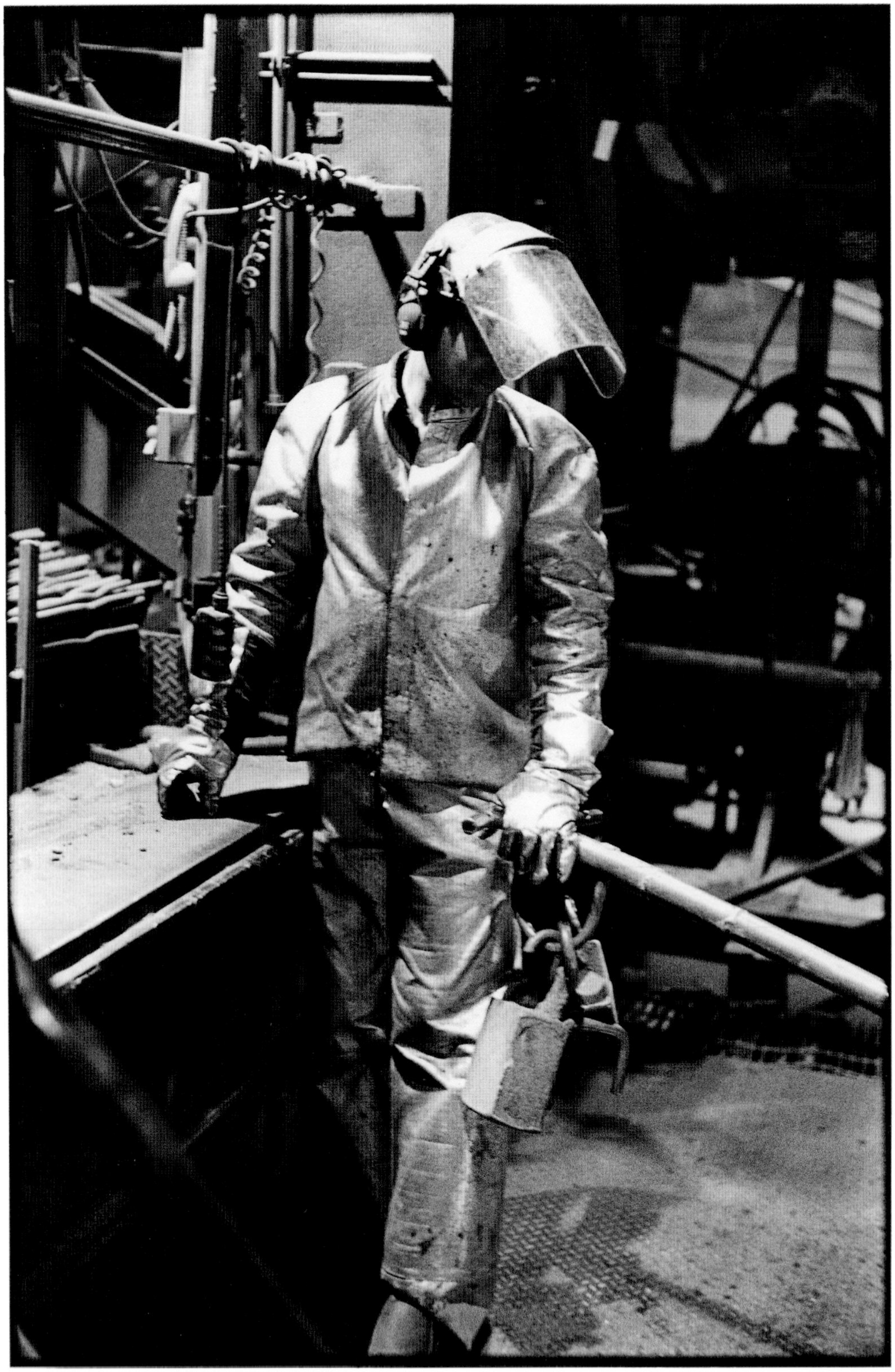

Tending furnace
Northland Steel

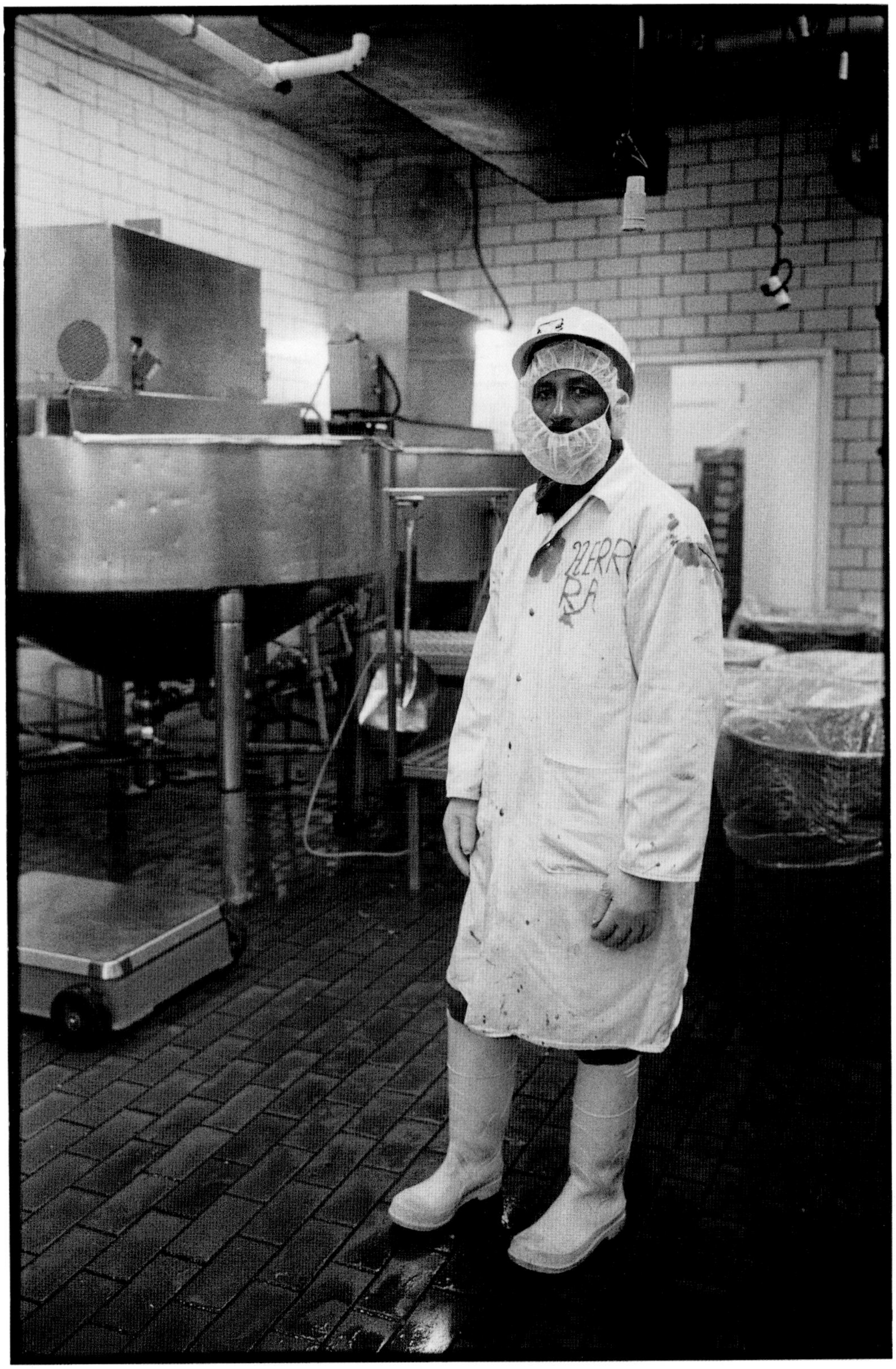

Chili cook room
GFI America

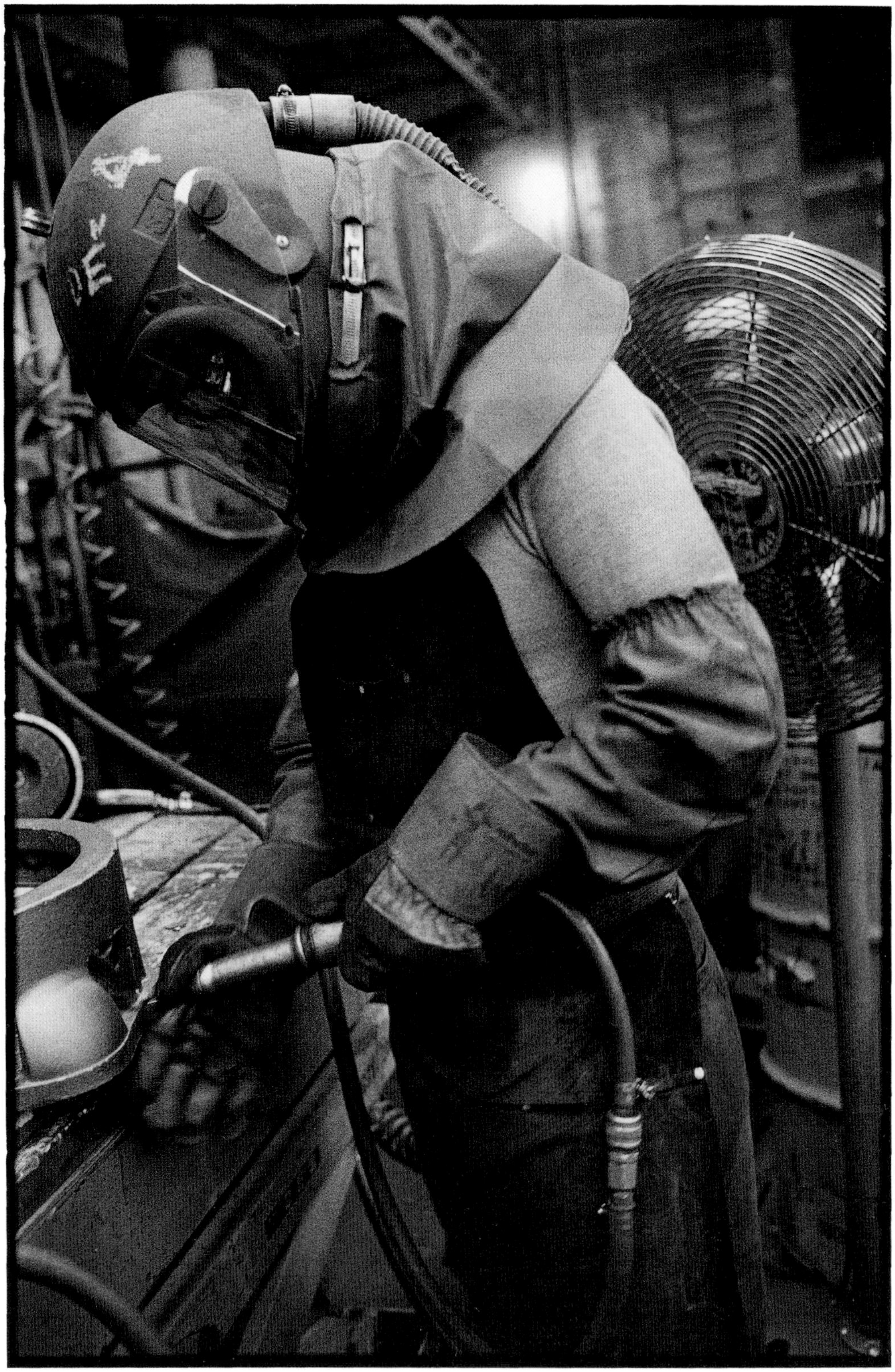

Grinder

Smith Foundry

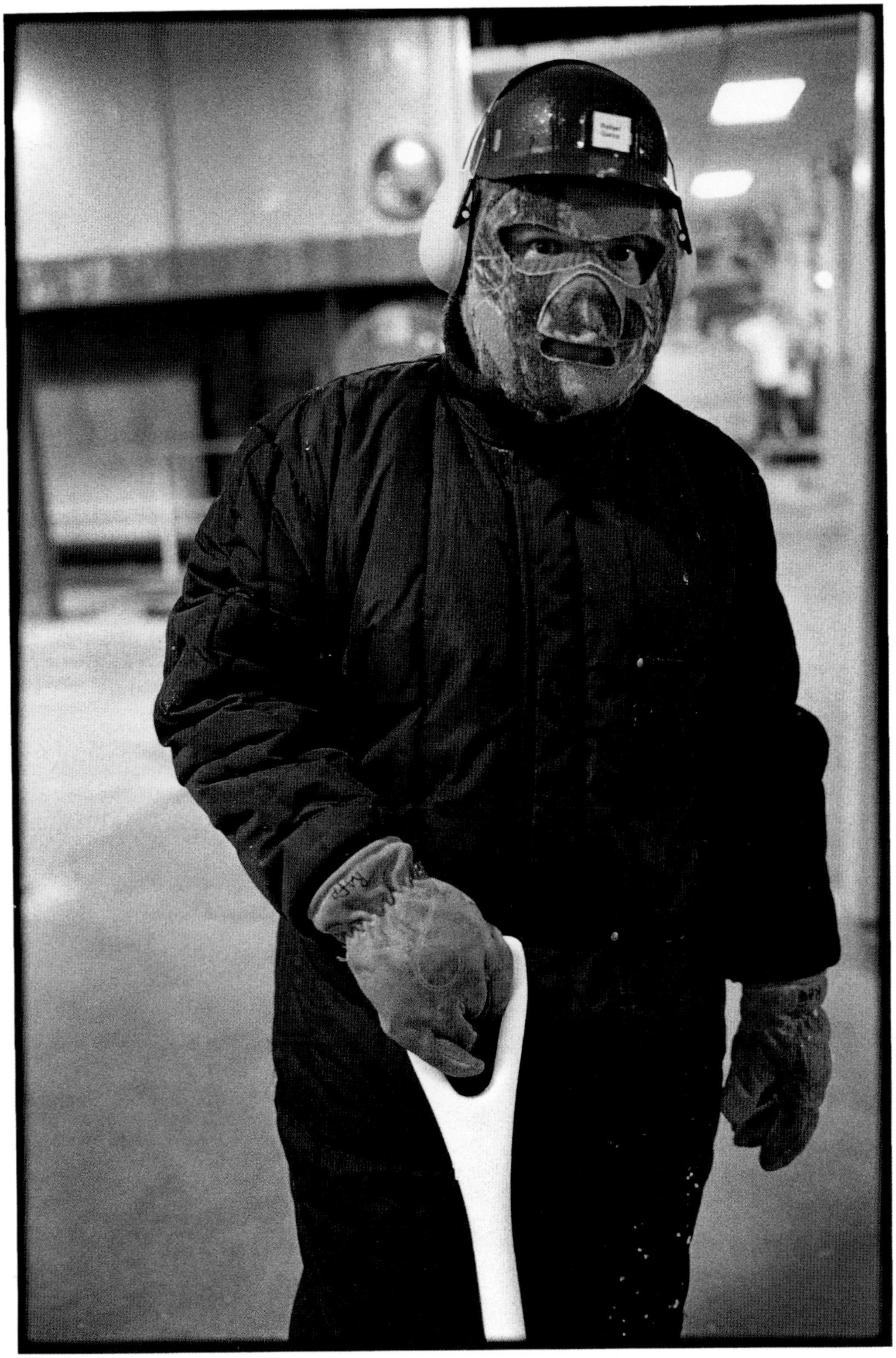

Freezer worker
Agrilink

“As a carpenter I’d put on a hard hat and go on the job site and interview right there with the supervisor. Here I had to get dressed up, make a resume, go in and see somebody that probably doesn’t know how to do the job I was going to do anyway and I don’t know how to do it. And from that point you get to go and see the supervisor. A whole new way of doing things.”

CHARLES OSTERFELD
ROSEMOUNT ENGINEERING

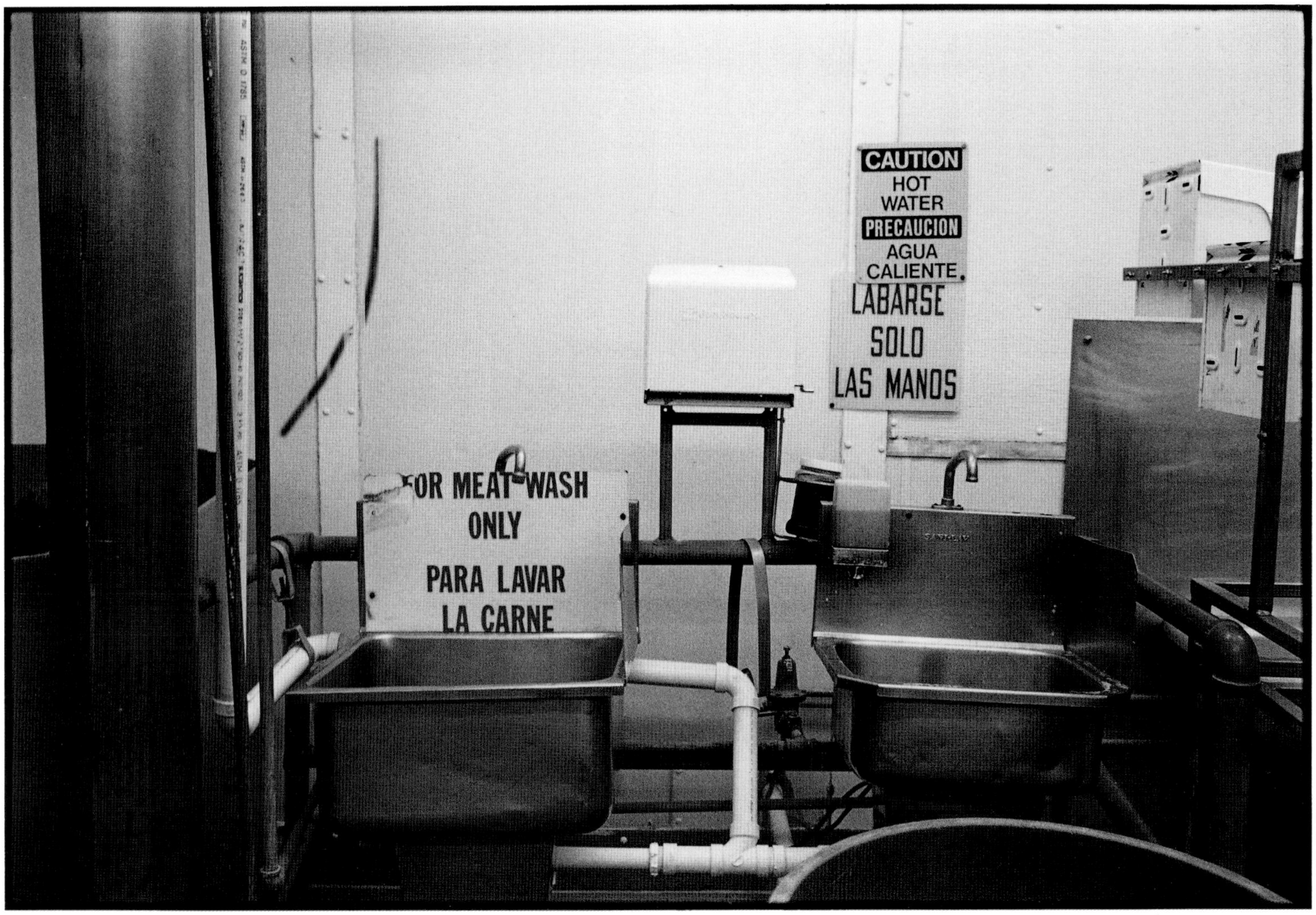

Sinks

GFI America

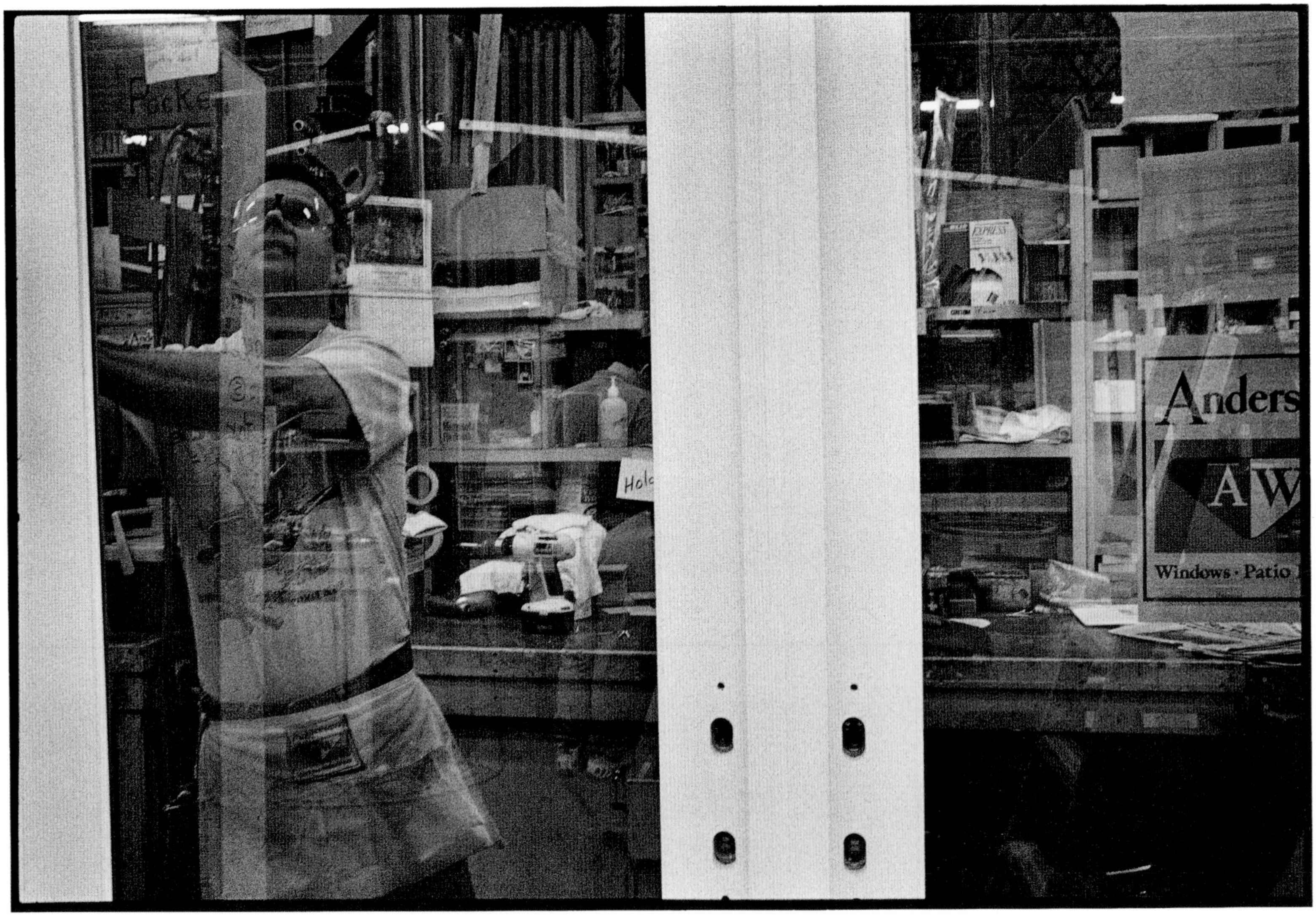

Window assembly
Andersen Window

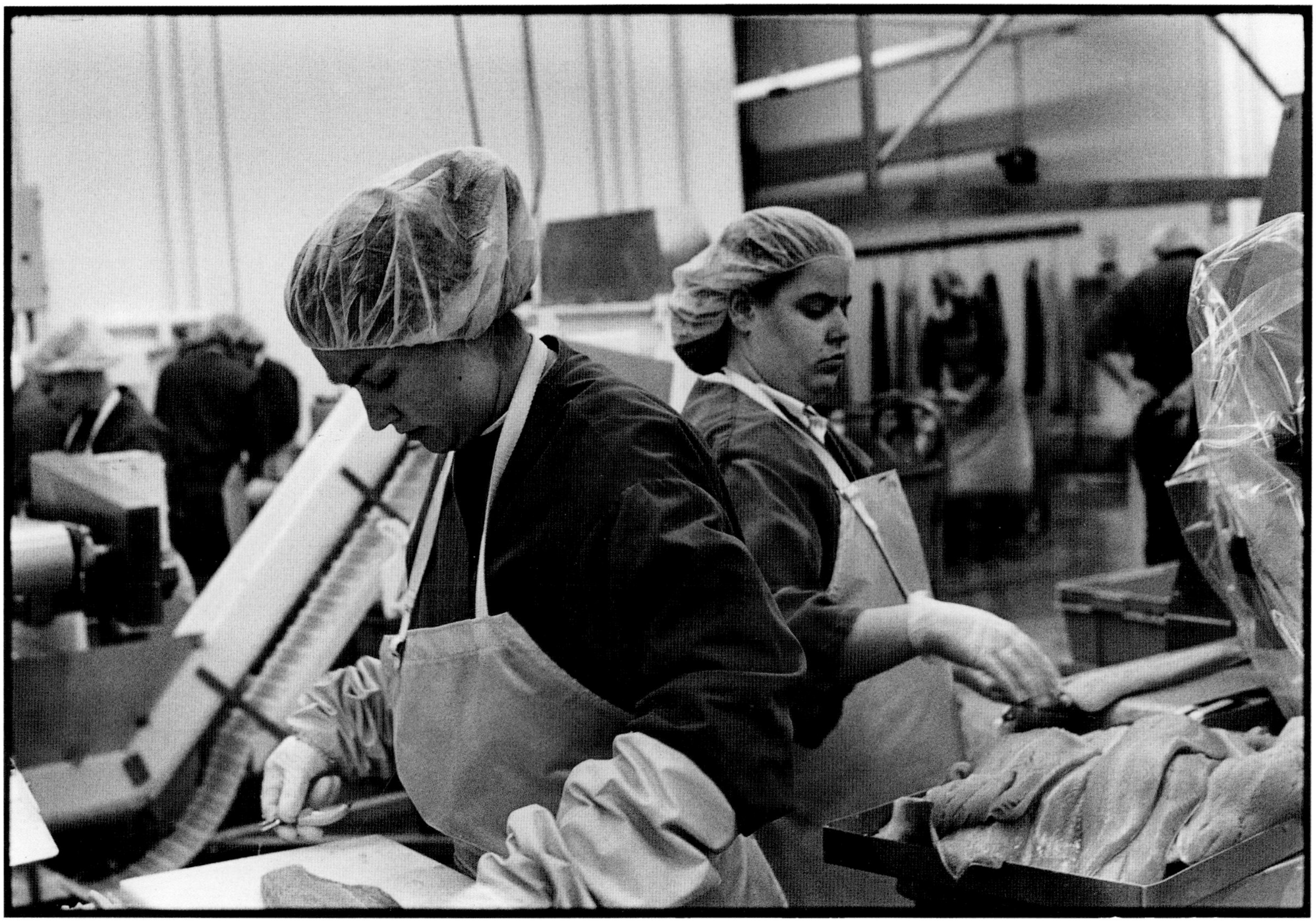

Weighing fish
Morey's Seafood

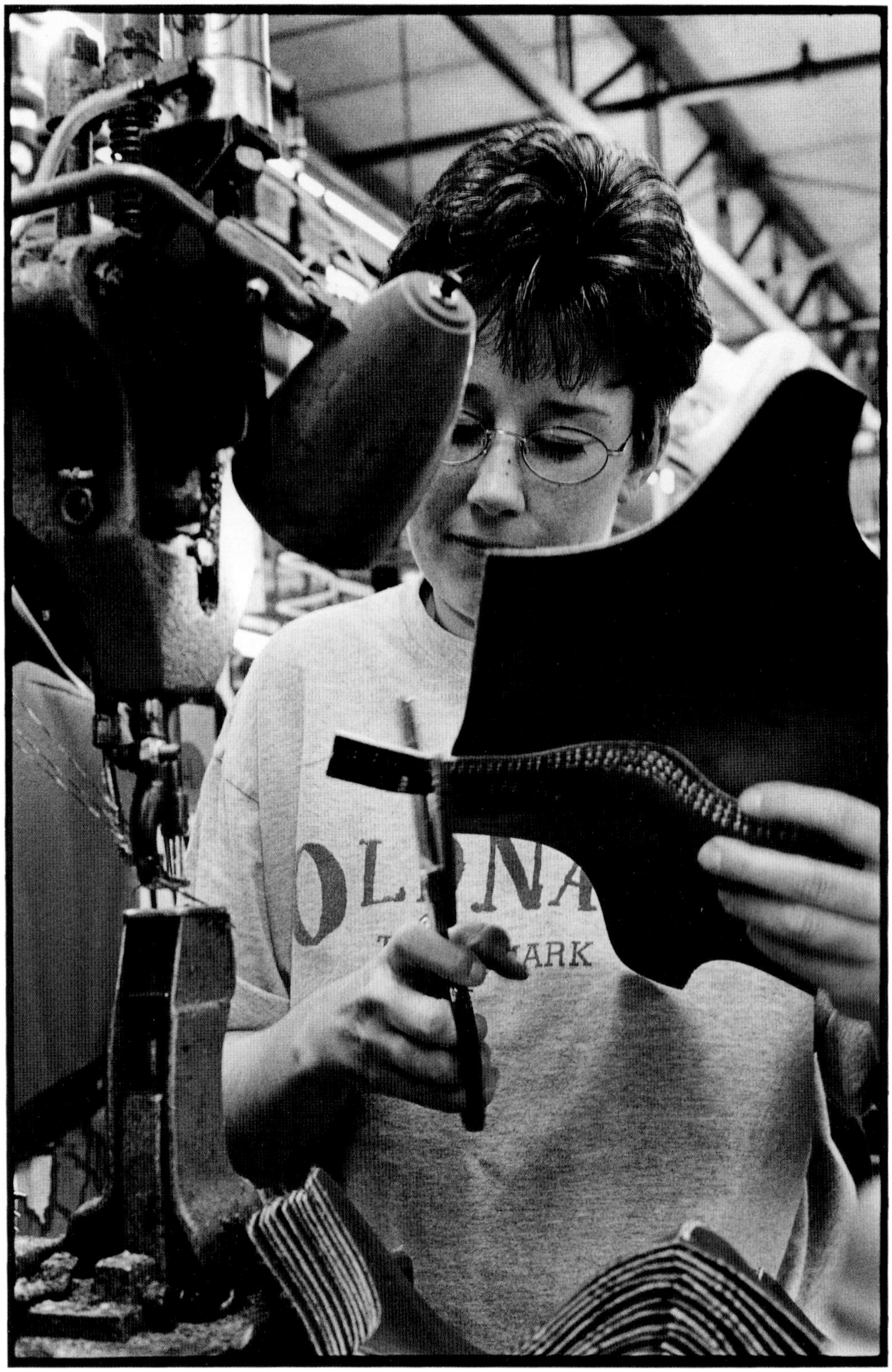

Cutting shoe pattern
Red Wing Shoe

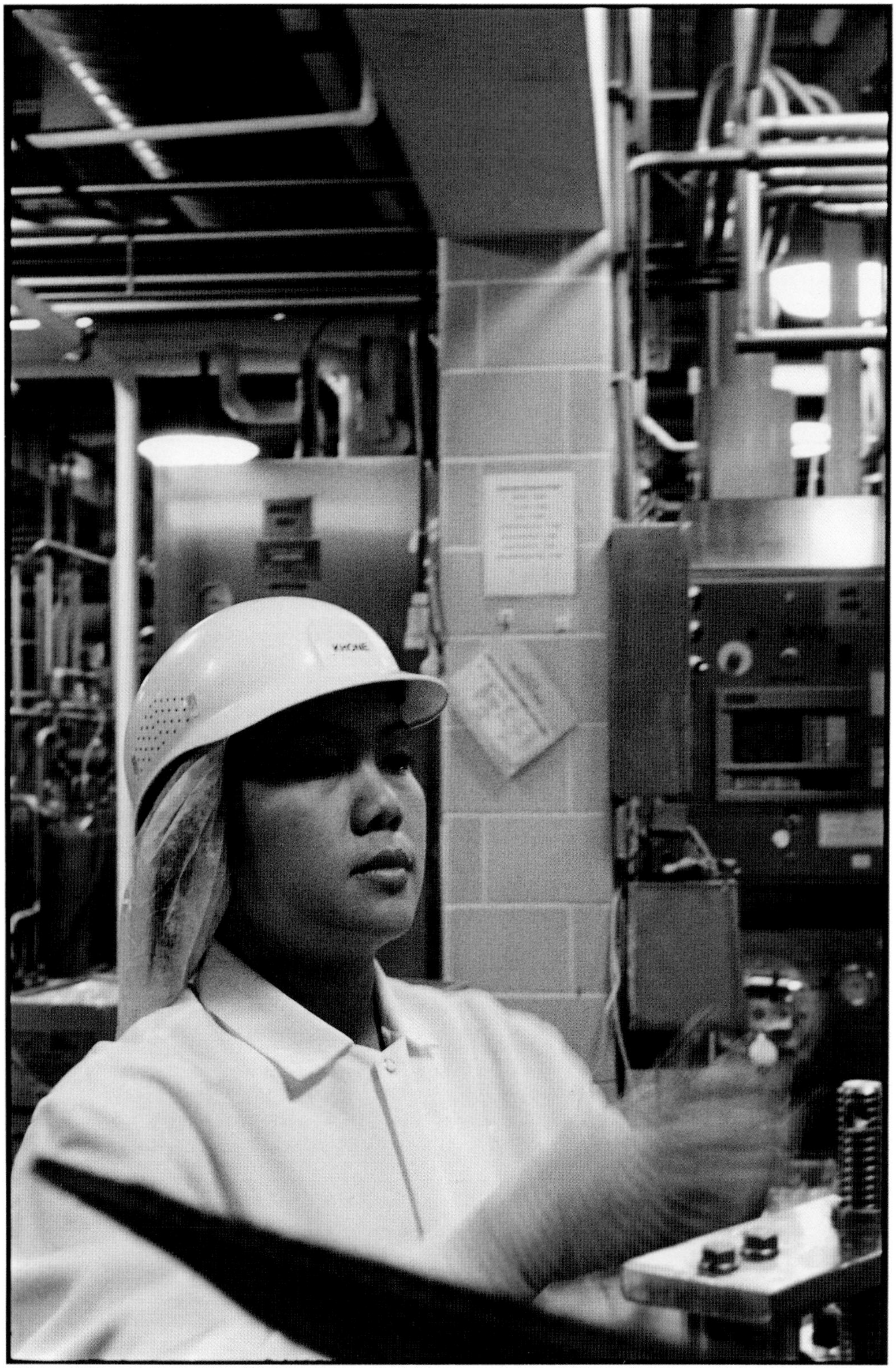

Ice cream maker
Schwan's

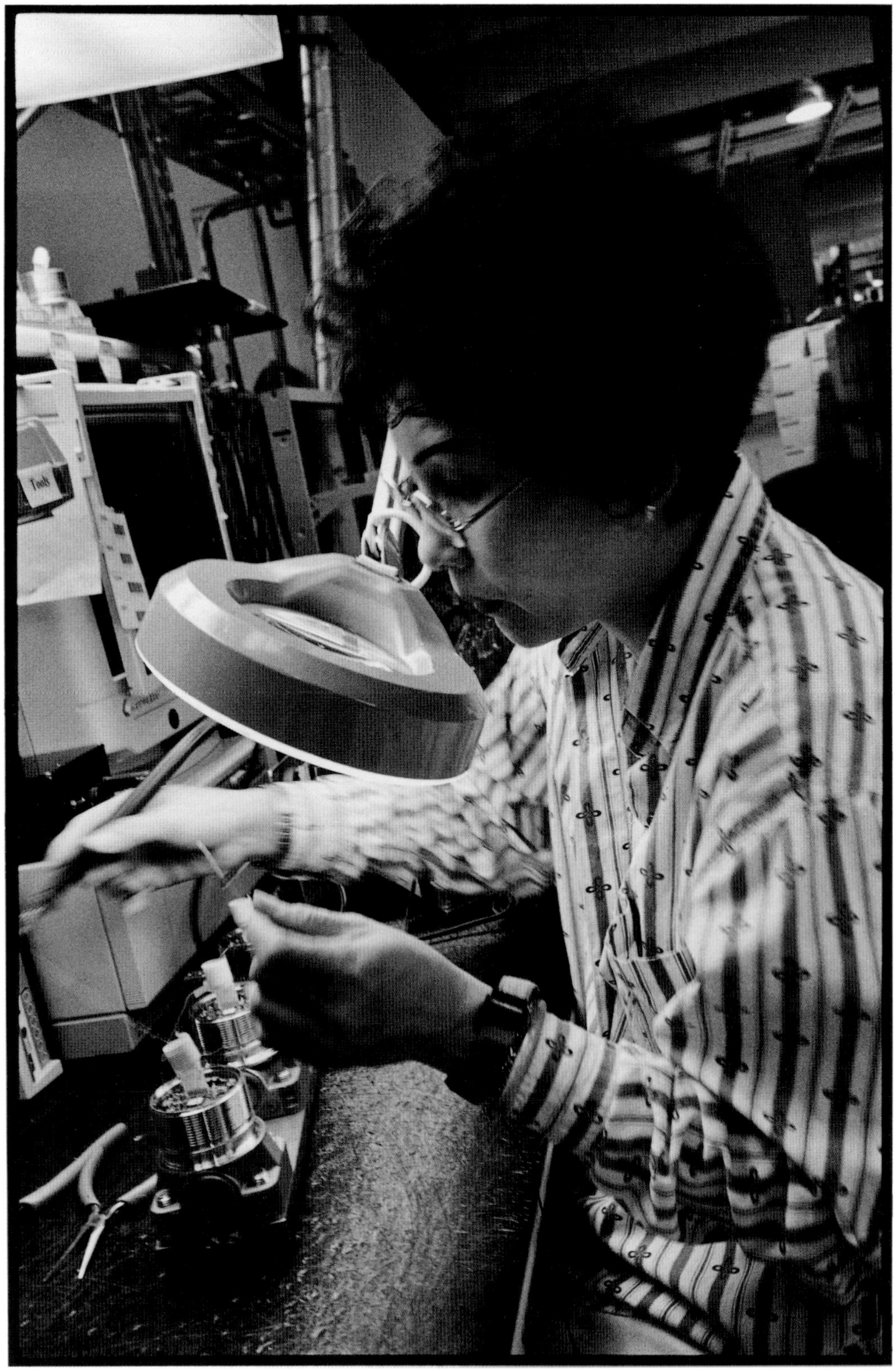

Parts assembly
Rosemount Engineering

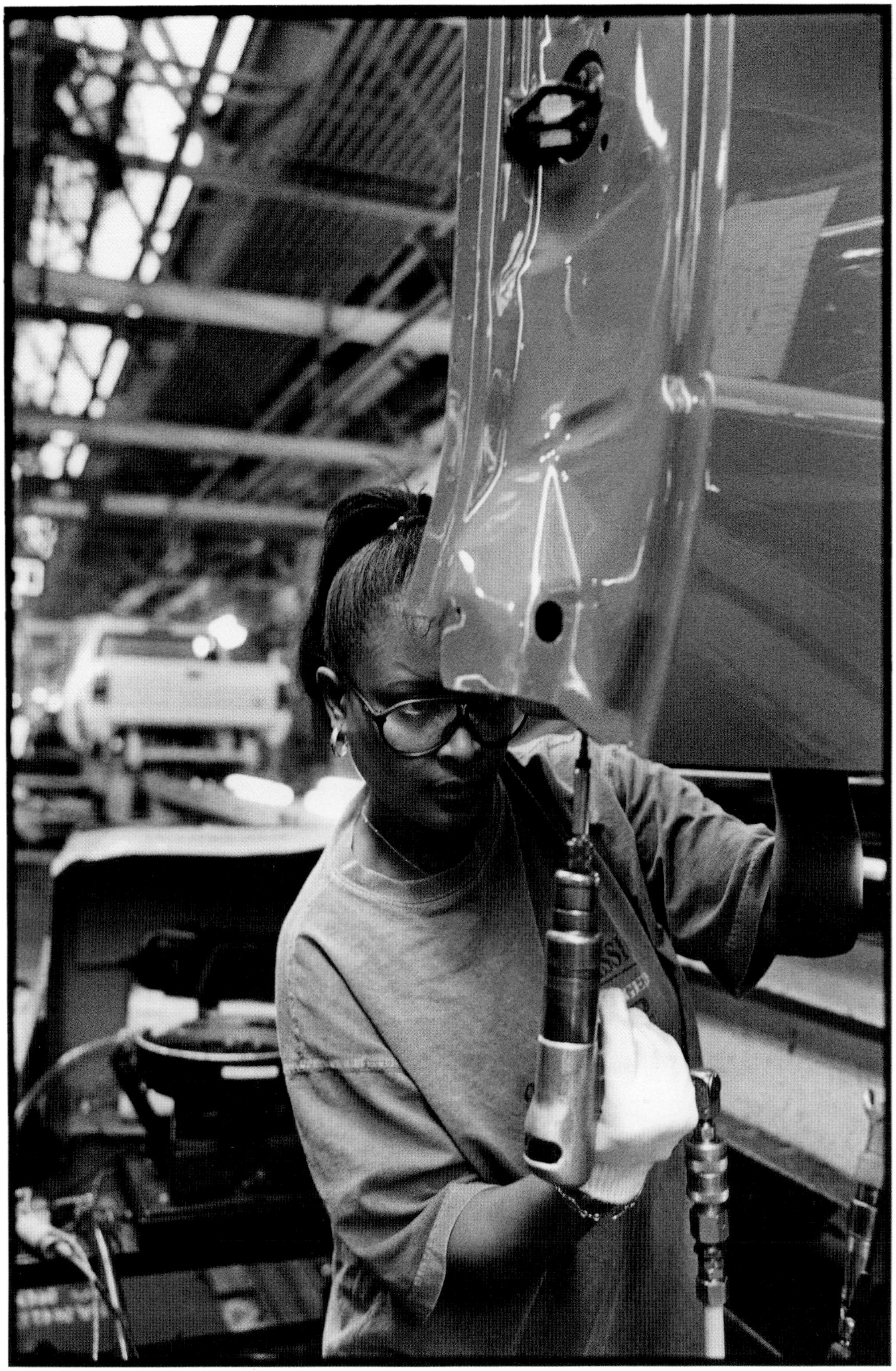

Truck assembly
Ford Motor Company

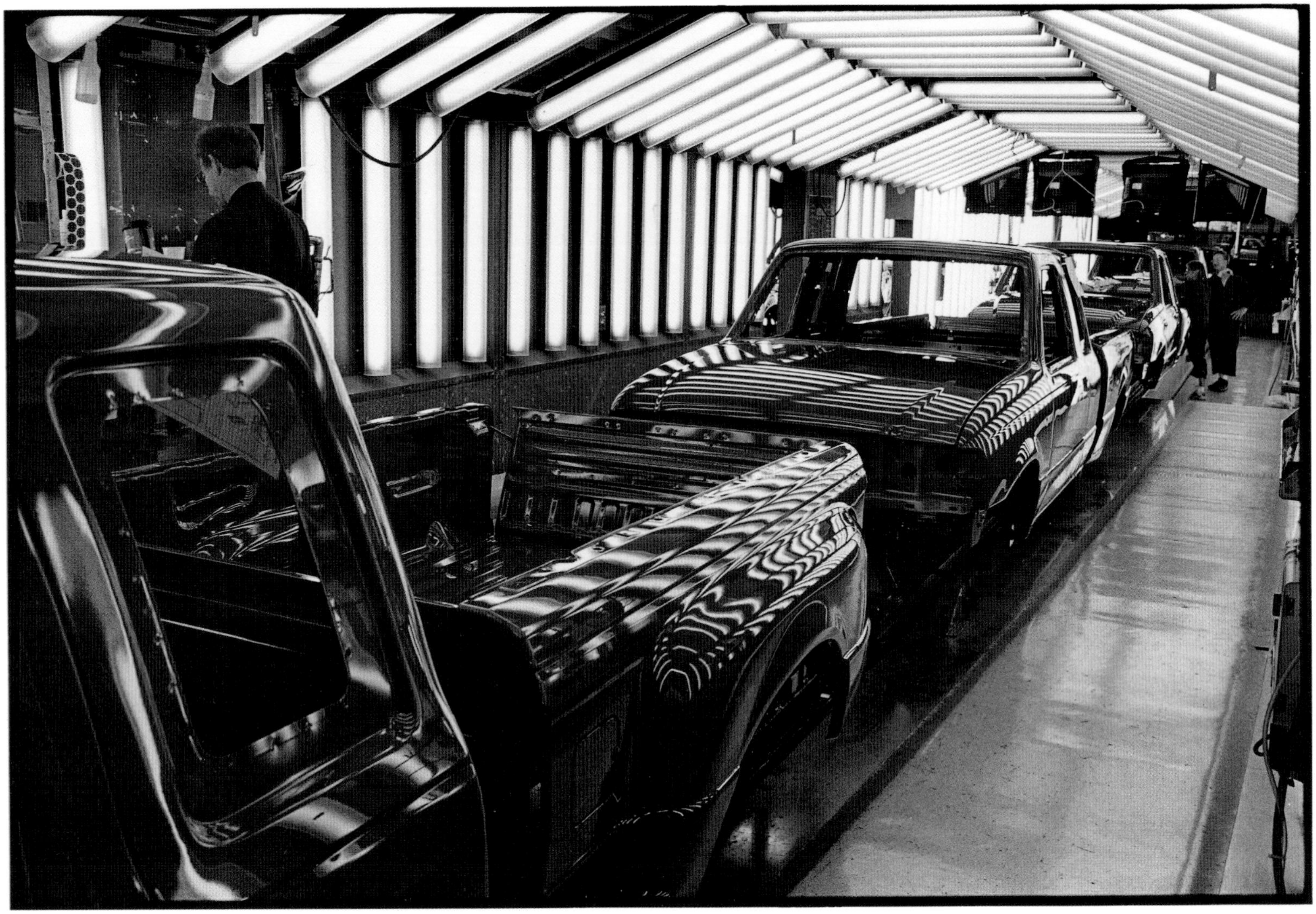

Inspection booth
Ford Motor Company

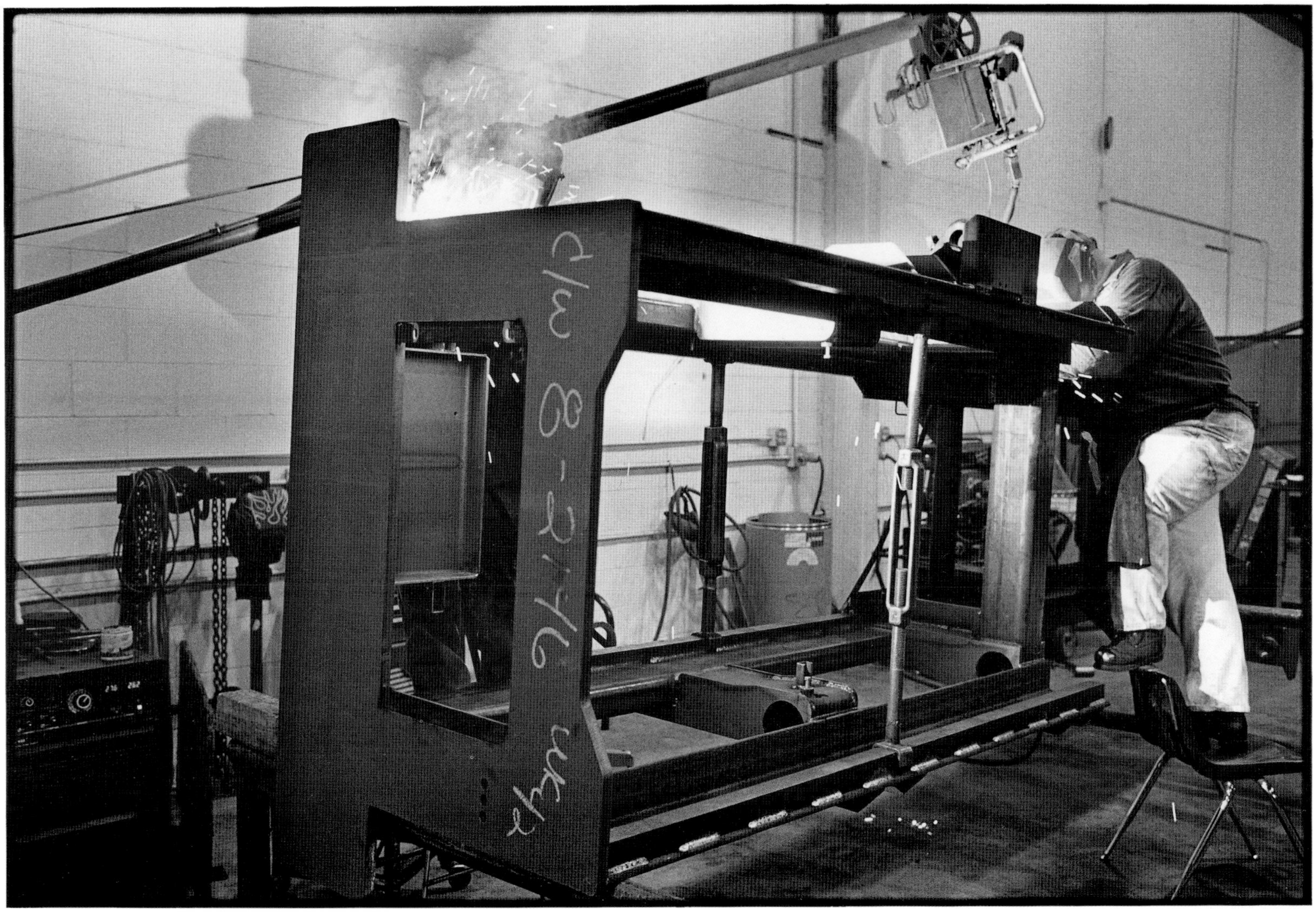

Welder
Lull International

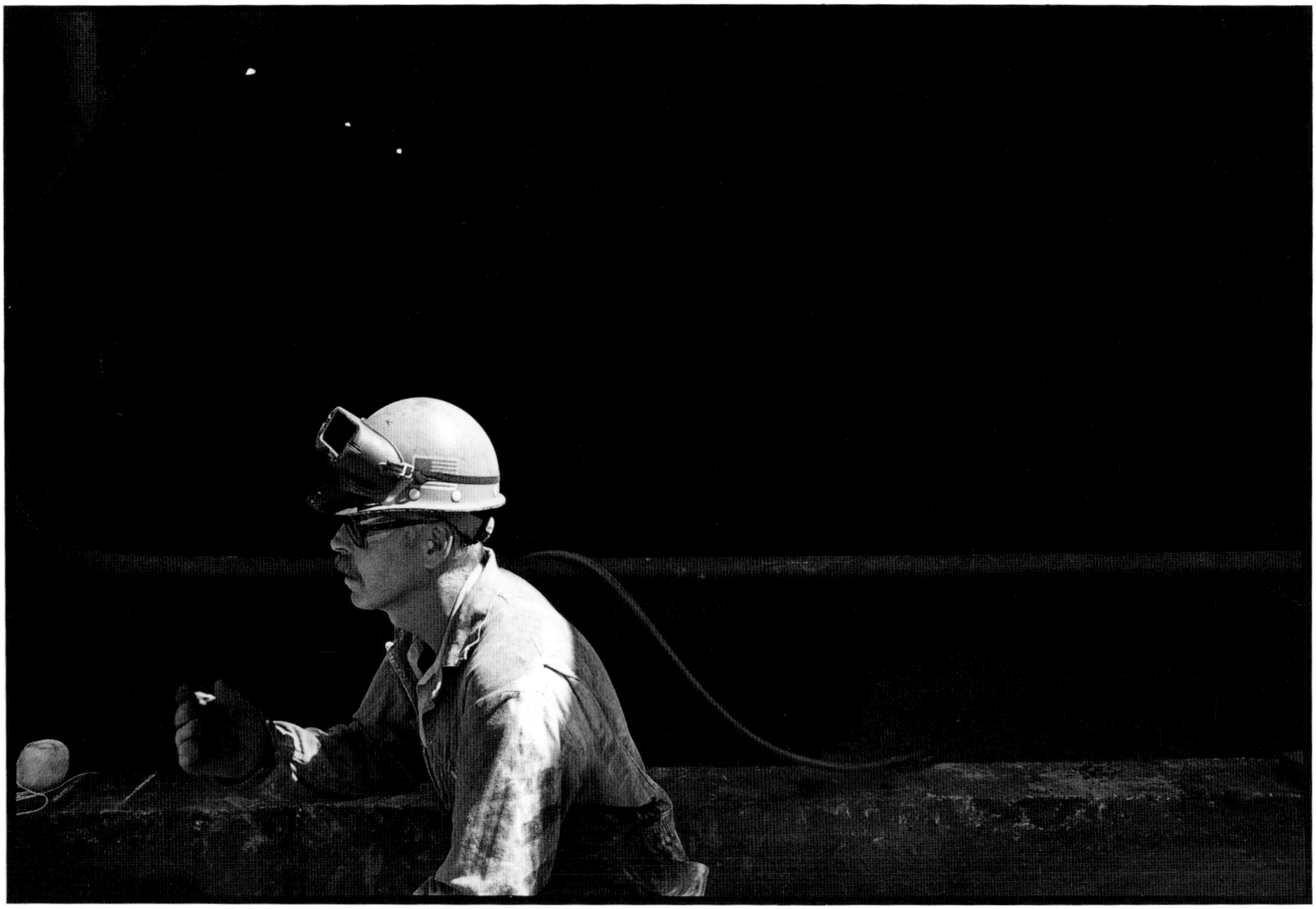

Night shift
Ispat Inland Mining

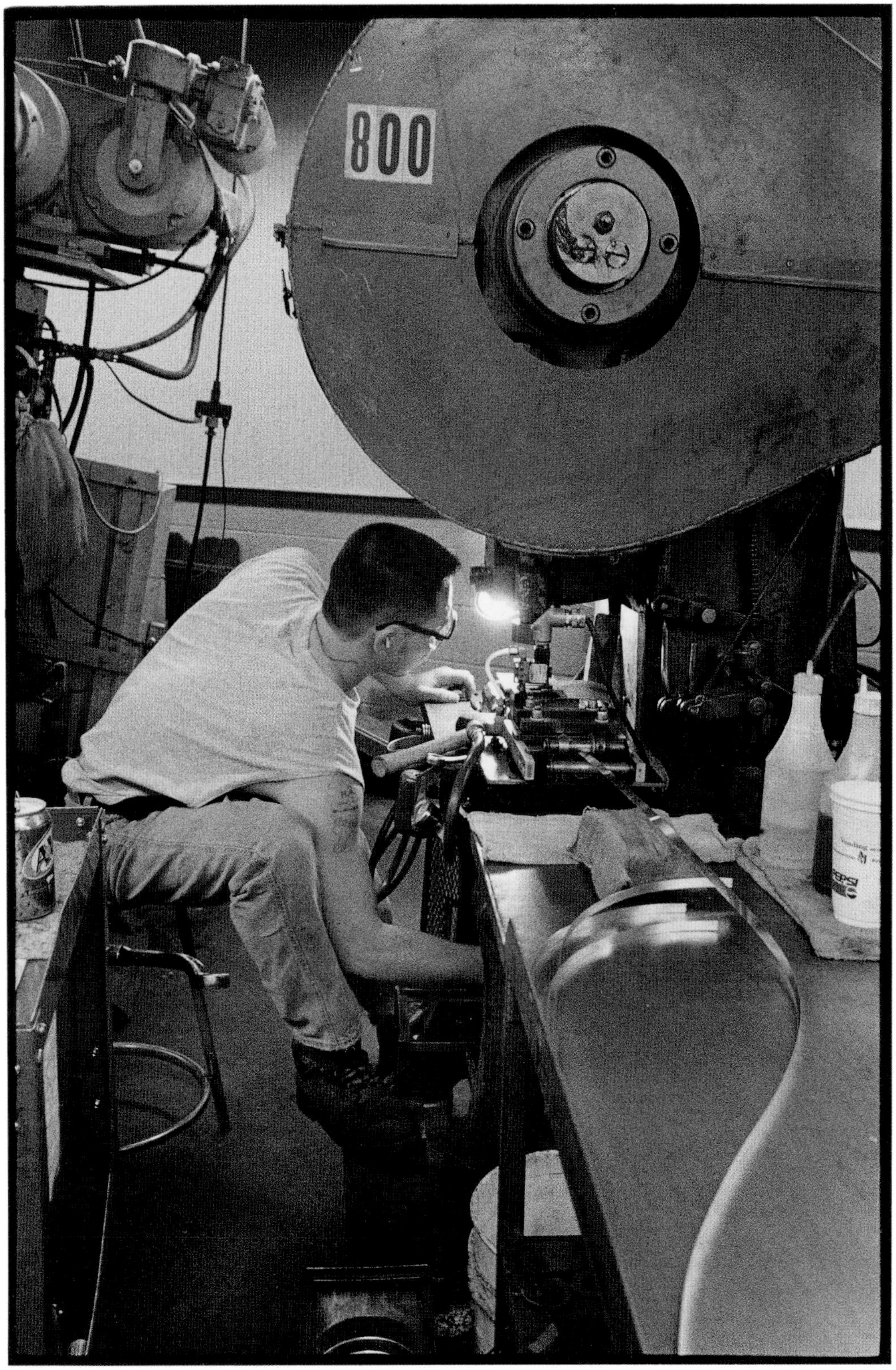

Stamping-machine operator
Boker's

"We have a lot of women working in manufacturing and they have to juggle between childcare and working. A lot of women come to work every day just so they can have the insurance. A lot of the people on the floor come to work so that they can have the health-care insurance for their children. A lot of their wages just go to childcare. Some of the facilities in town open up at 6:00, a lot of the women have to be here at 6:05, 6:10, 6:15."

JANE QUADE
RED WING SHOE

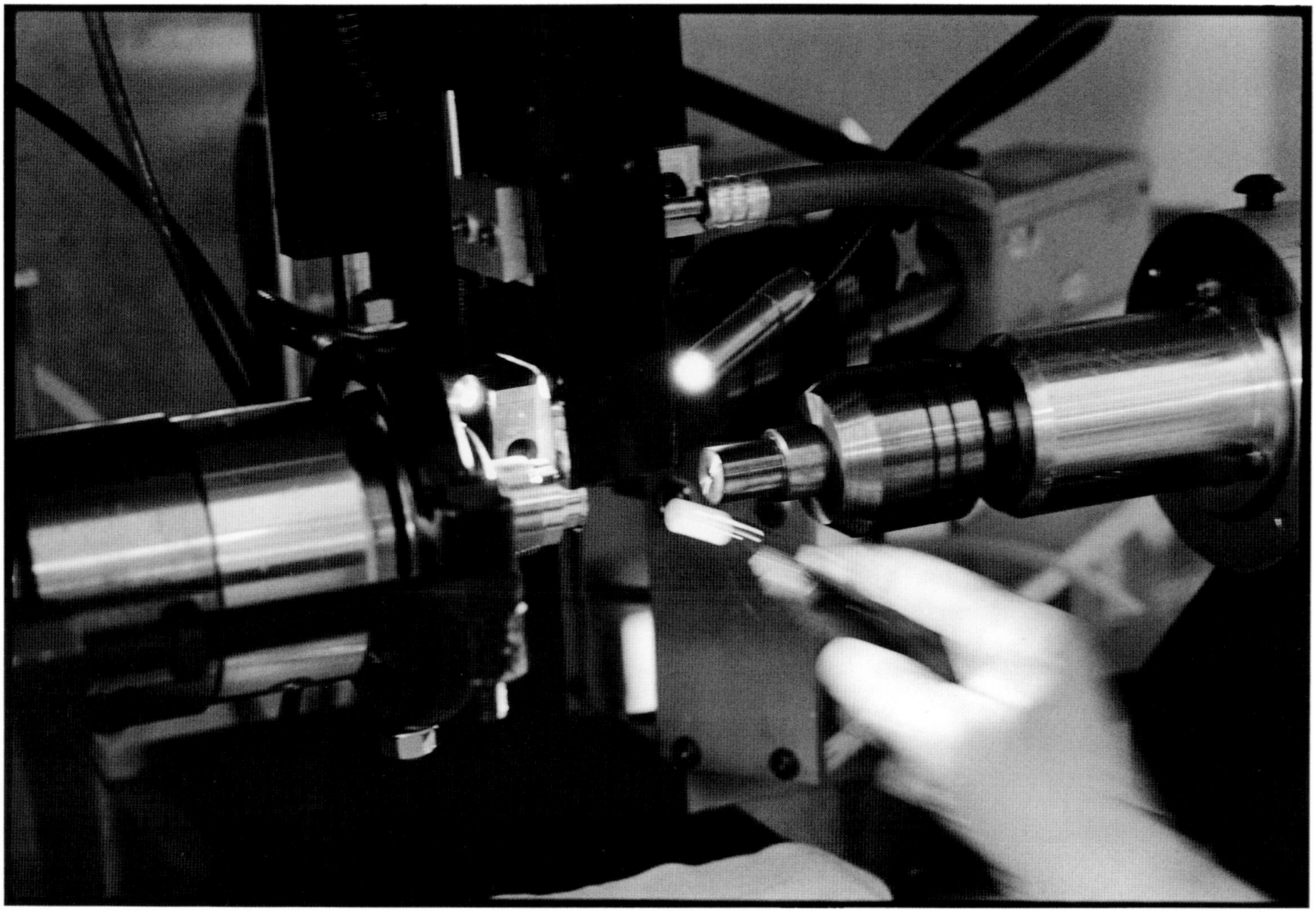

Fabricating parts
Rosemount Engineering

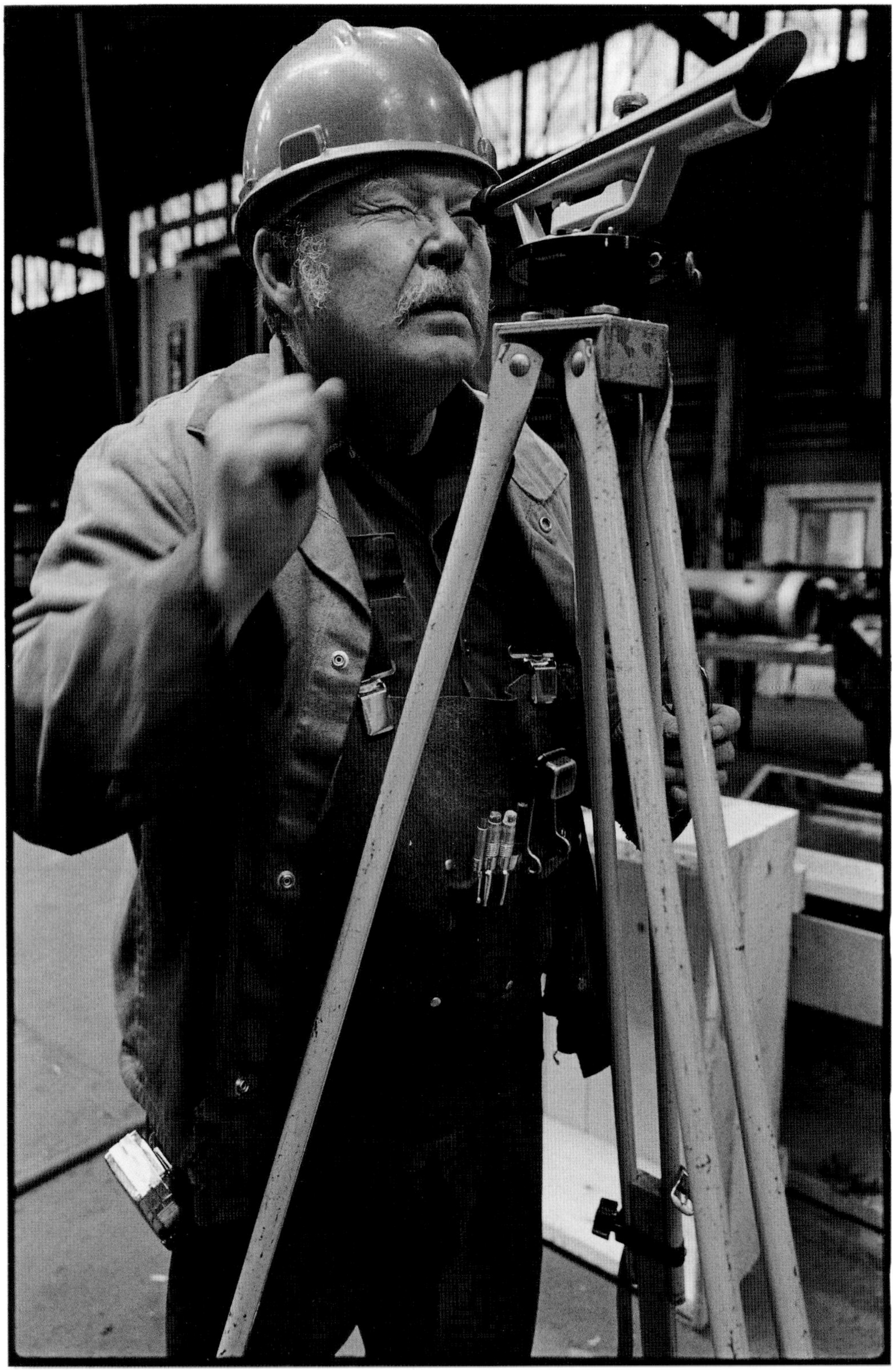

Measuring pipes
BendTec

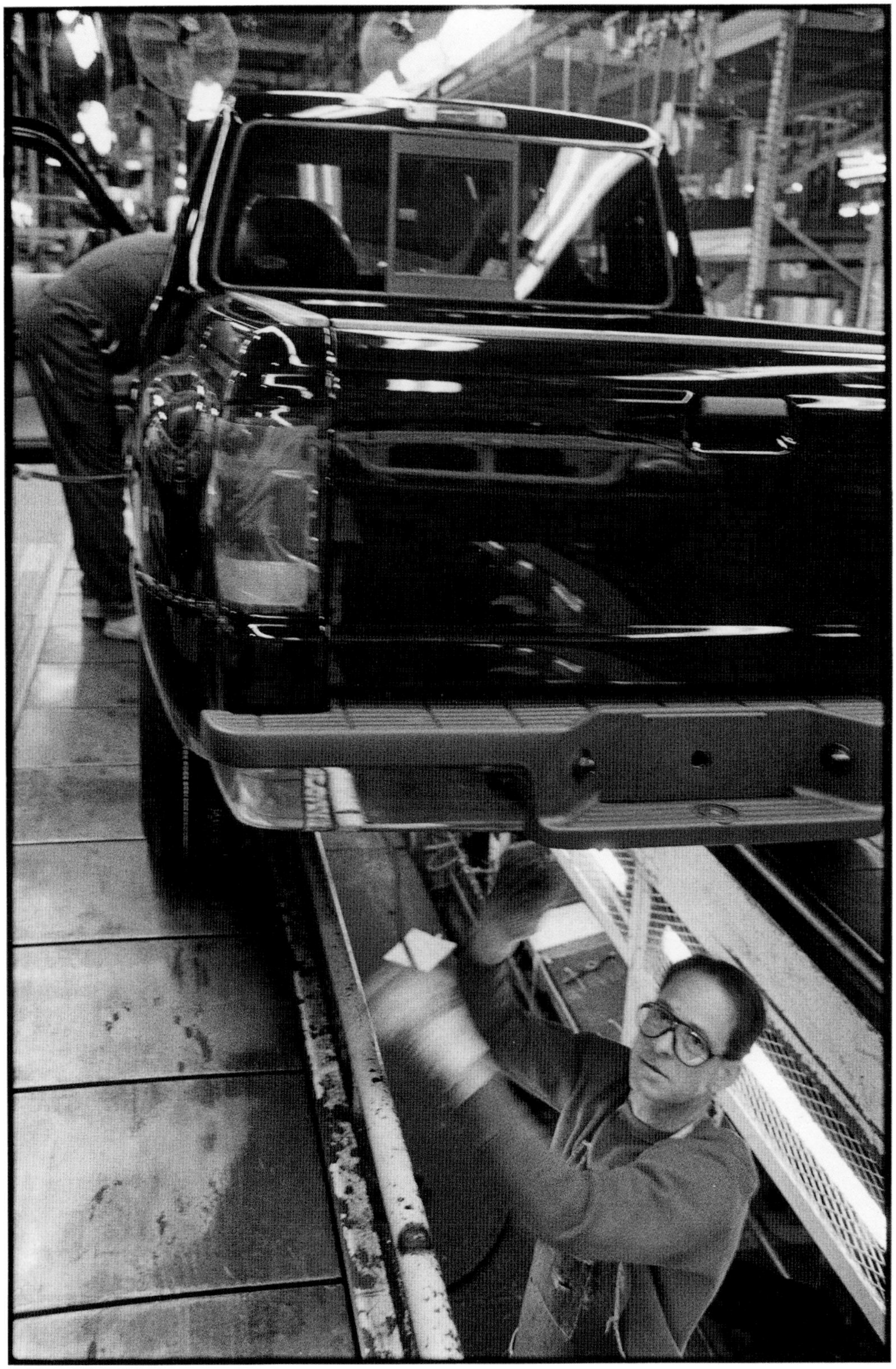

Truck assembly
Ford Motor Company

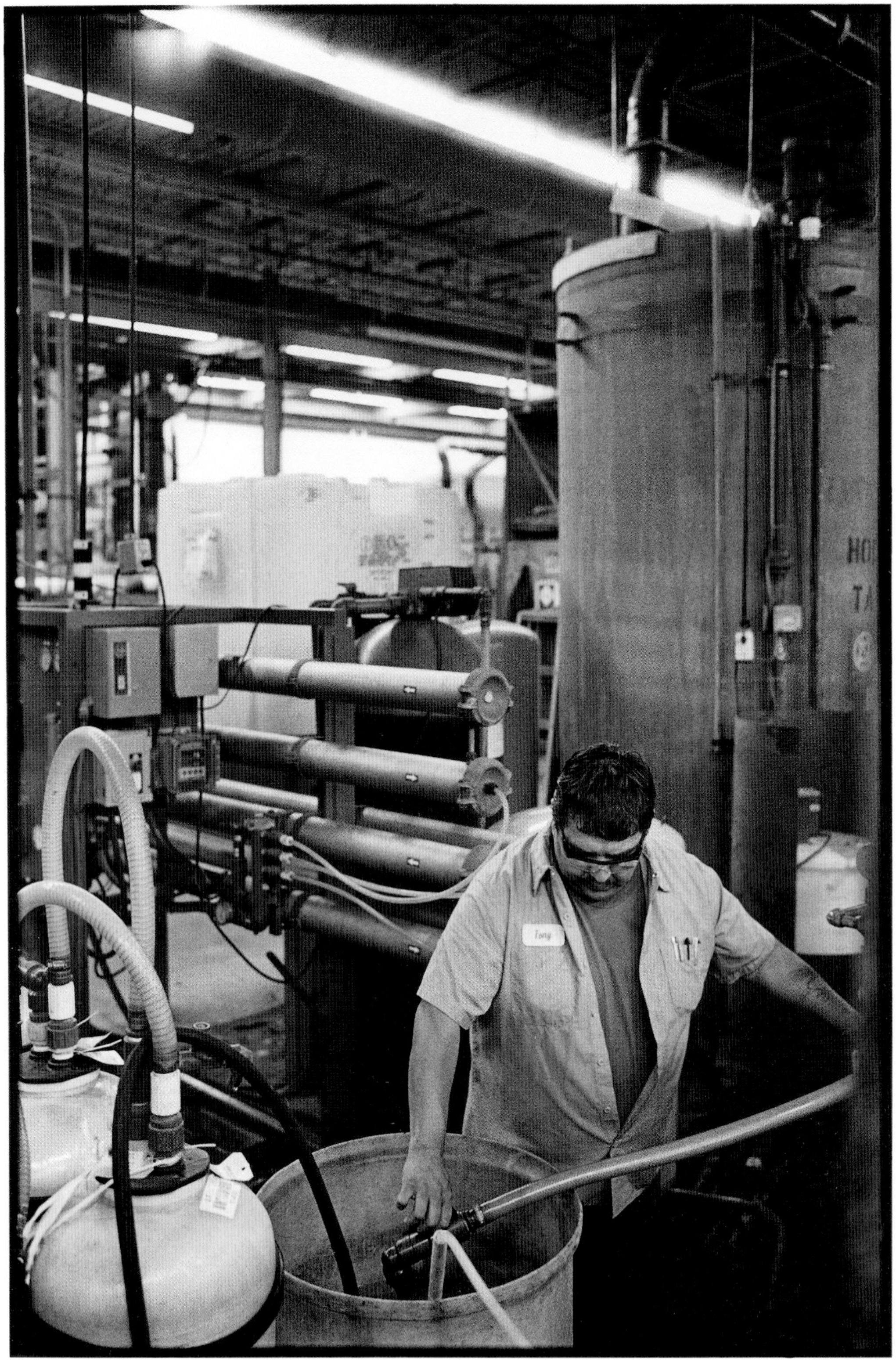

Measuring electroplate solution
Nico Products

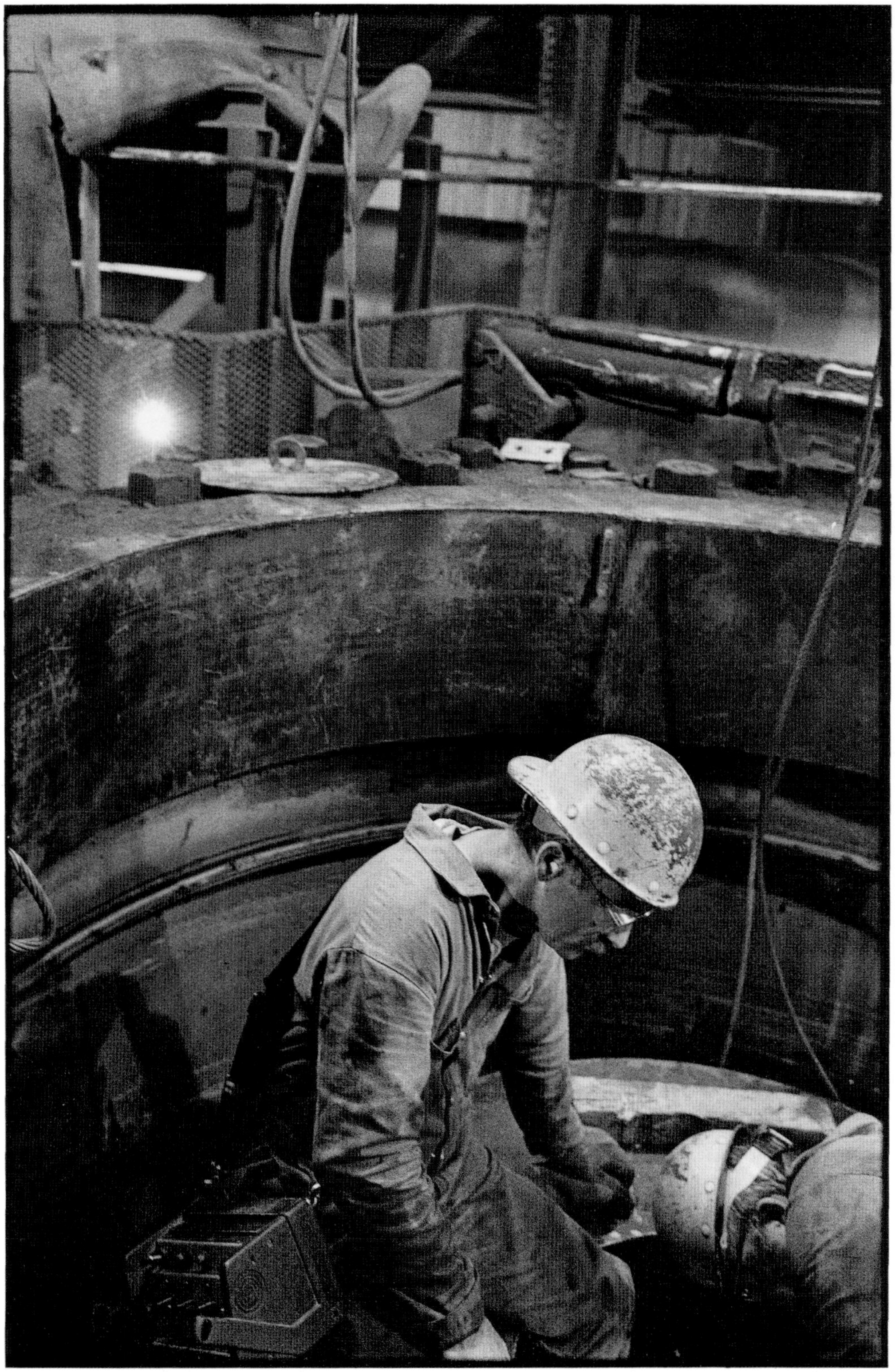

Machine repair
Ispat Inland Mining

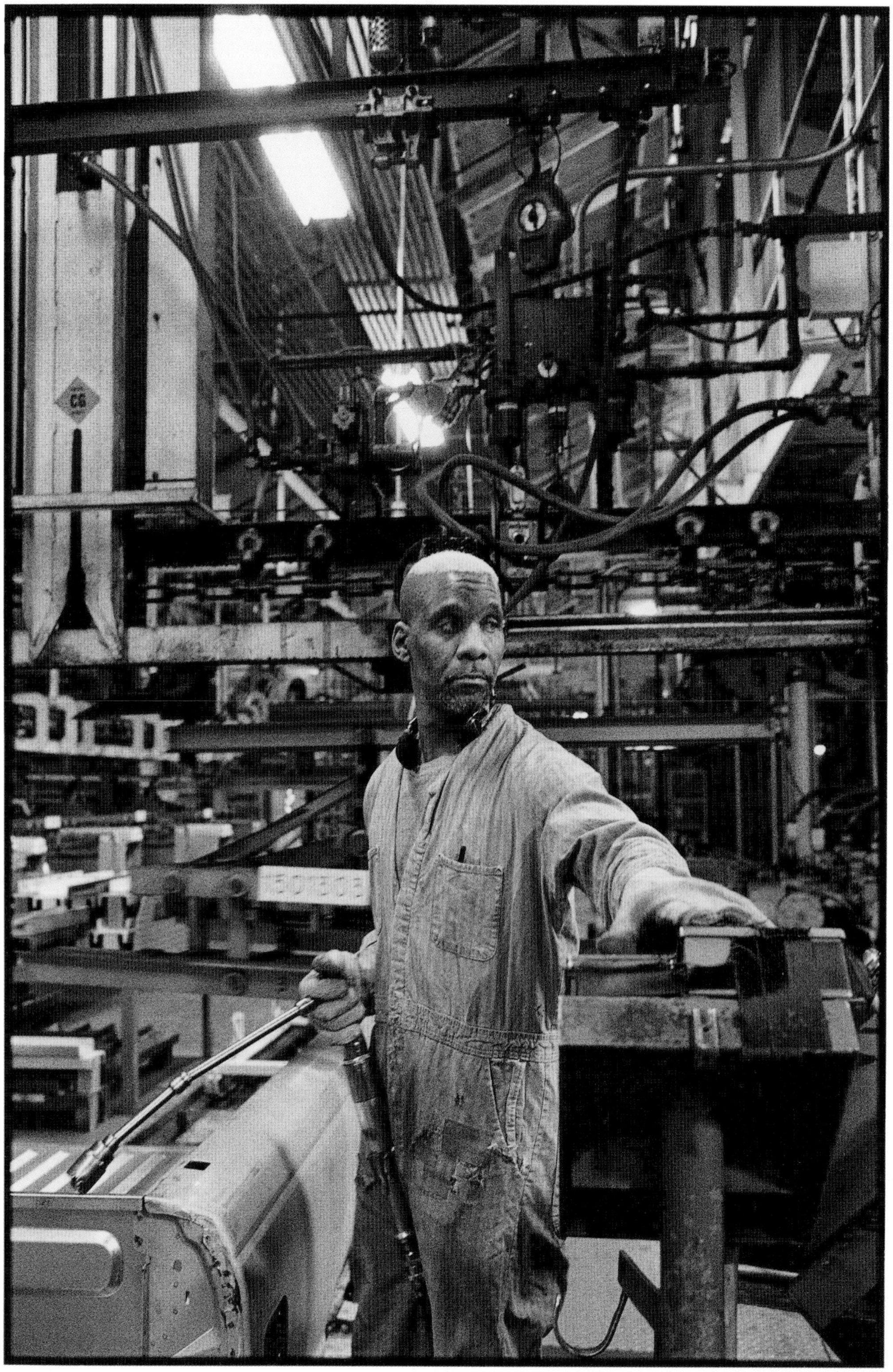

Assembly worker
Ford Motor Company

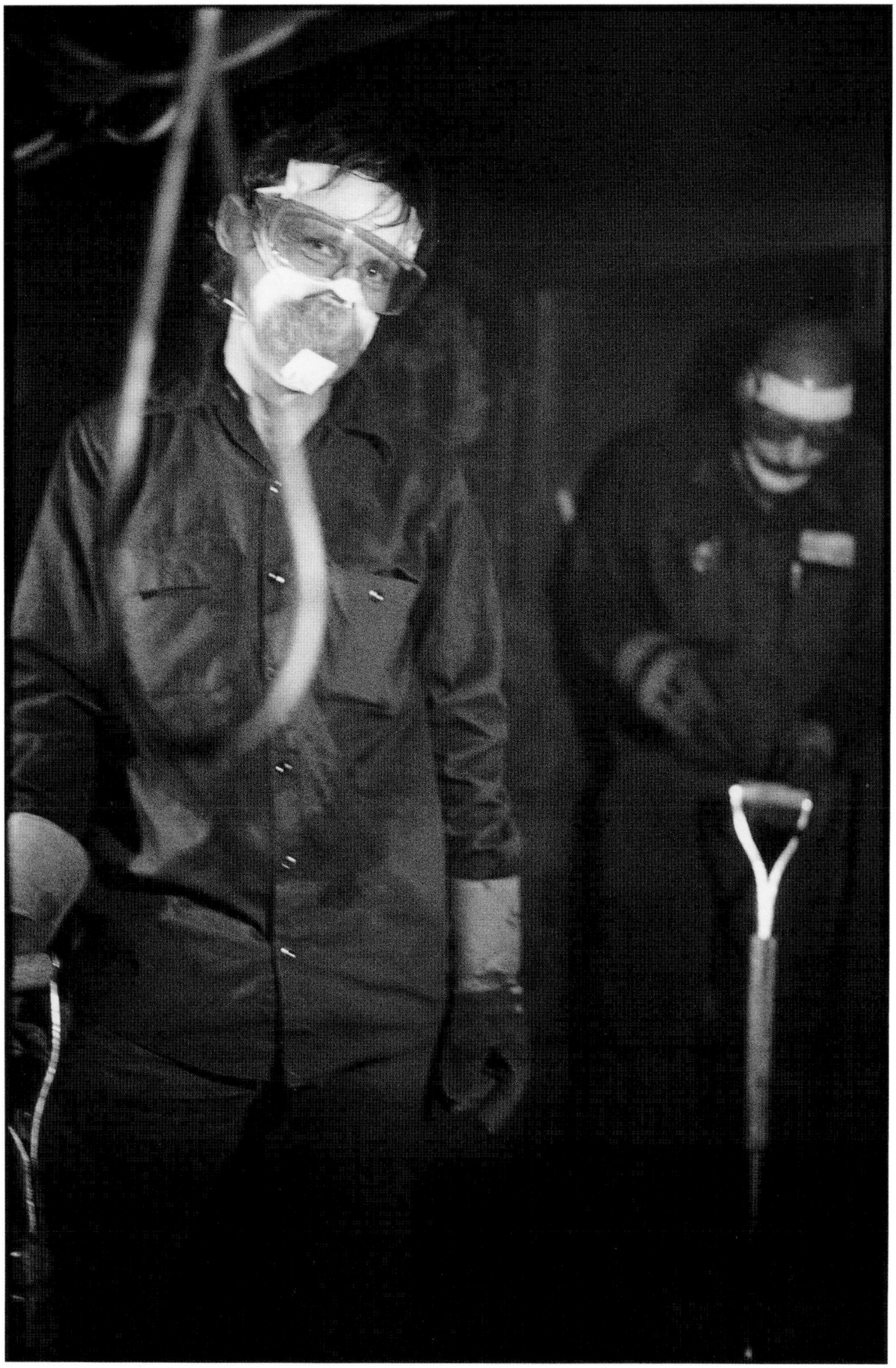

Laborer
Smith Foundry

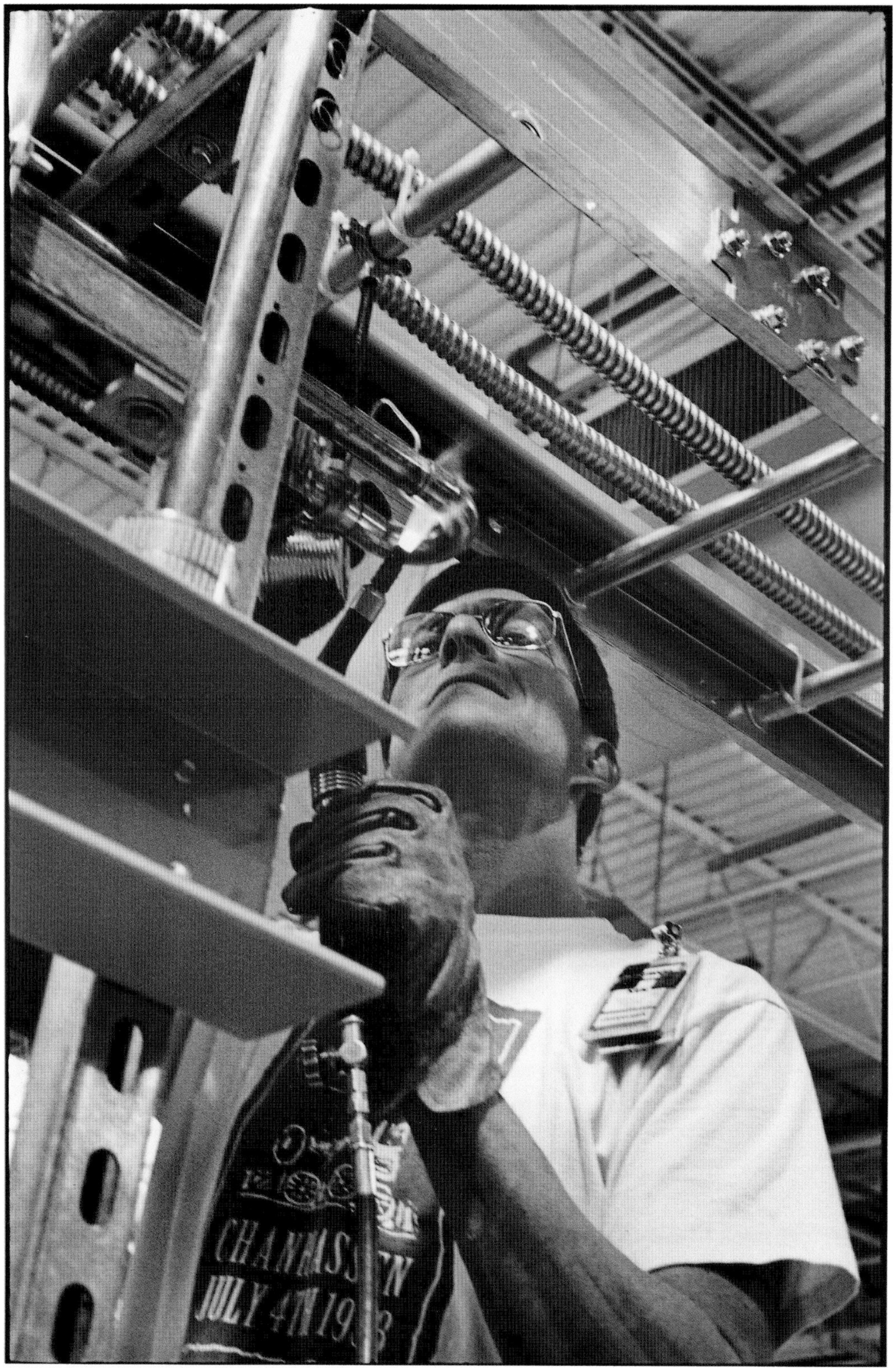

Contract plumber
Rosemount Engineering

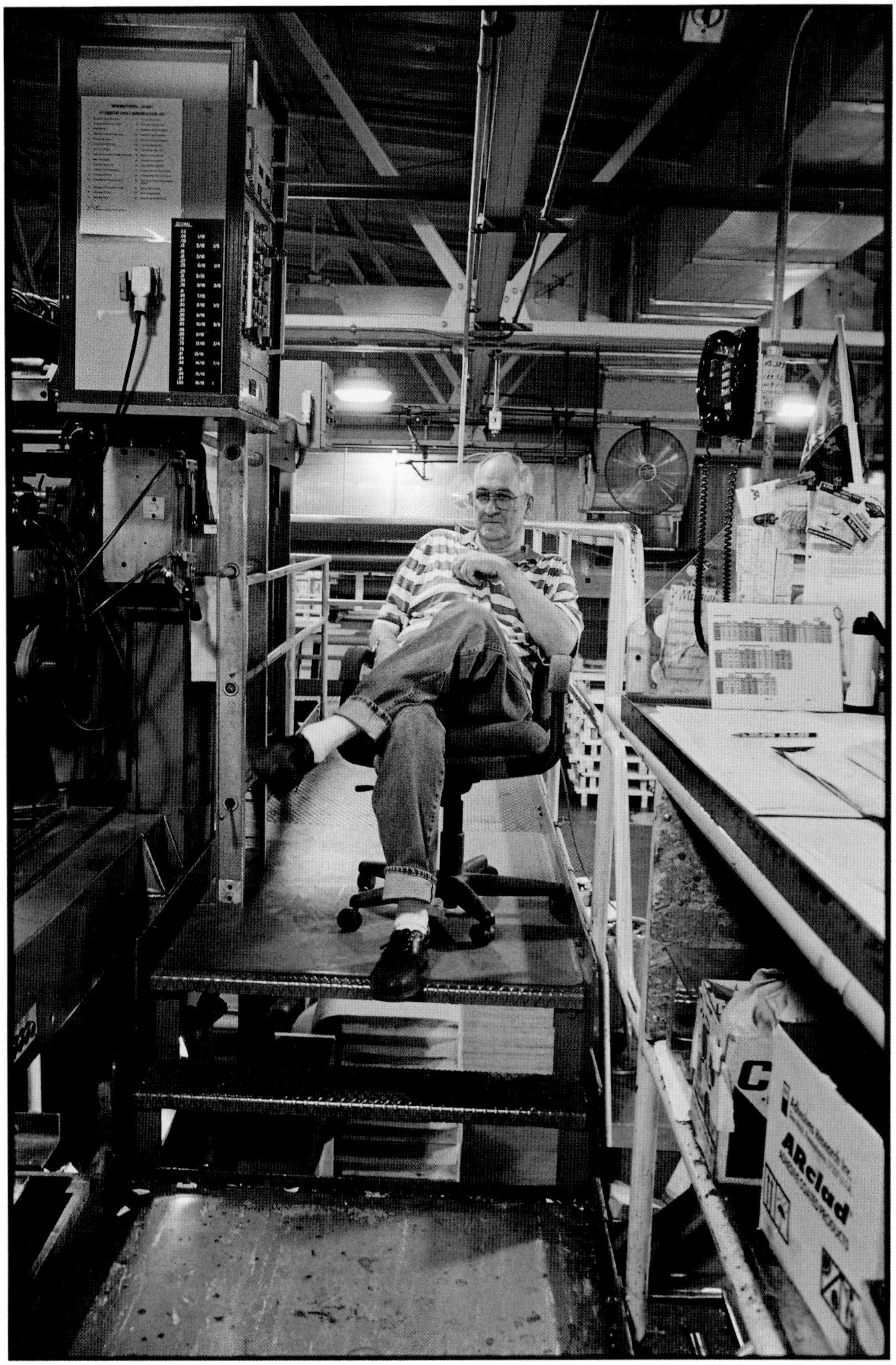

Machine operator
Potlatch

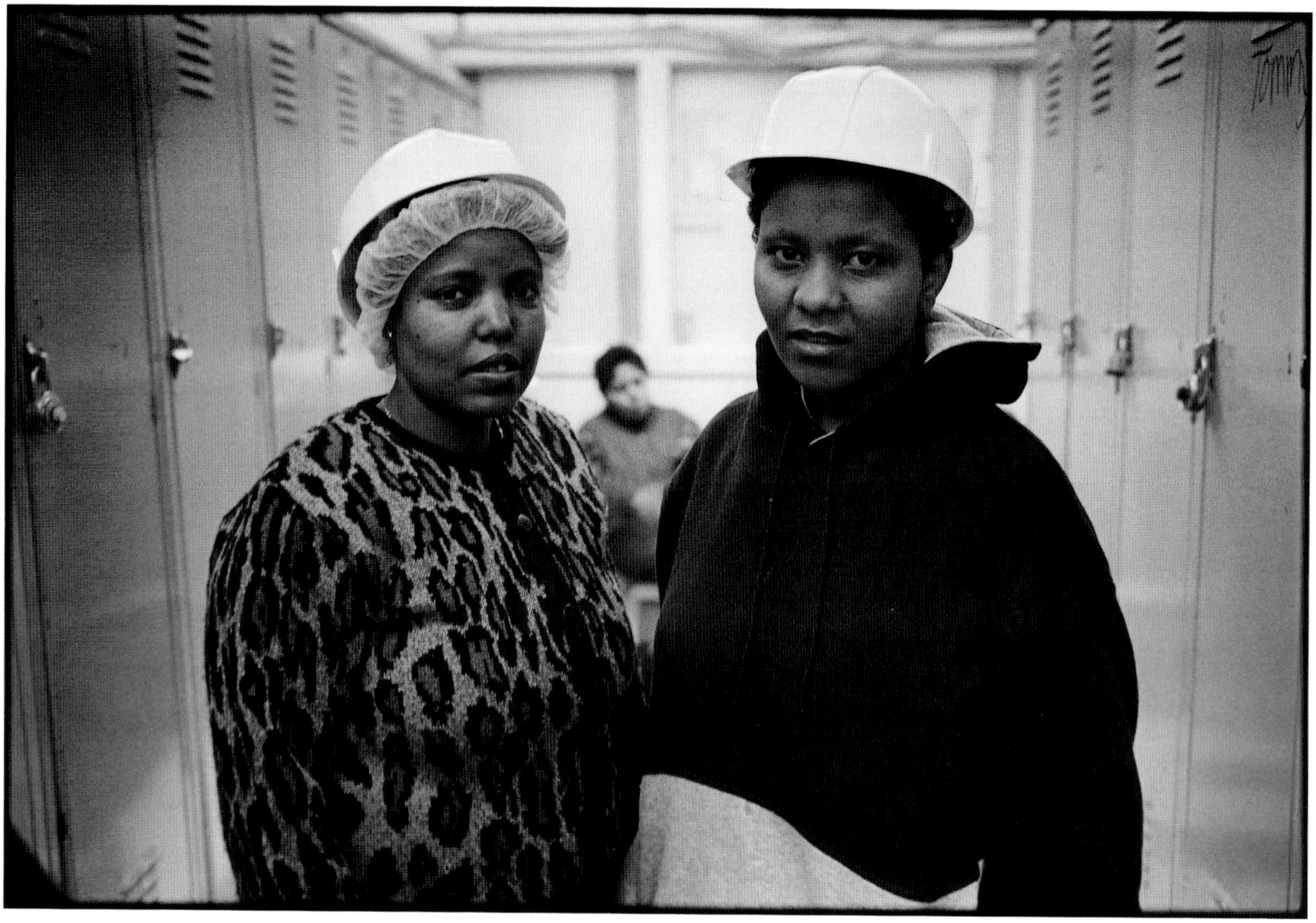

Lunchroom
GFI America

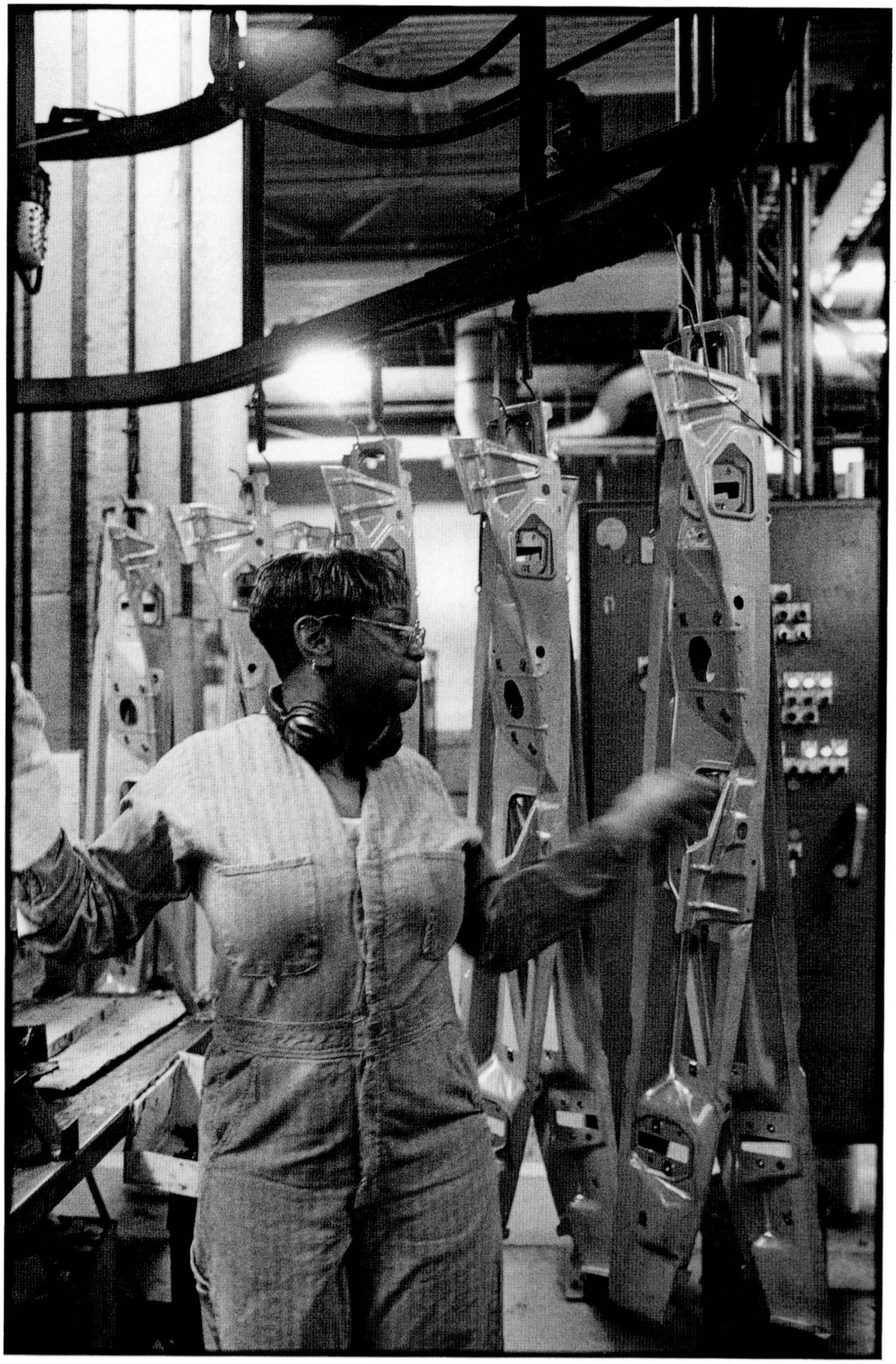

Assembly worker
Ford Motor Company

"One of the problems we face is there always seems to be someone new—different. I don't know, it seemed like we had a lot of Vietnamese and then all of a sudden that kind of stopped and we had a lot of Mexicans and now we have a lot of Somalis. And that's good. It enables us to learn different cultures, different languages."

CHARLES OSTERFELD
ROSEMOUNT ENGINEERING

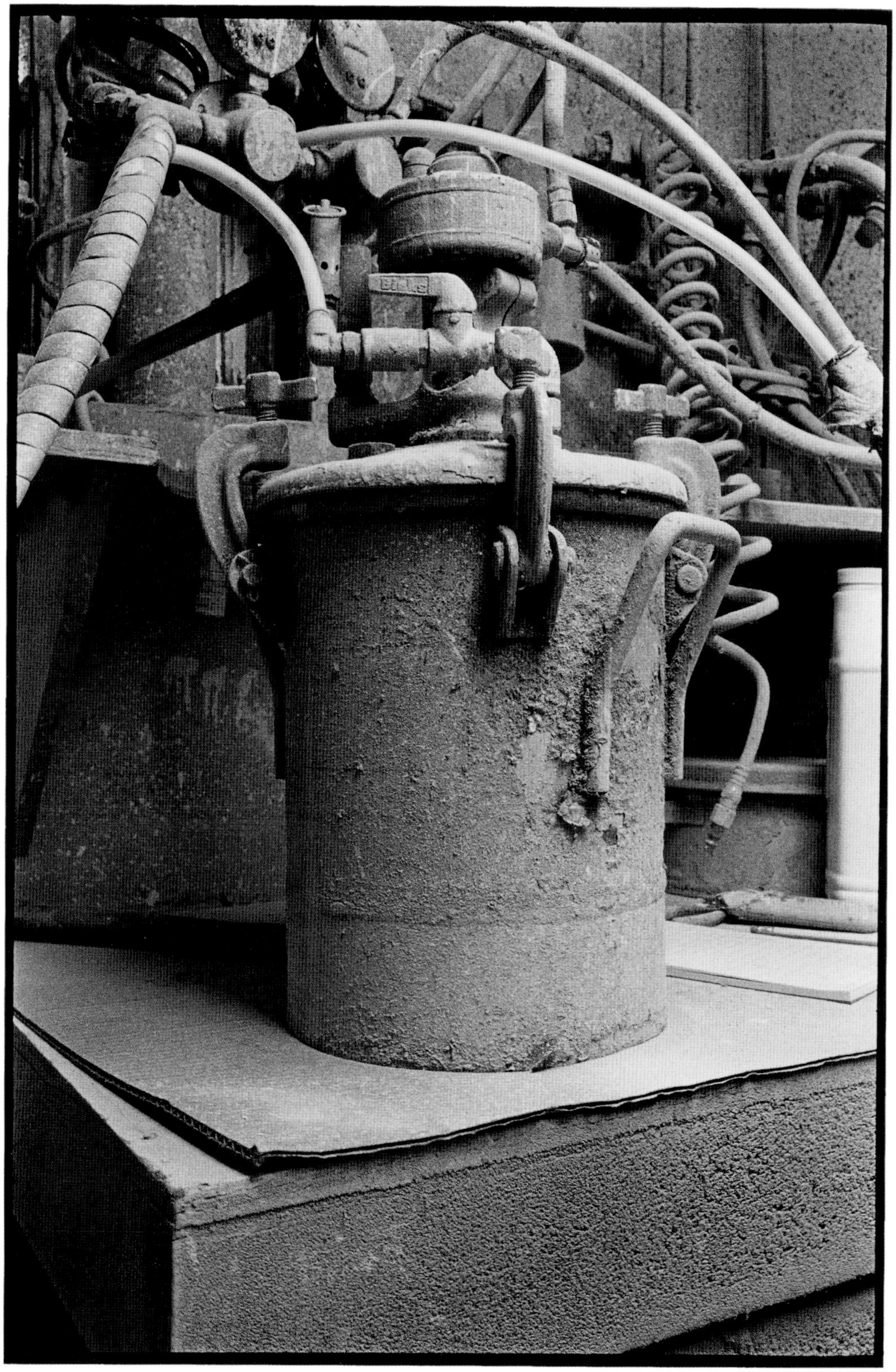

Paint room
Andersen Window

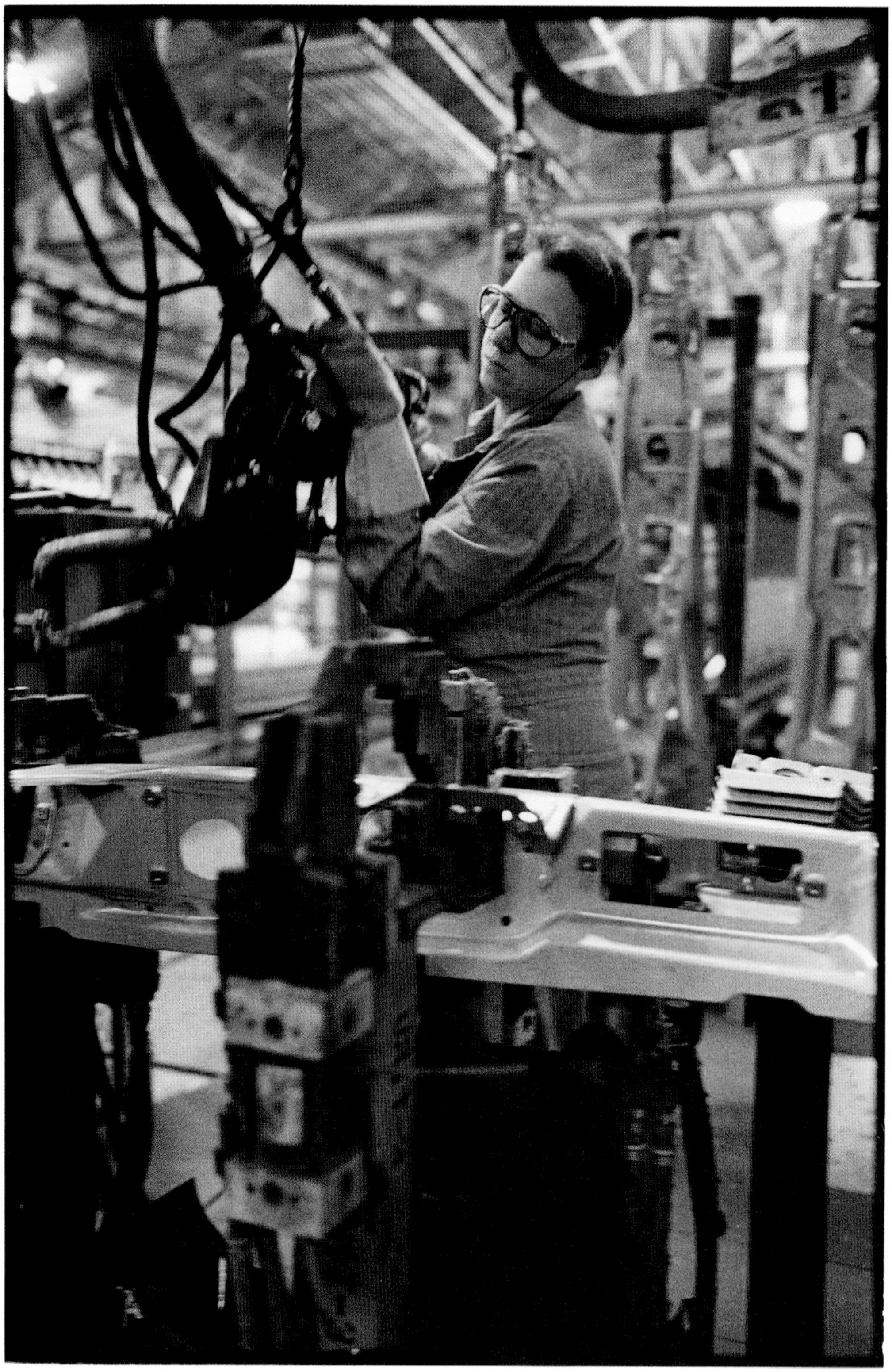

Assembly worker
Ford Motor Company

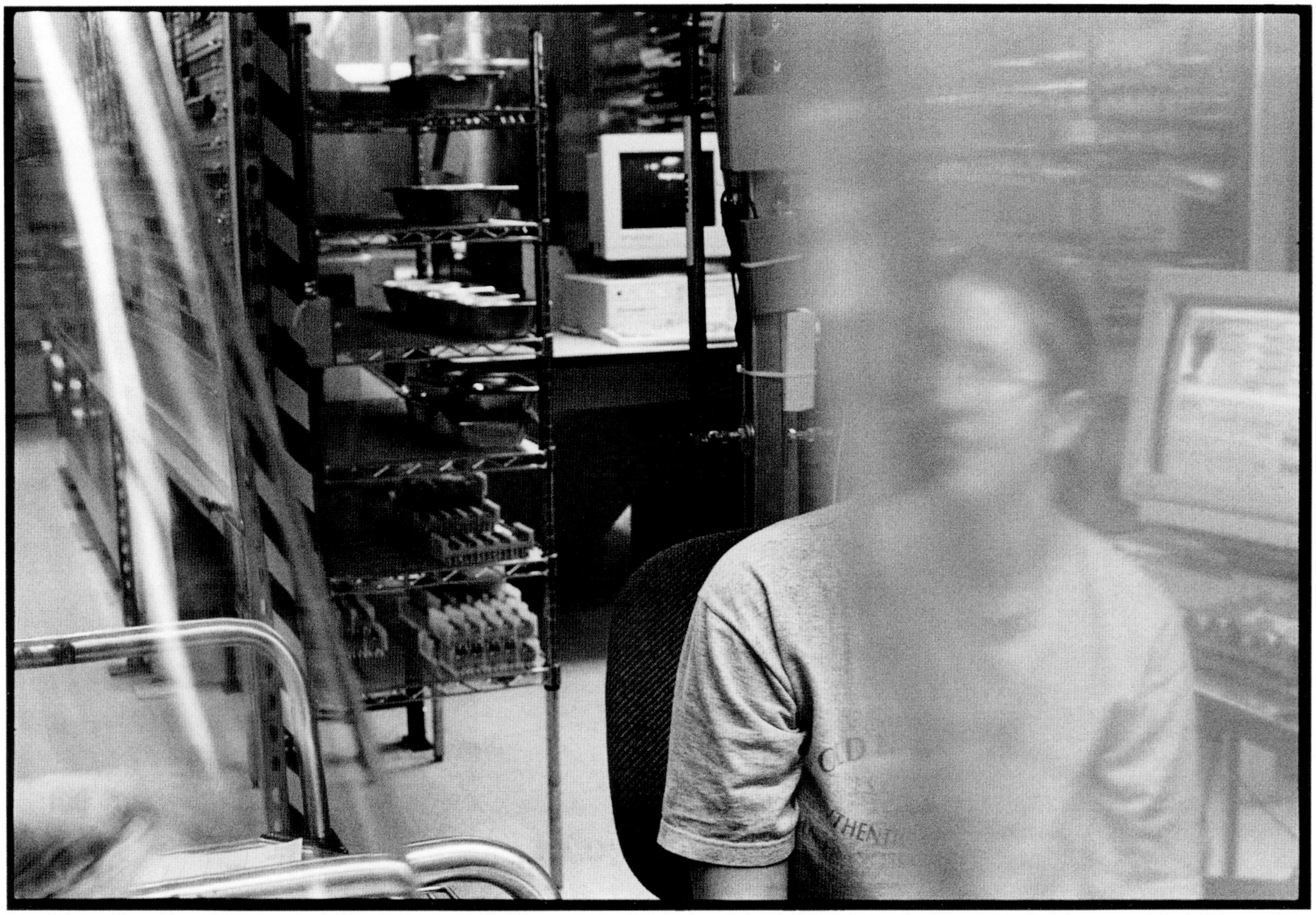

Assembly worker
Rosemount Engineering

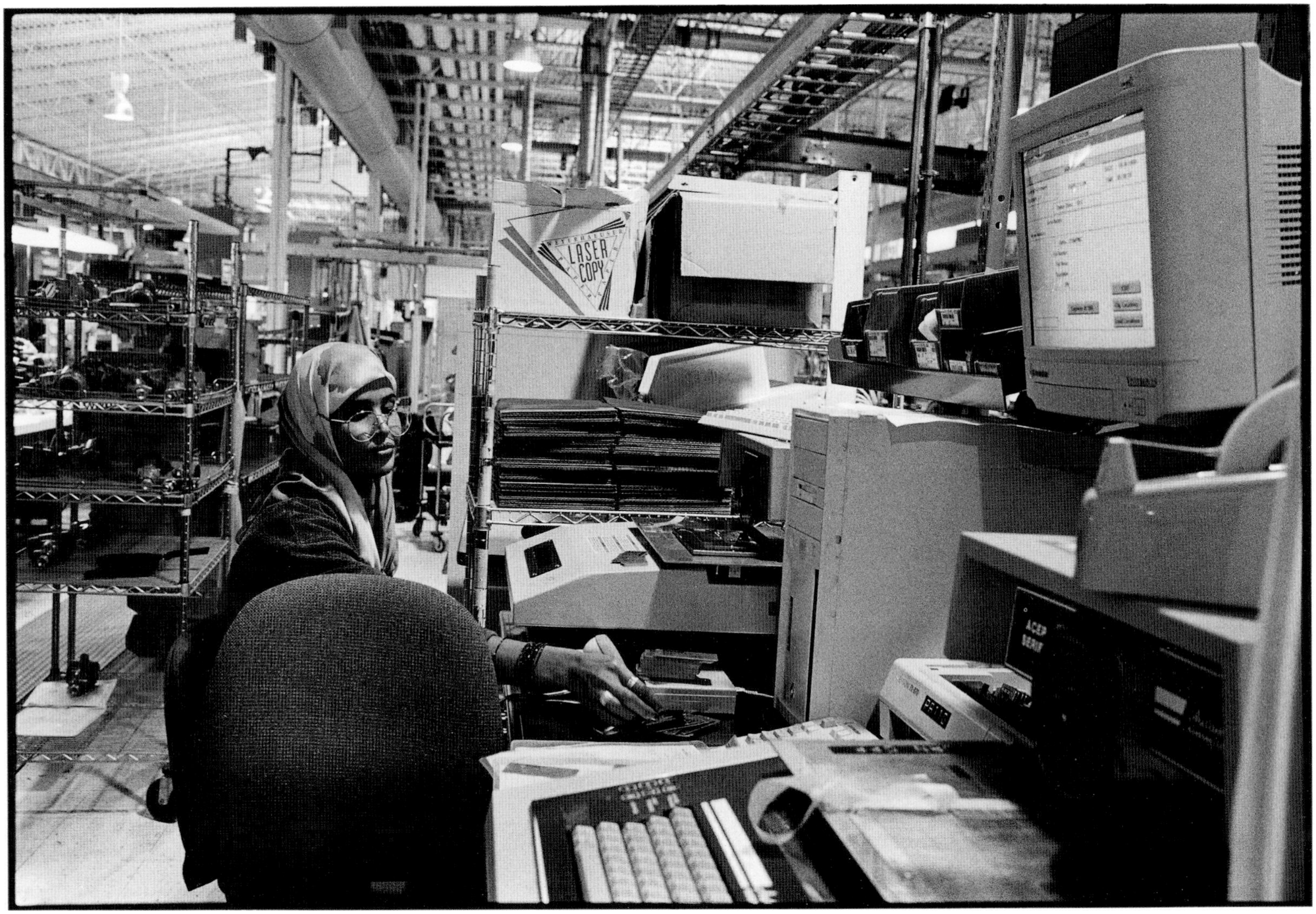

Parts inspection
Rosemount Engineering

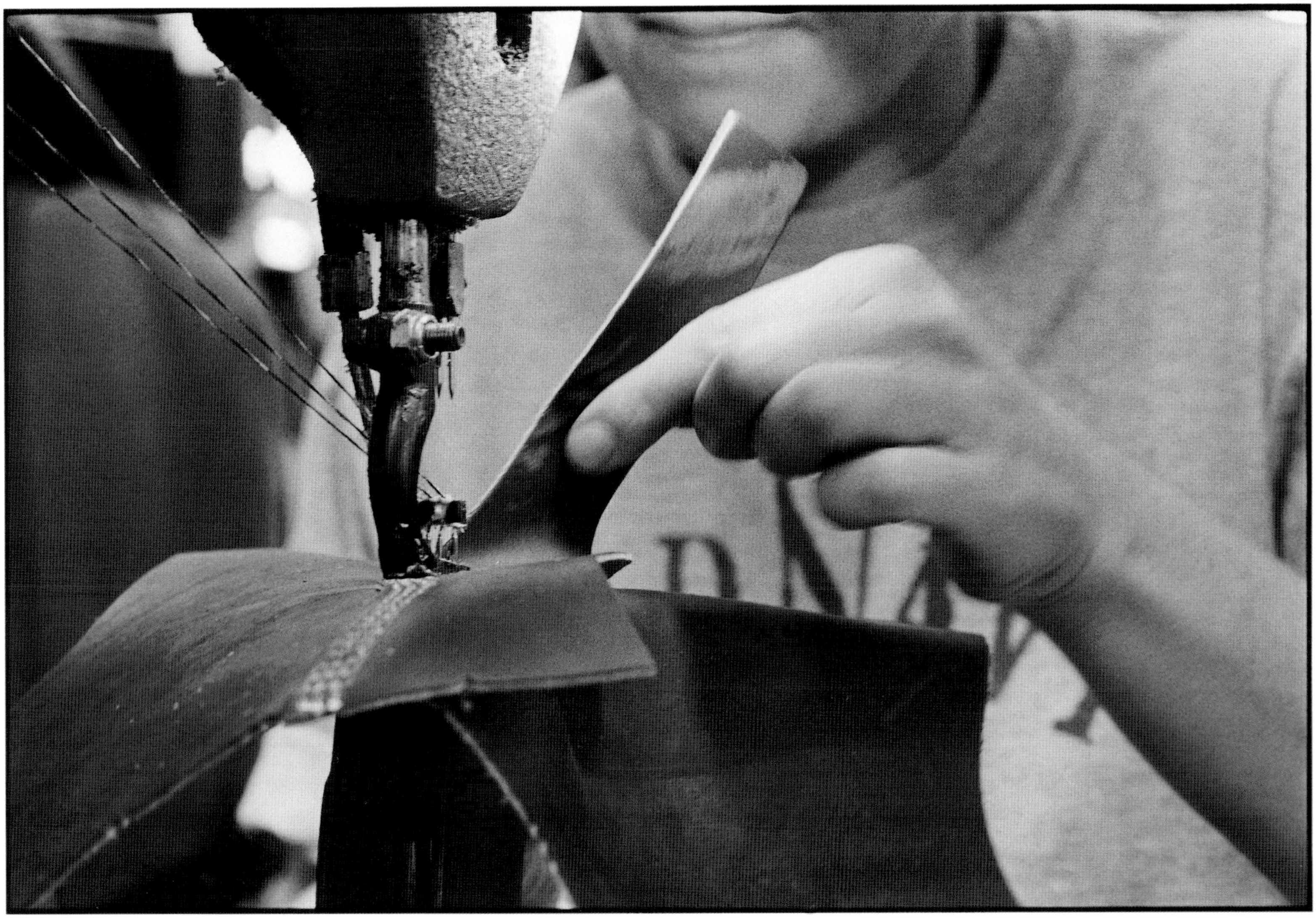

Sewing machine operator
Red Wing Shoe

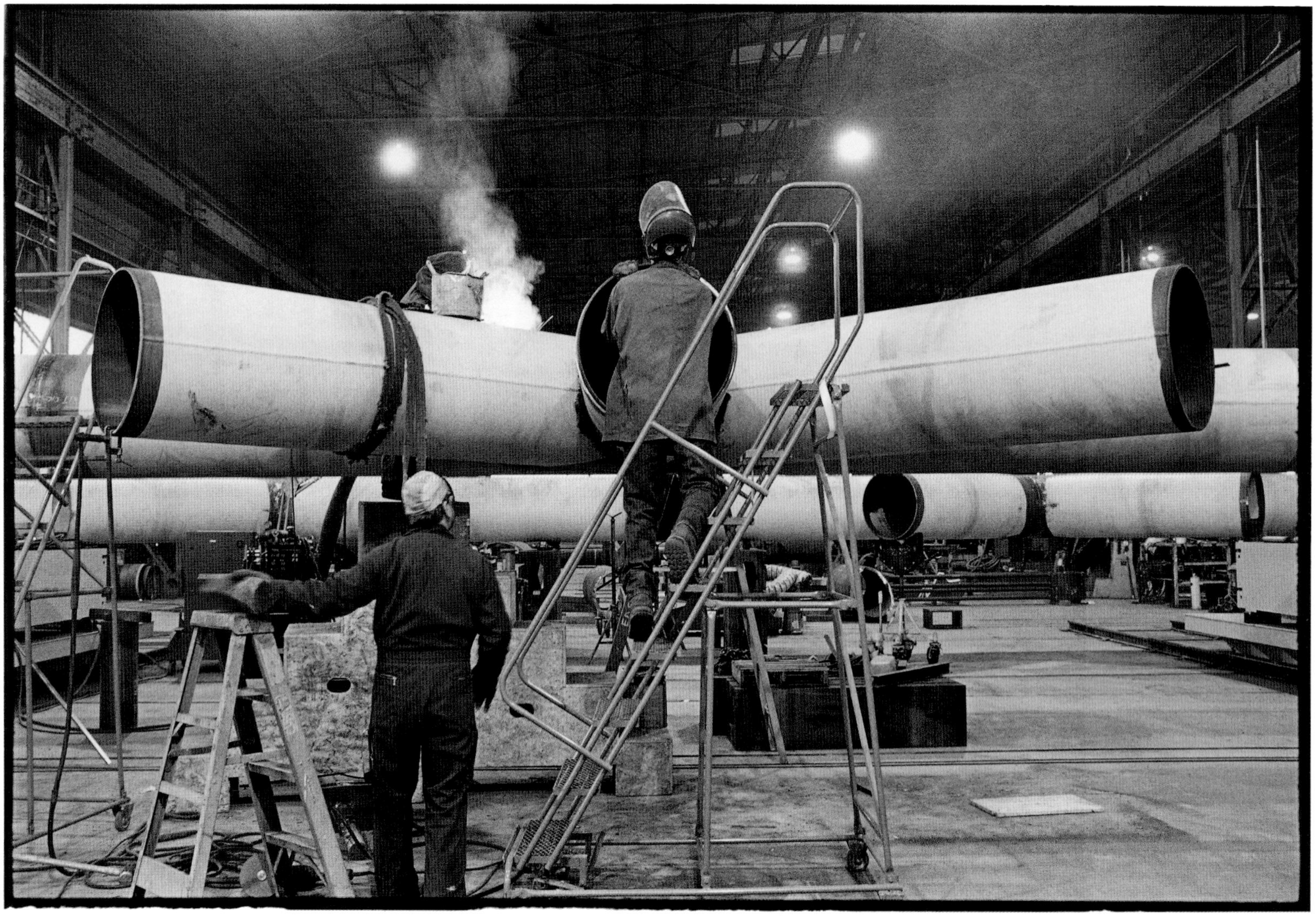

Pipe welding
BendTec

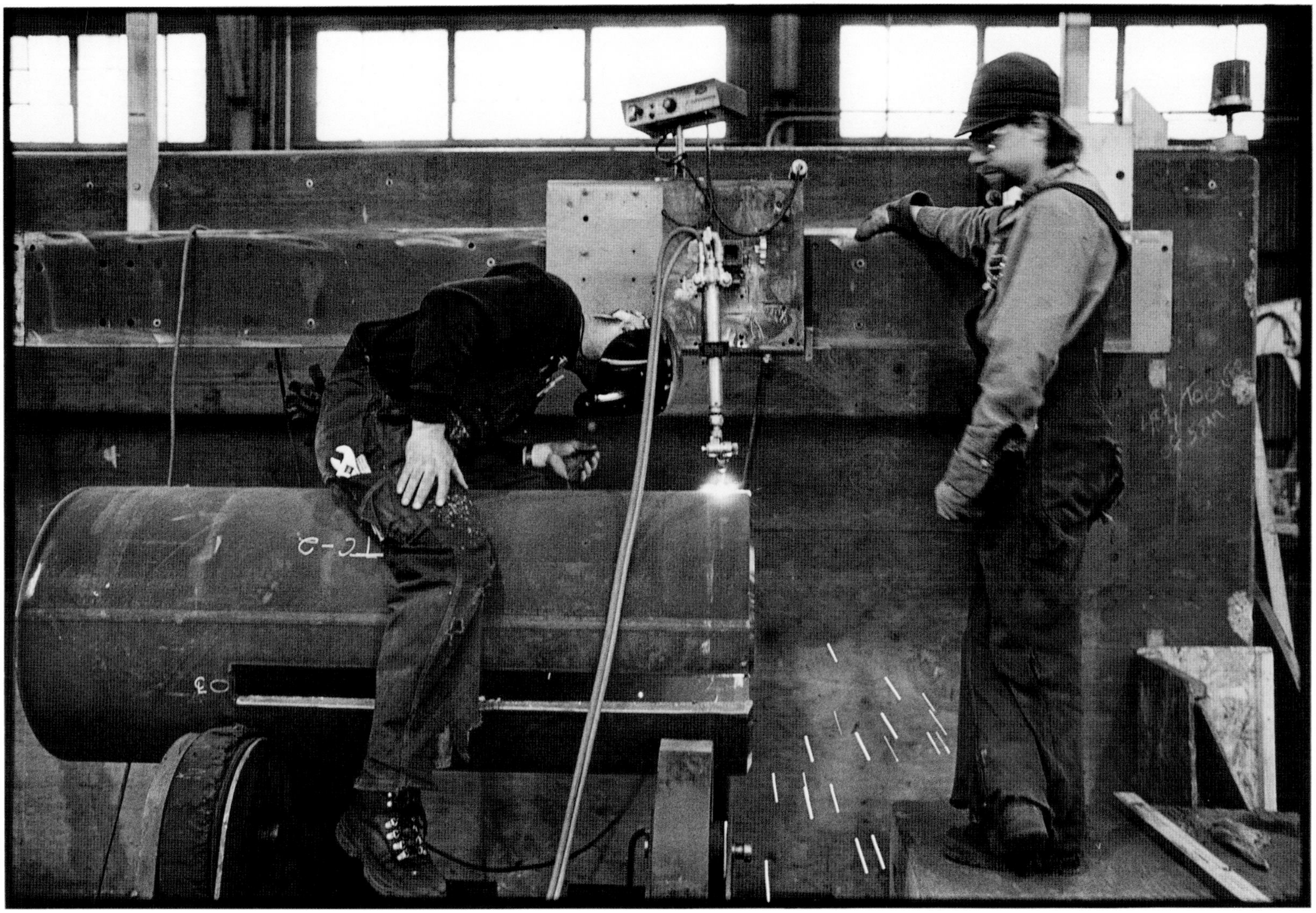

Cutting pipes
BendTec

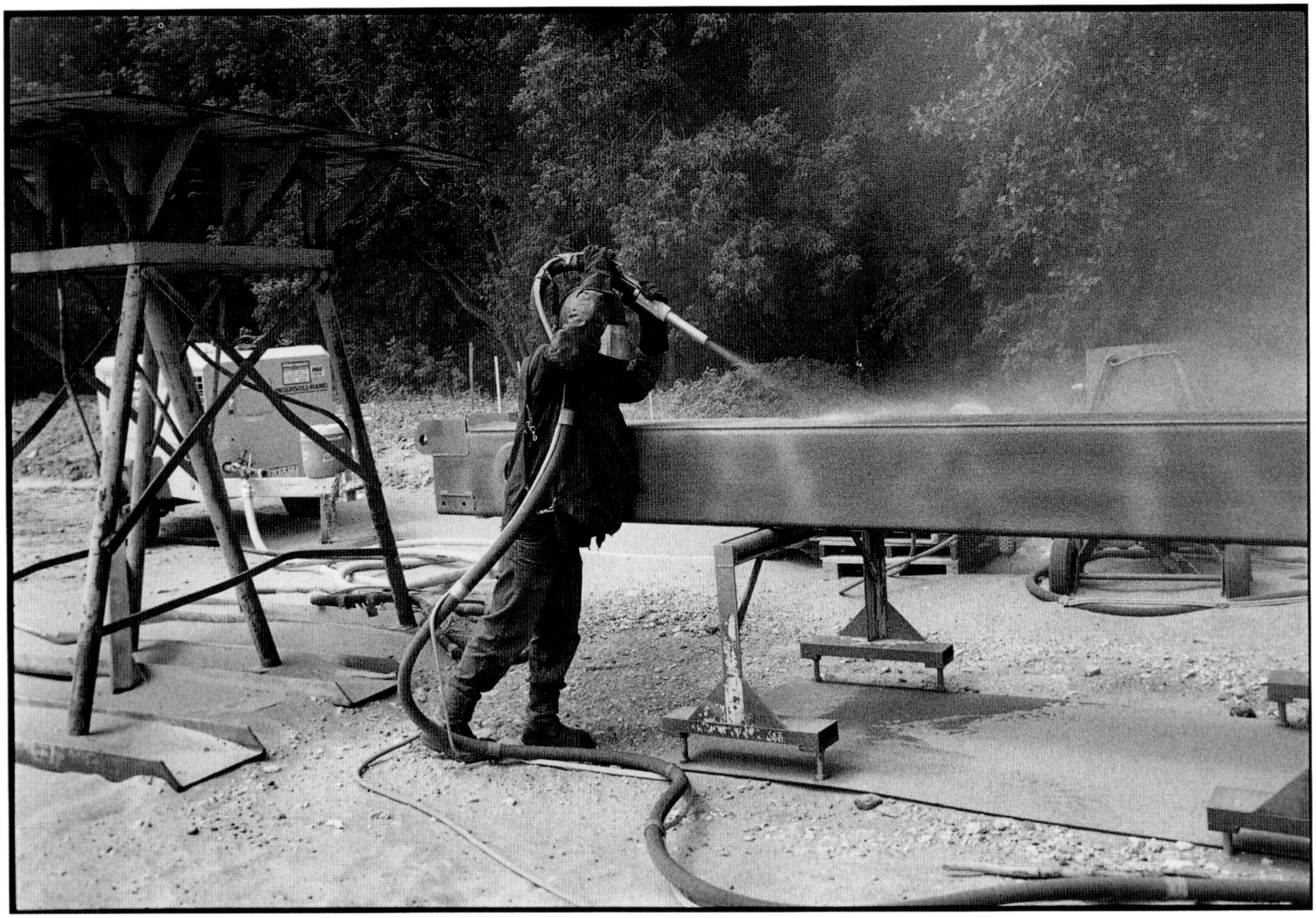

Sandblasting
Lull International

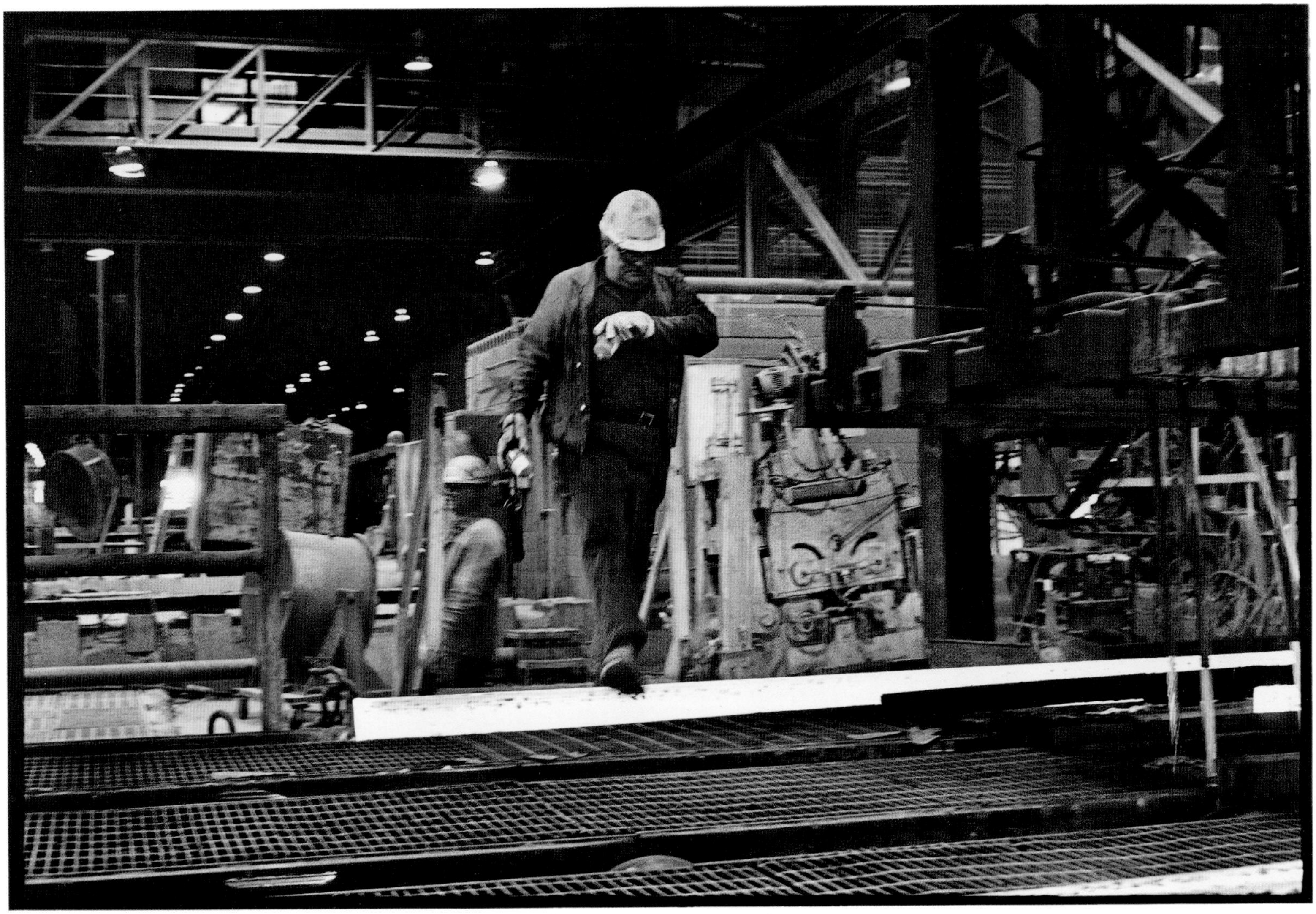

Walking over hot steel
North Star

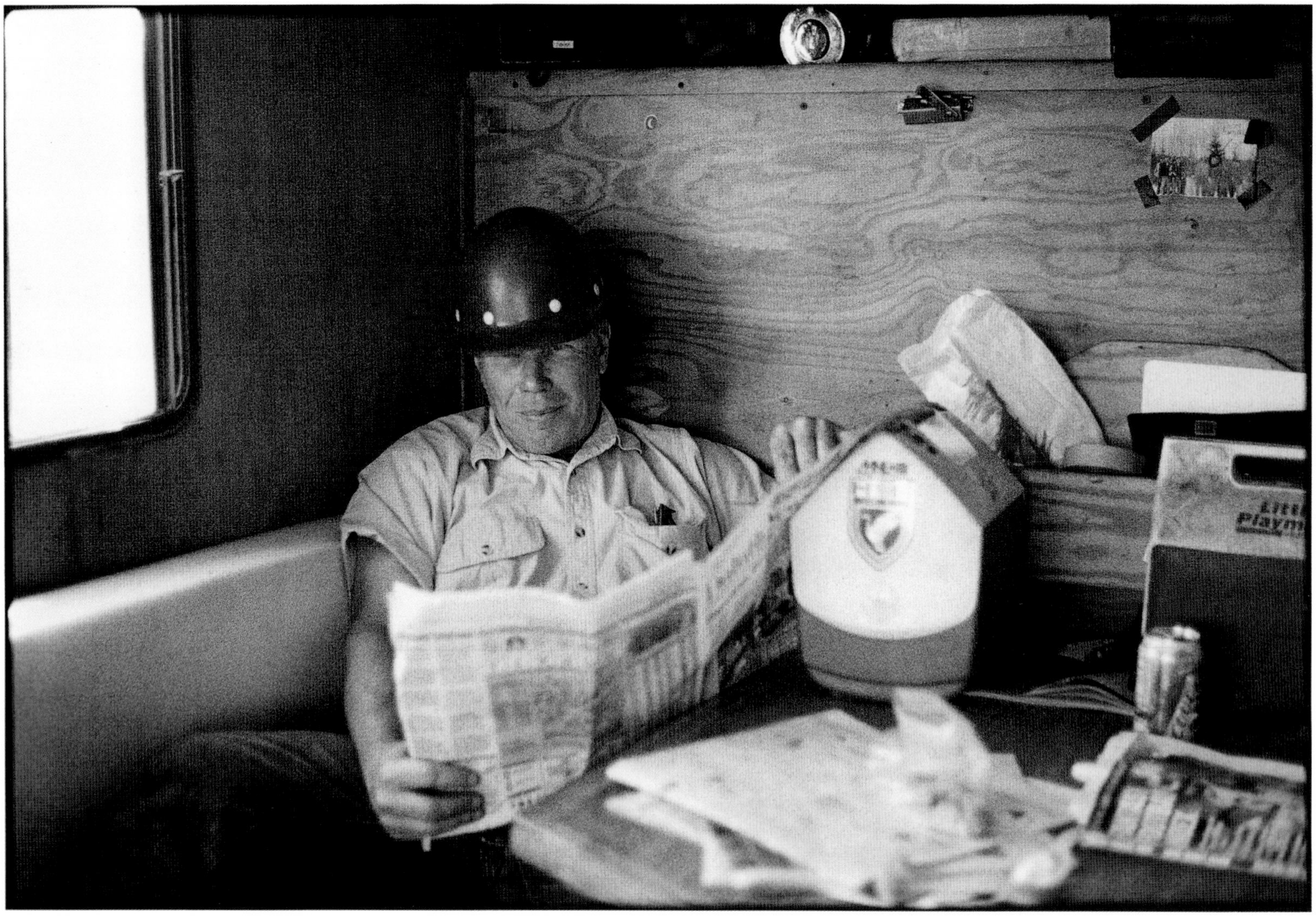

Rest break
Ispat Inland Mining

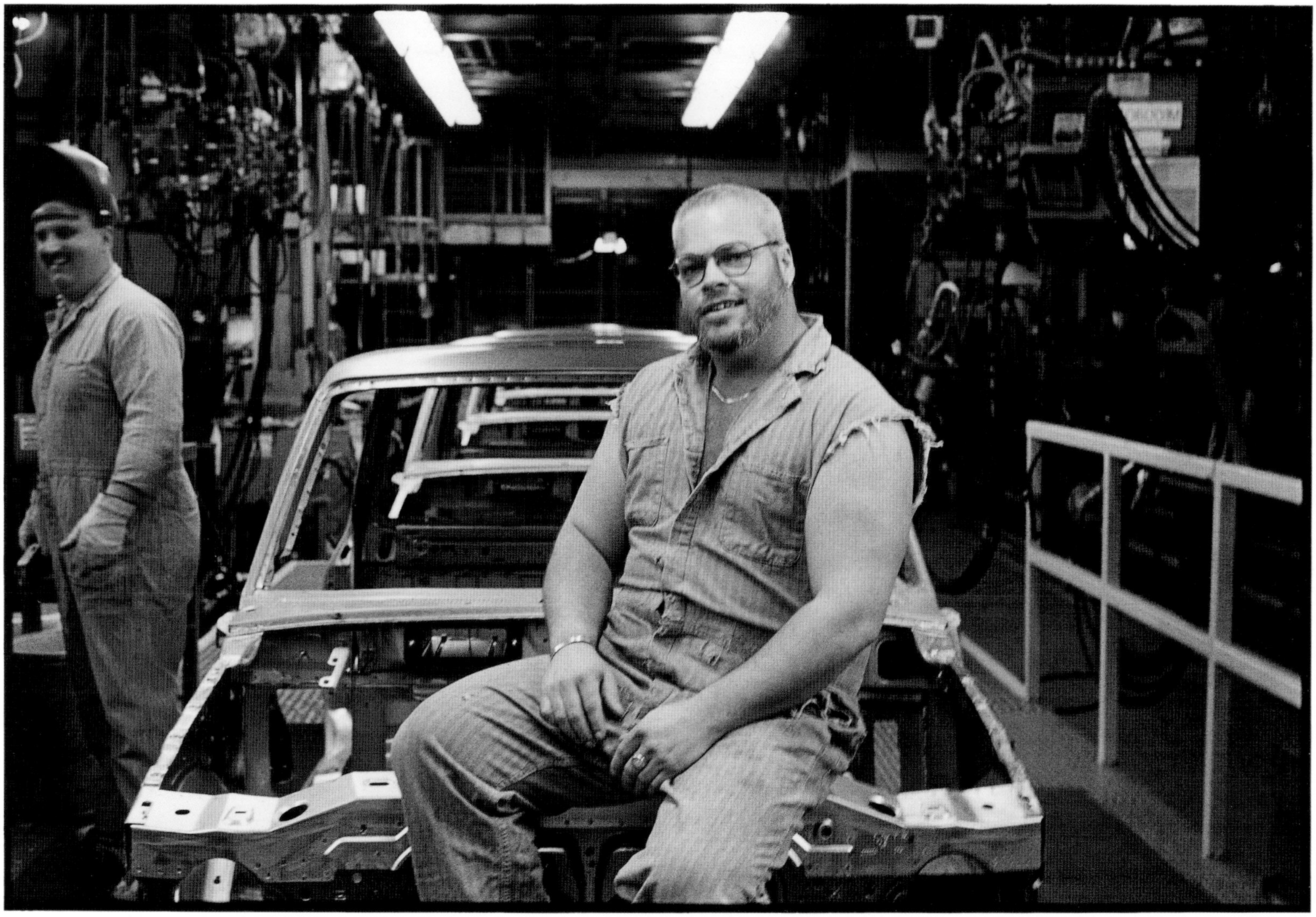

Assembly worker
Ford Motor Company

"Okay, I'm going to tell you like it is, they say, 'You got a white man's job.' They ask me, How long do I think I'm going to be able to keep that job? I guess they had another black guy on this job I was on and the reason he was pulled off it was because he didn't come to work every day. But since then, they were pointing out to me—which is true—you had a couple white guys that the majority of the time they were not here, but there was no mention of taking them off the job. So it's kind of hard to deny it. It is very hard to deny it because when they tell you that, you've seen it. It makes you wonder."

ANONYMOUS WORKER

"I sometimes see some have to work harder than others to get the respect and the pay that others get. Some come in the door and don't even do half the work that you do. And you can see a person that, especially when they are talking to you, that they are trying to understand and they can't figure you out. It's like you're labeled—because of color. You're automatically looked at as being lazy. And that's something I've never been in my life is lazy."

CLARENCE (SONNY) DOBBINS
SMITH FOUNDRY

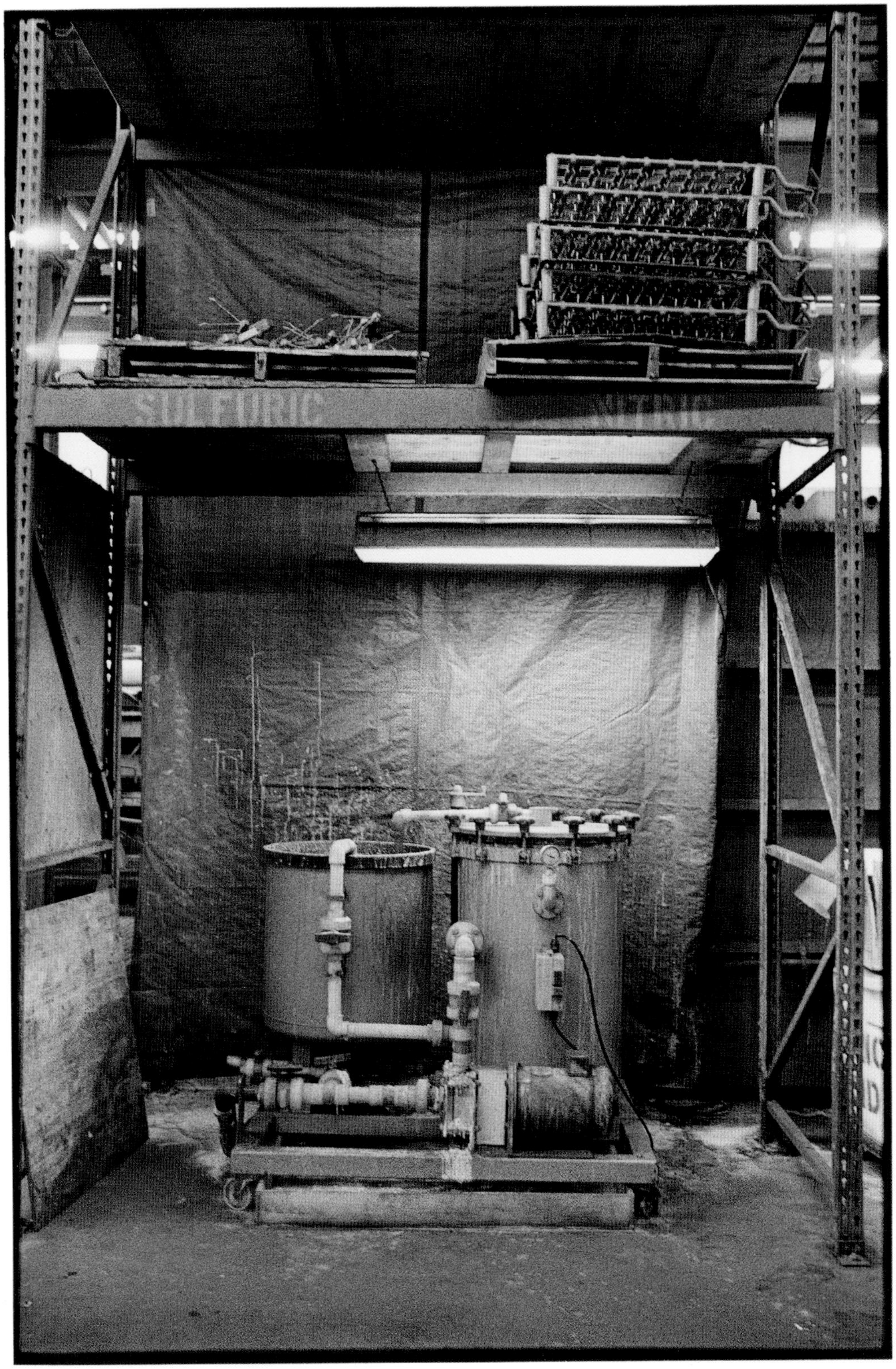

Storage bins

Nico Products

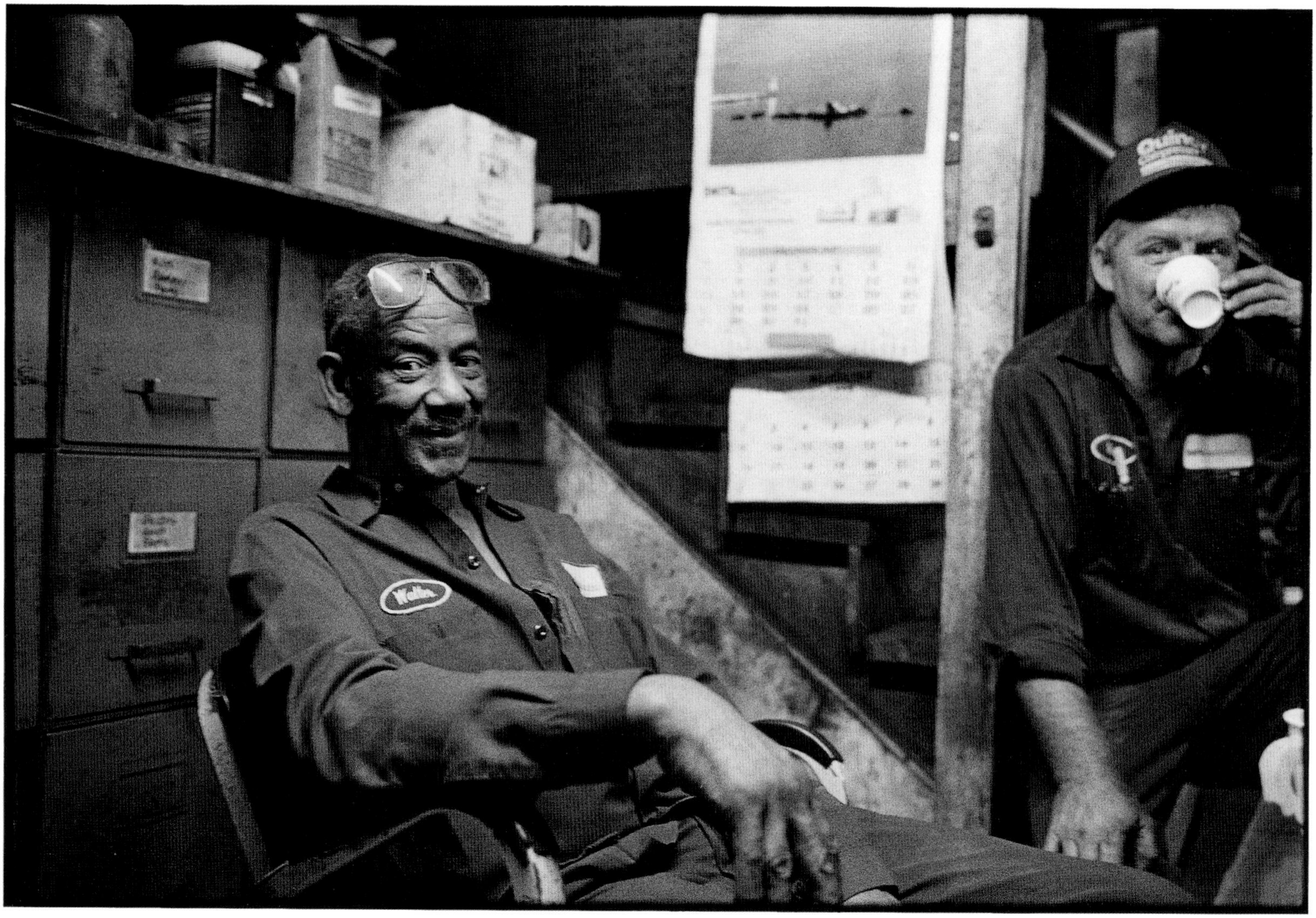

Rest break
Smith Foundry

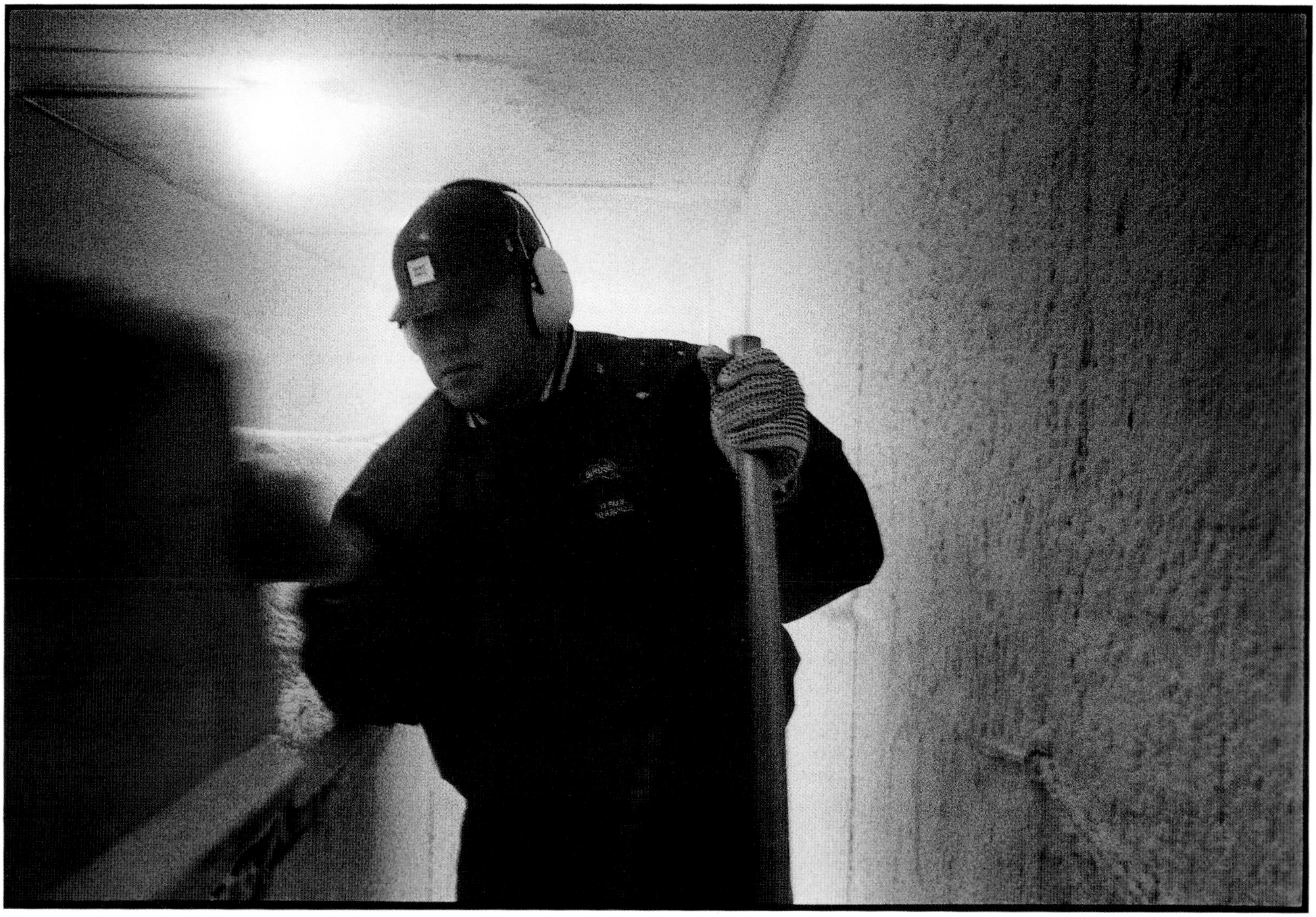

Inside freezer
Agrilink

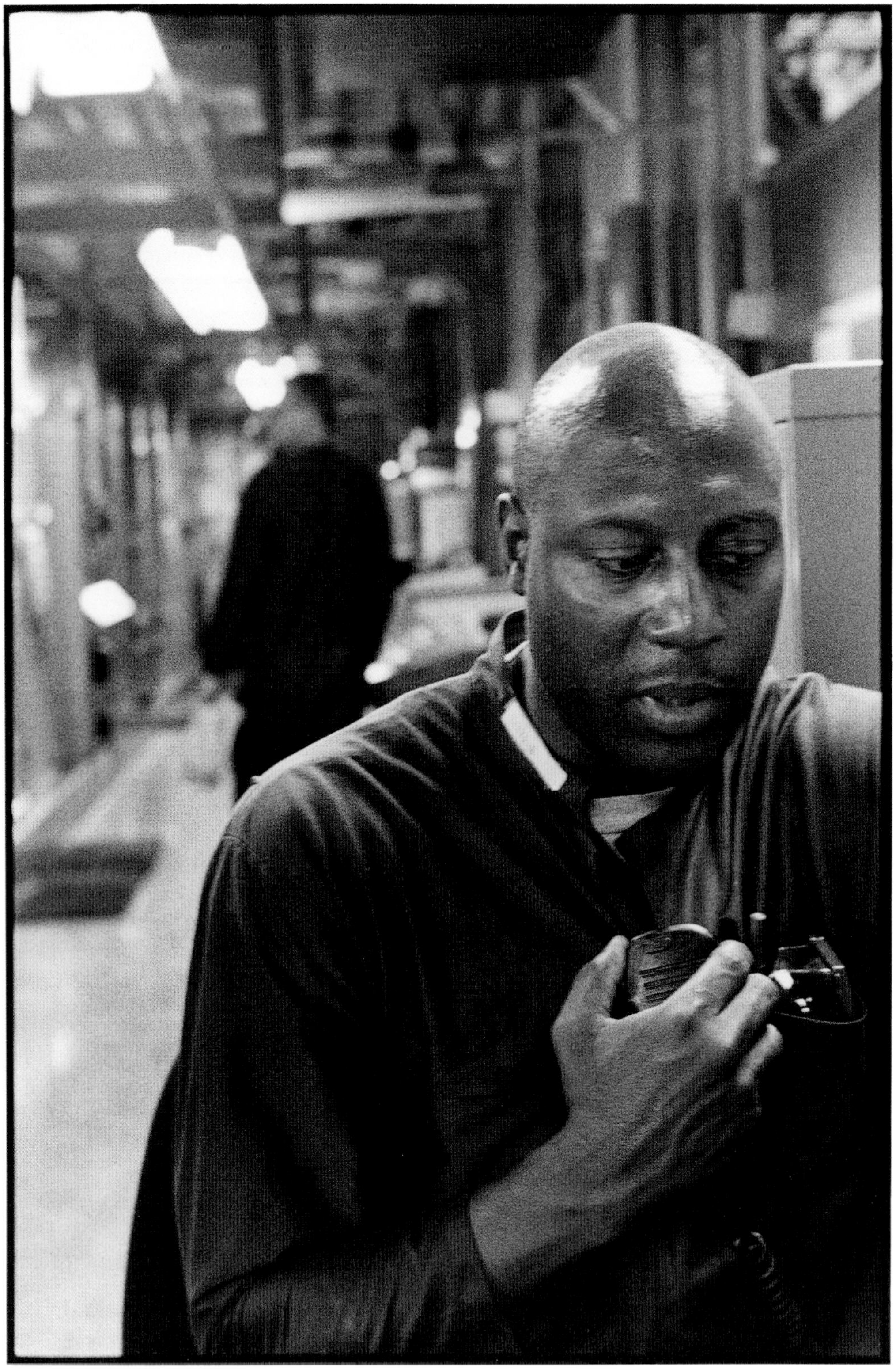

Paint-department supervisor
Ford Motor Company

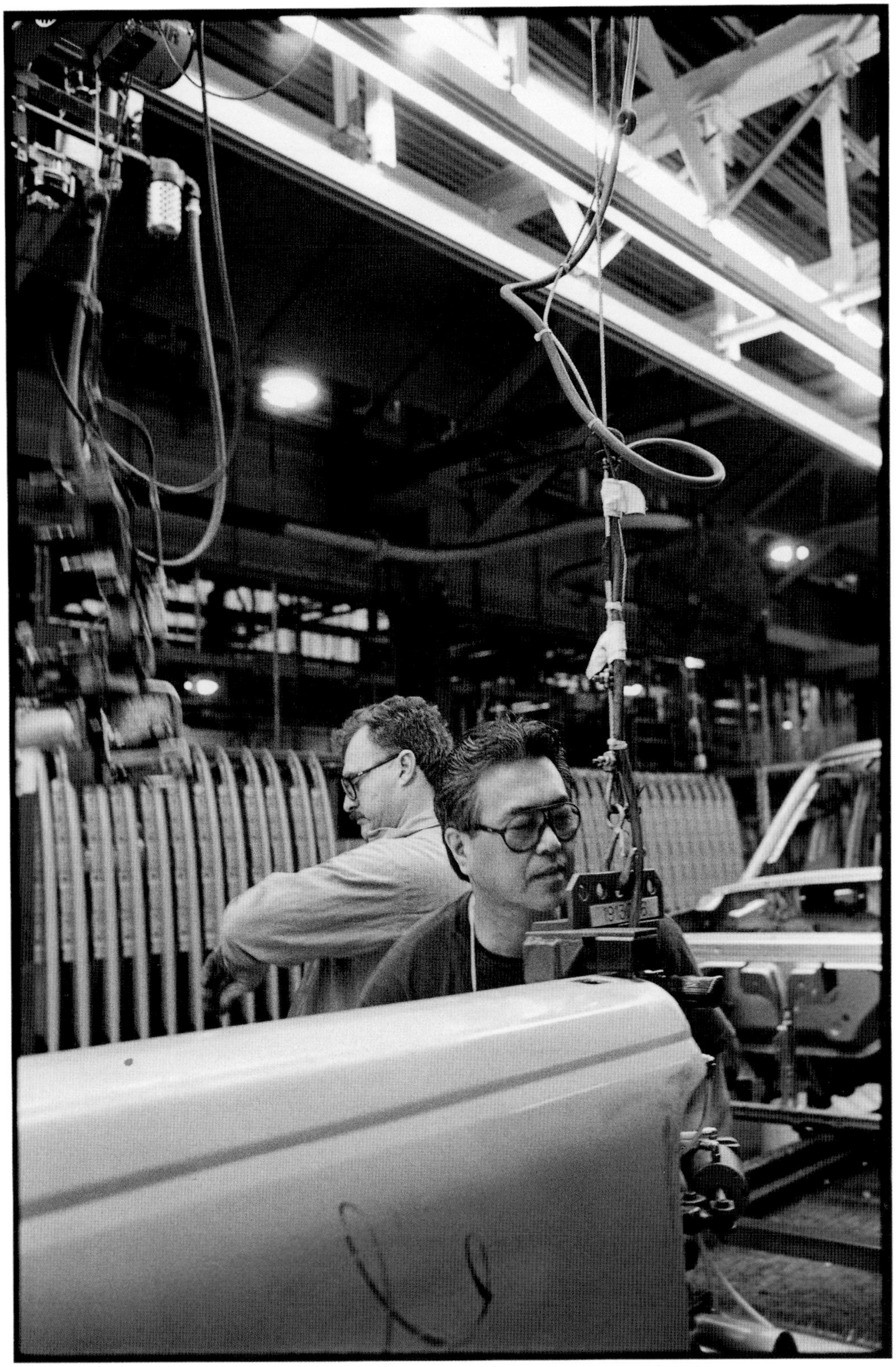

Assembly workers
Ford Motor Company

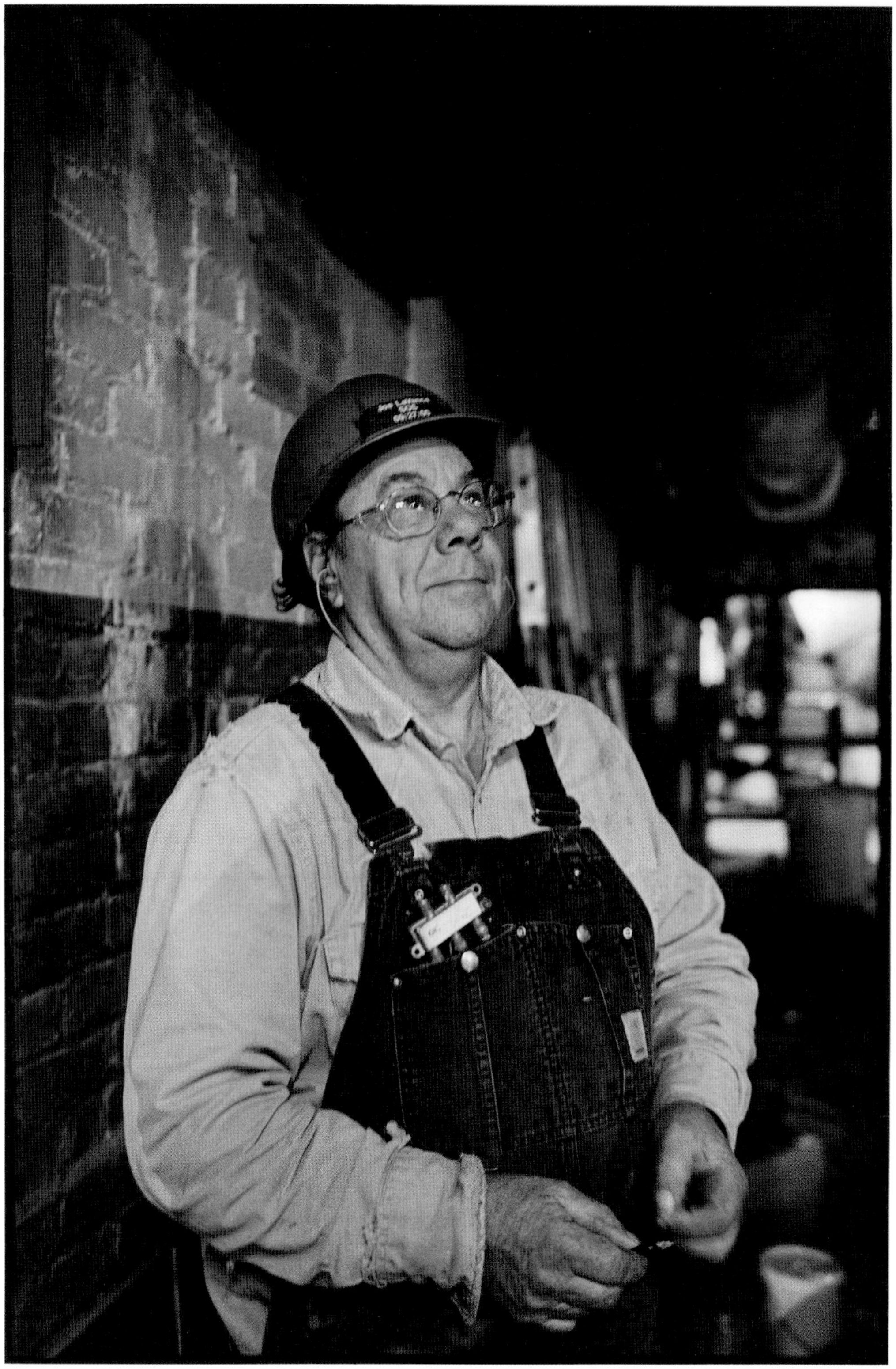

Trades worker
Potlatch

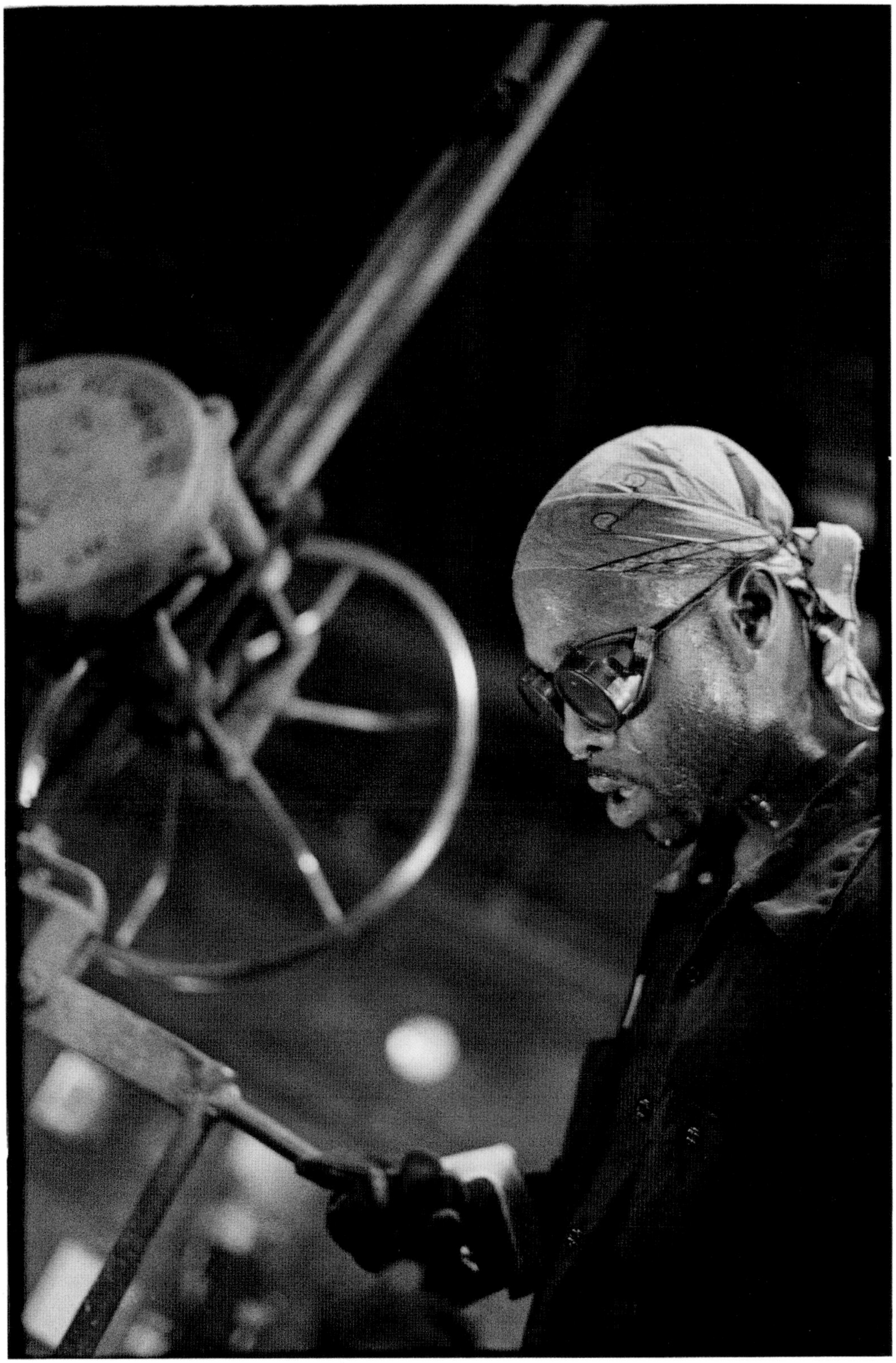

Pouring molten steel
Smith Foundry

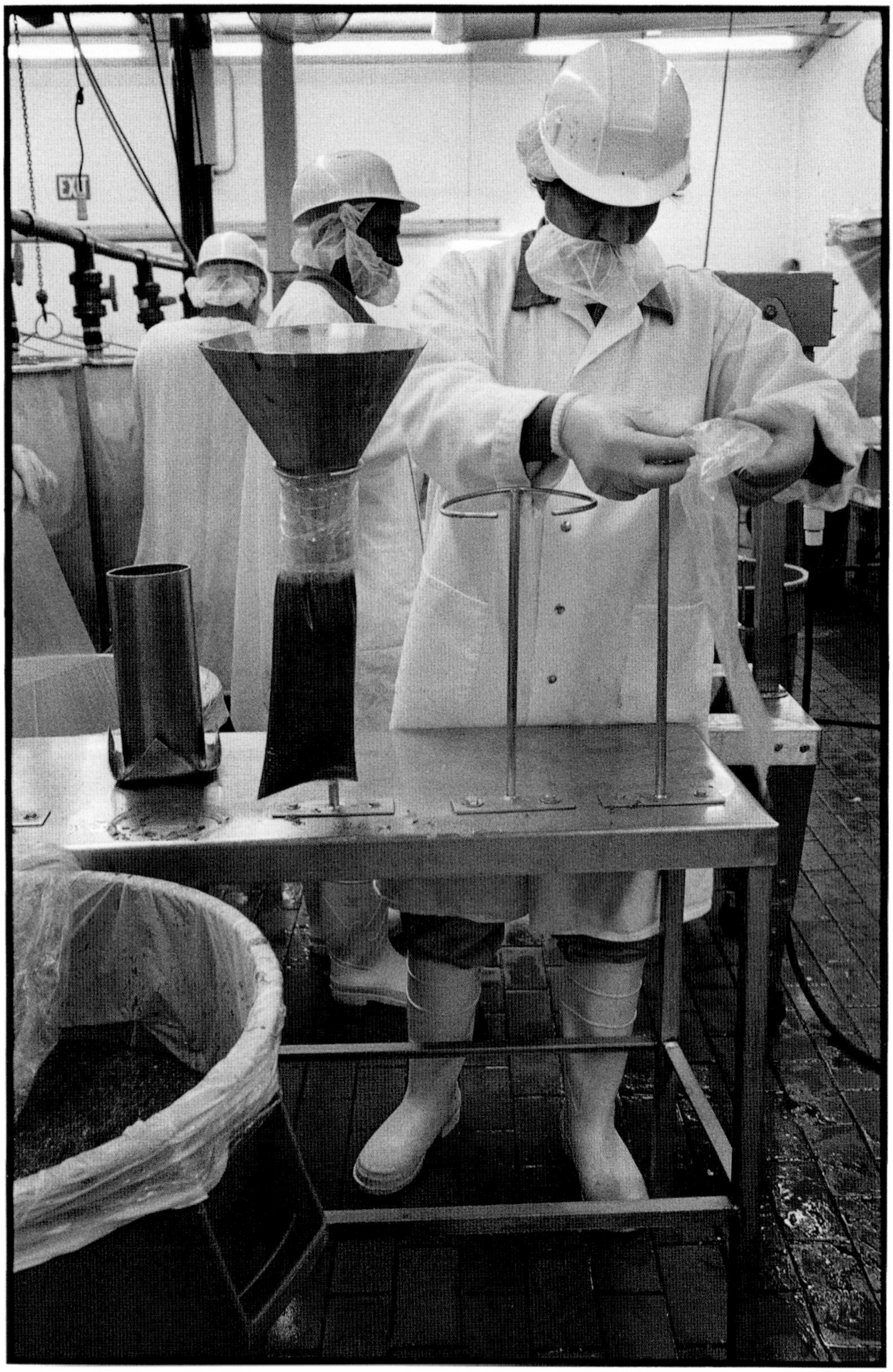

Chili cook room
GFI America

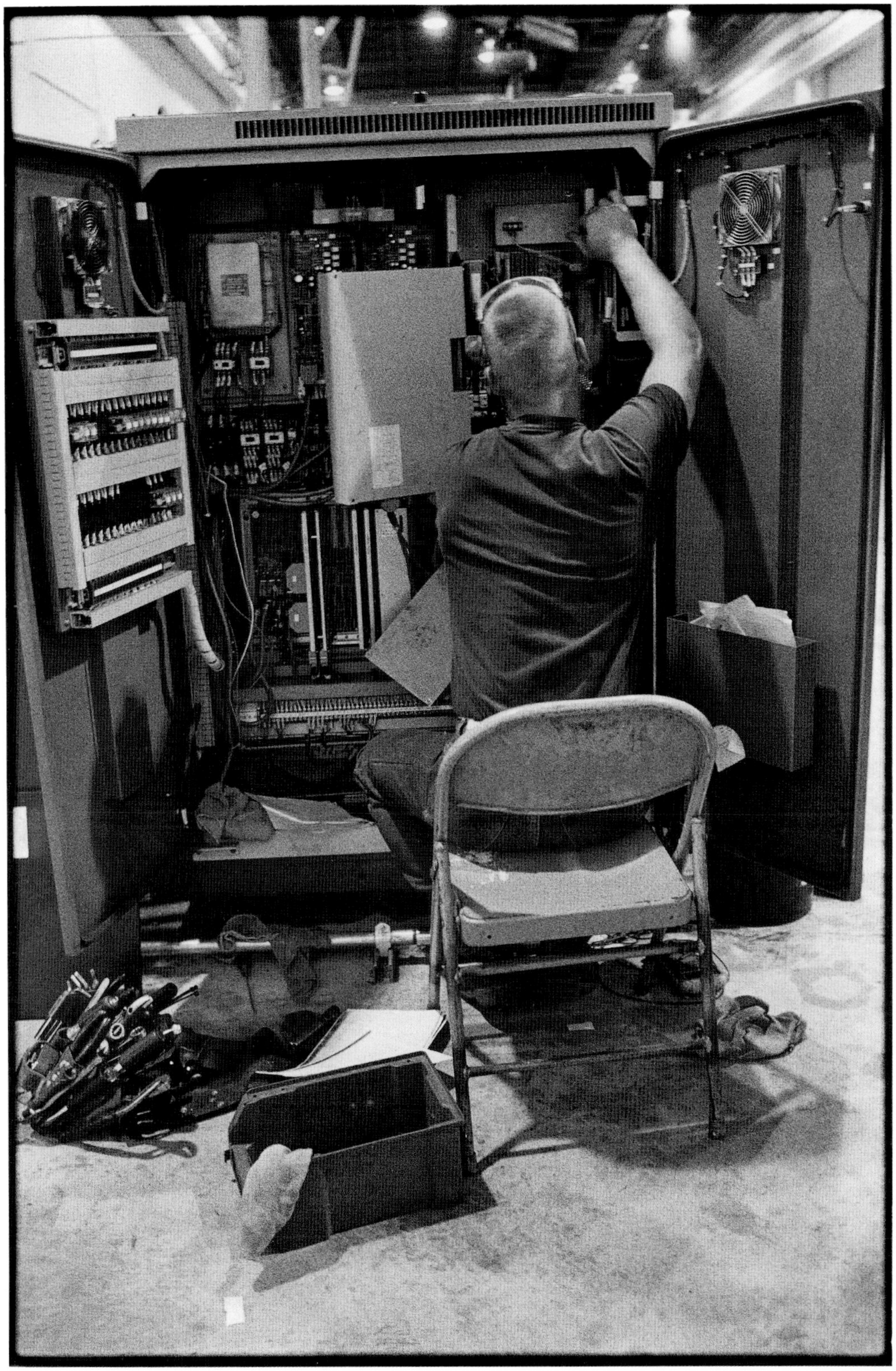

Electronics repair
Lull International

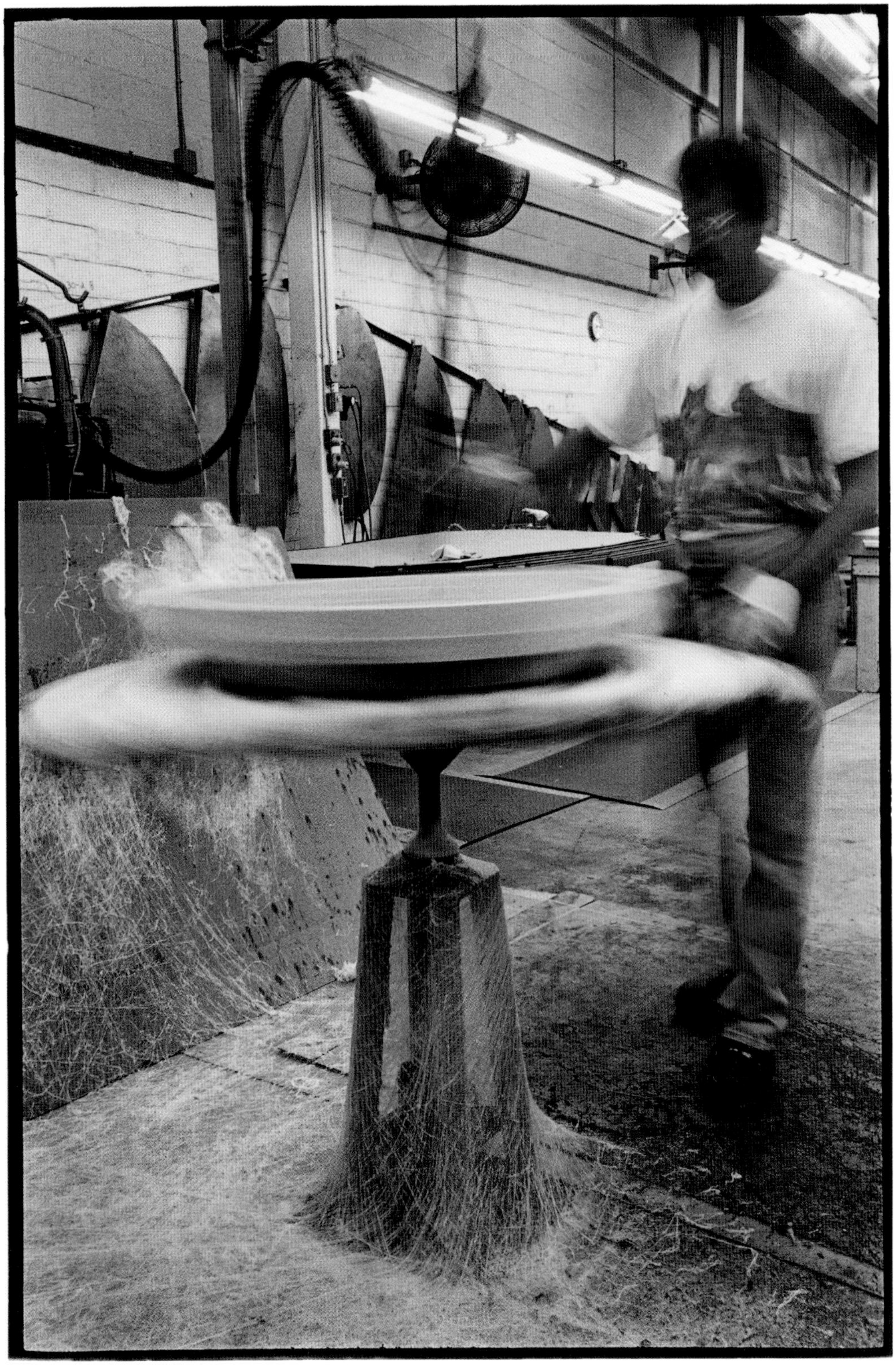

Machine operator
Andersen Window

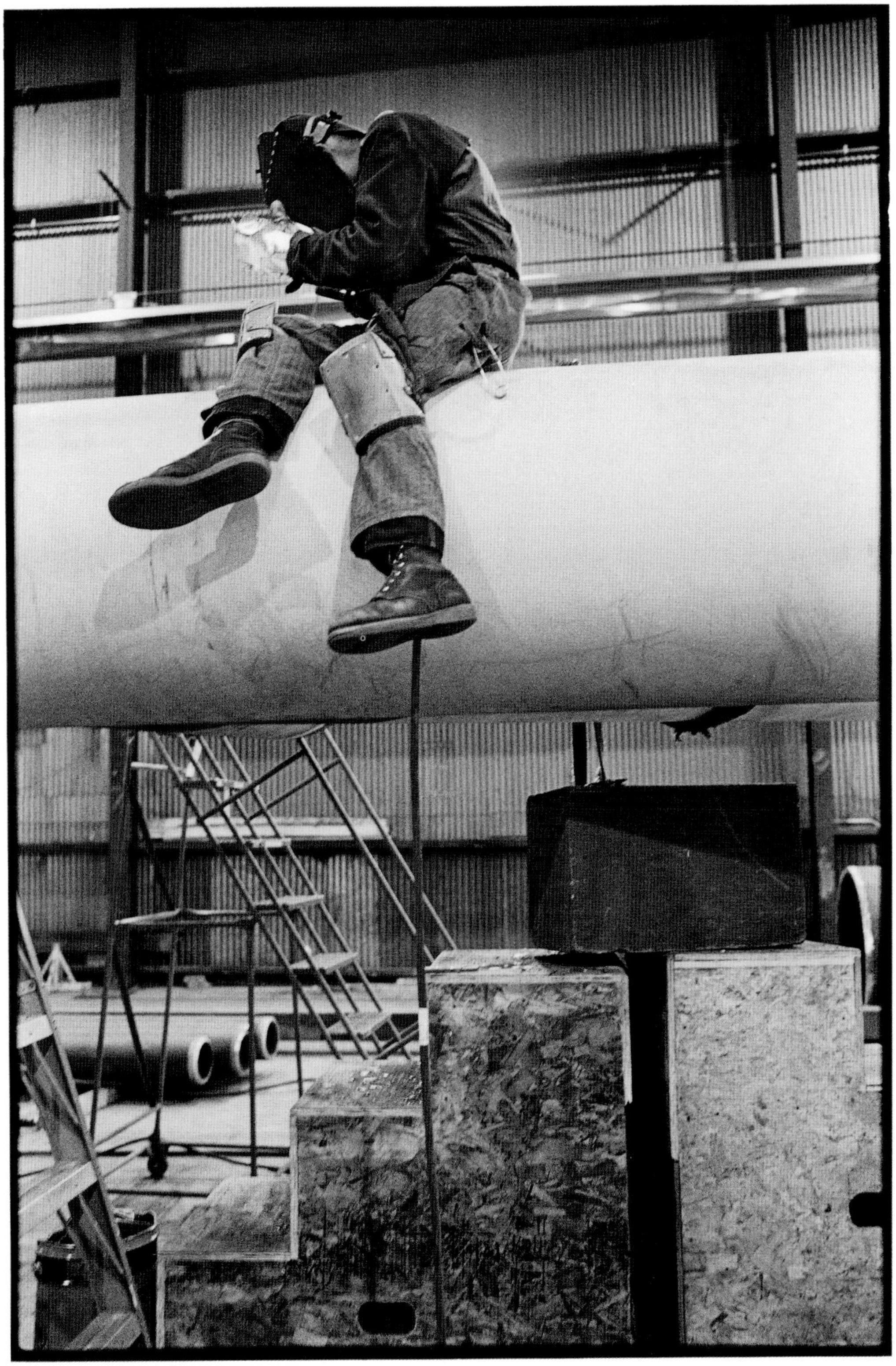

Welder
BendTec

“And it’s a little scary. You go in there, you’re different from everyone else—you’re in a wheelchair—and you don’t . . . they don’t know how to communicate with you and you don’t know how to communicate with them.

“I’m a big guy, and I was big then. And here’s this big guy and he’s in a wheelchair and he can’t hardly do everything that an able-bodied person a third of my size can do. But after you’ve been there for a couple of days, and the people that work around you know that they don’t have to be quite as attentive. They don’t have to get you this, get you that. Give him a little space and he can do it himself.”

CHARLES OSTERFELD
ROSEMOUNT ENGINEERING

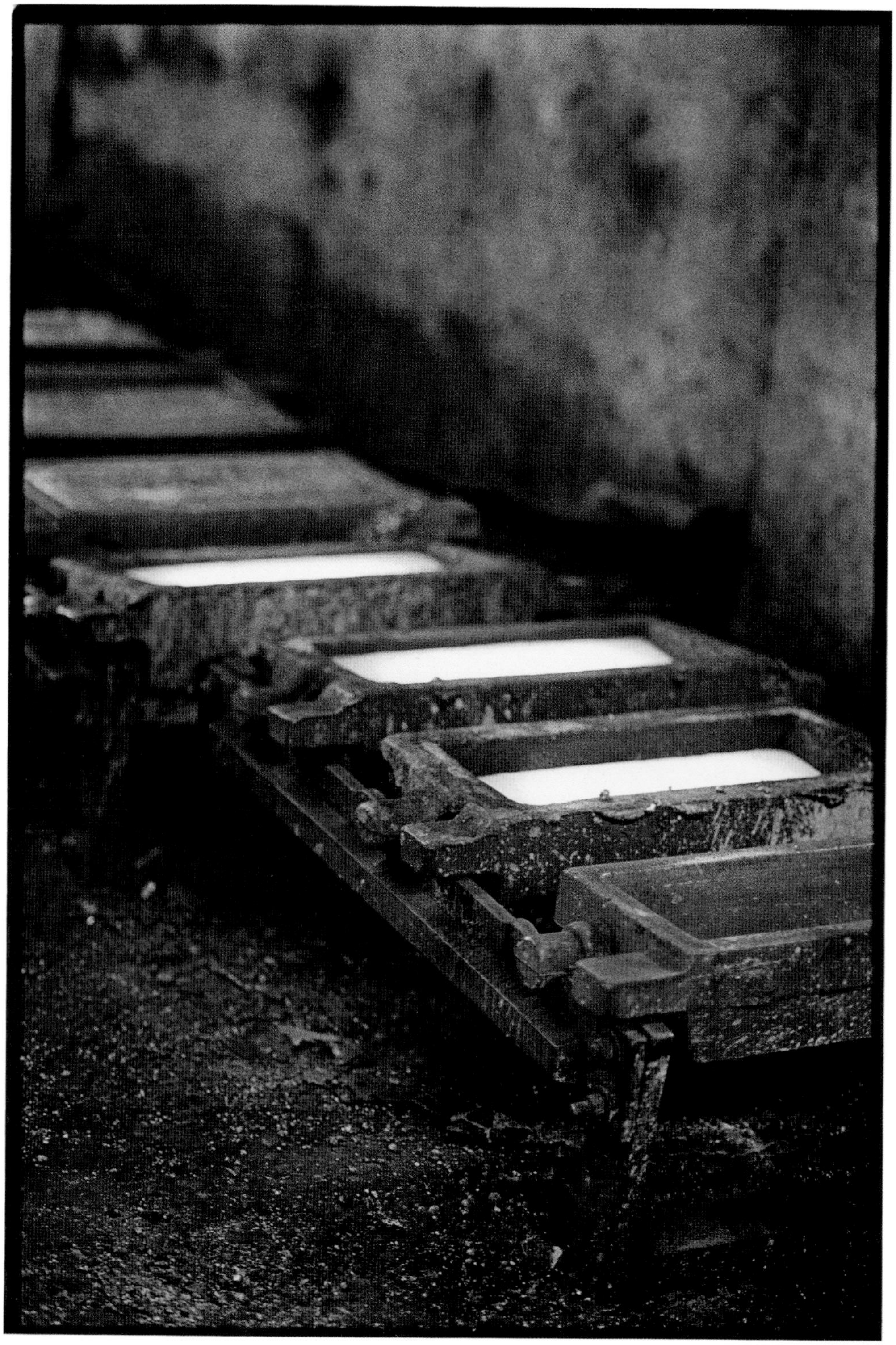

Molten steel in molds

Smith Foundry

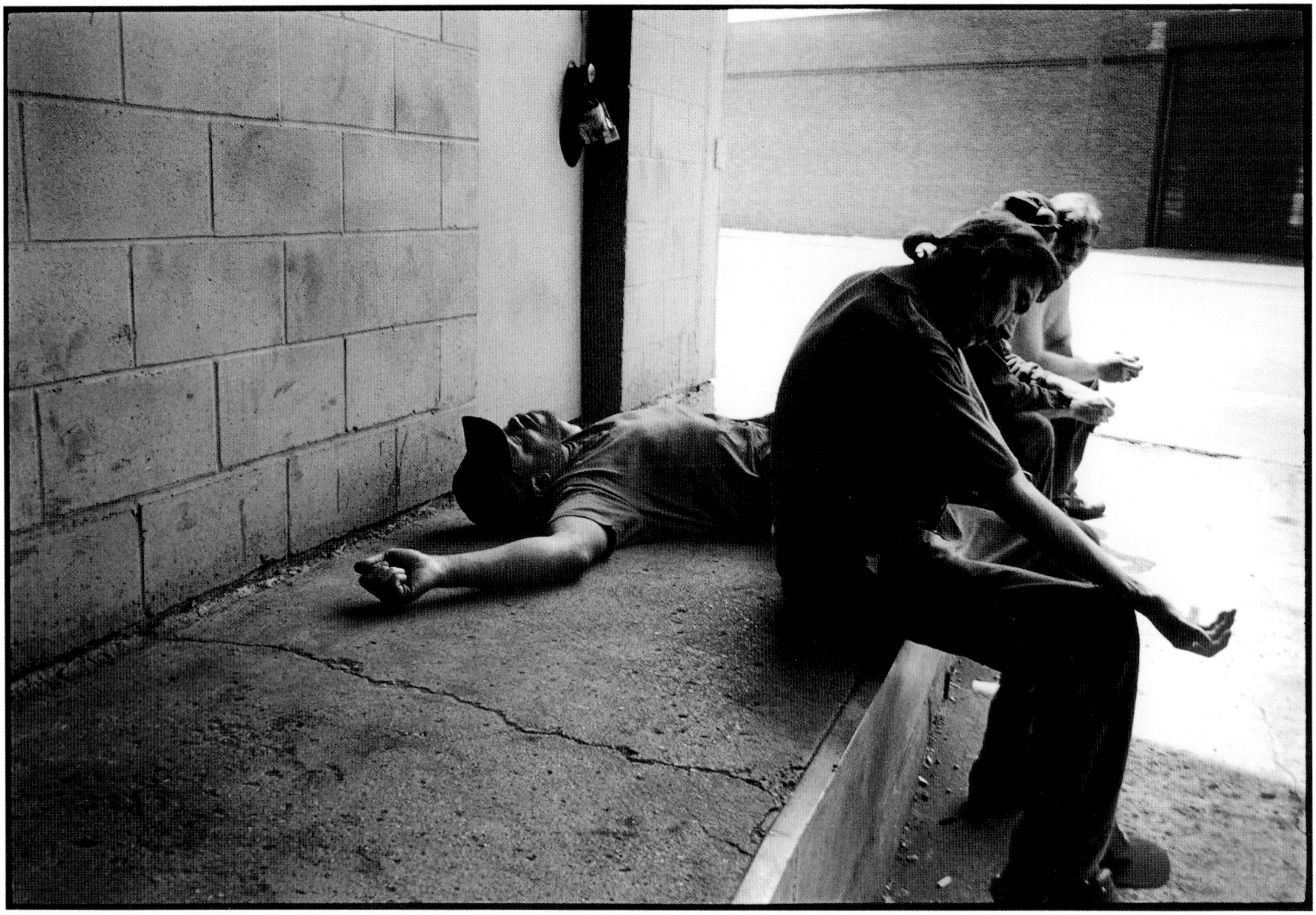

Rest break on hot day
Acme Foundry

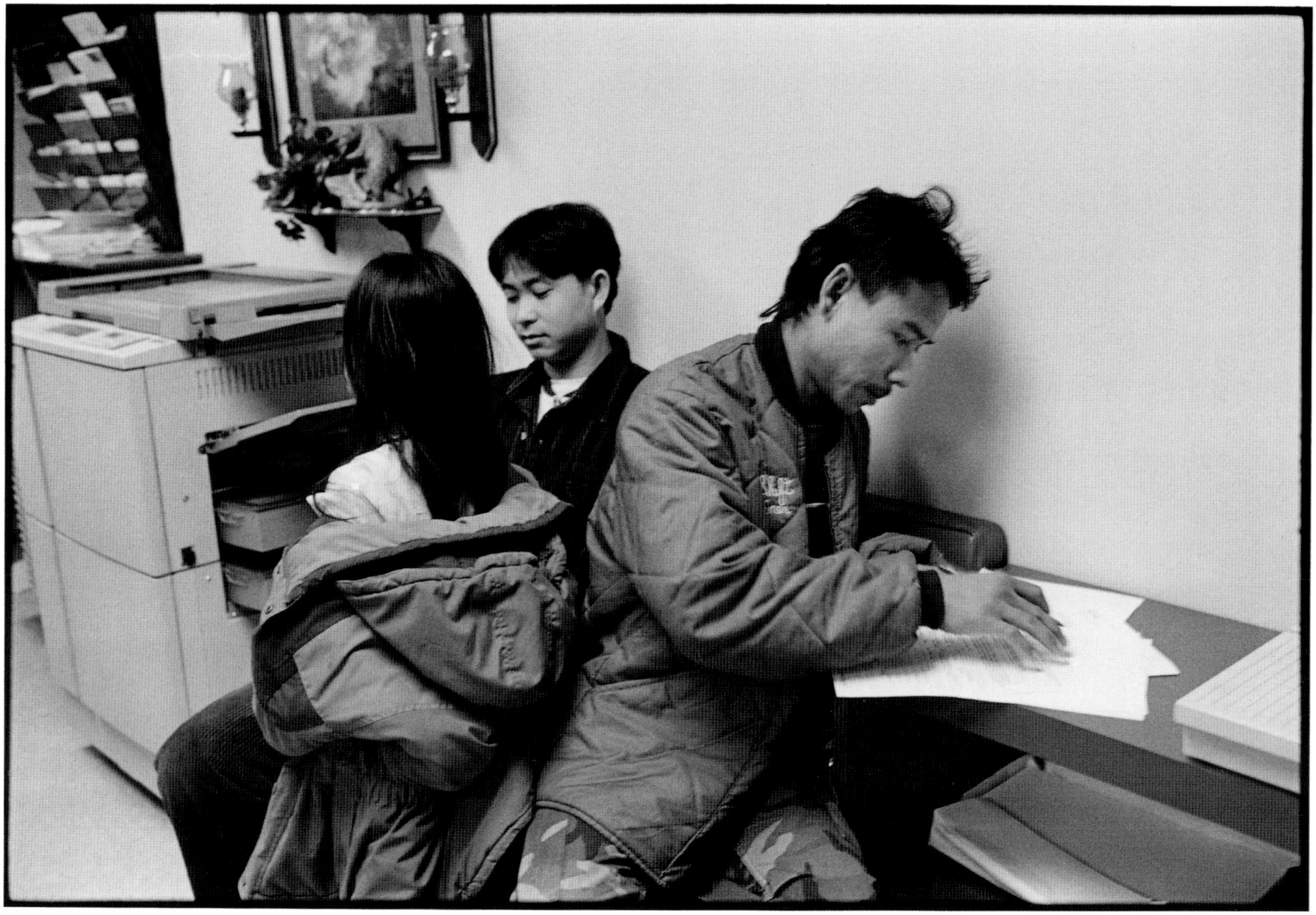

Job applicant

Toro

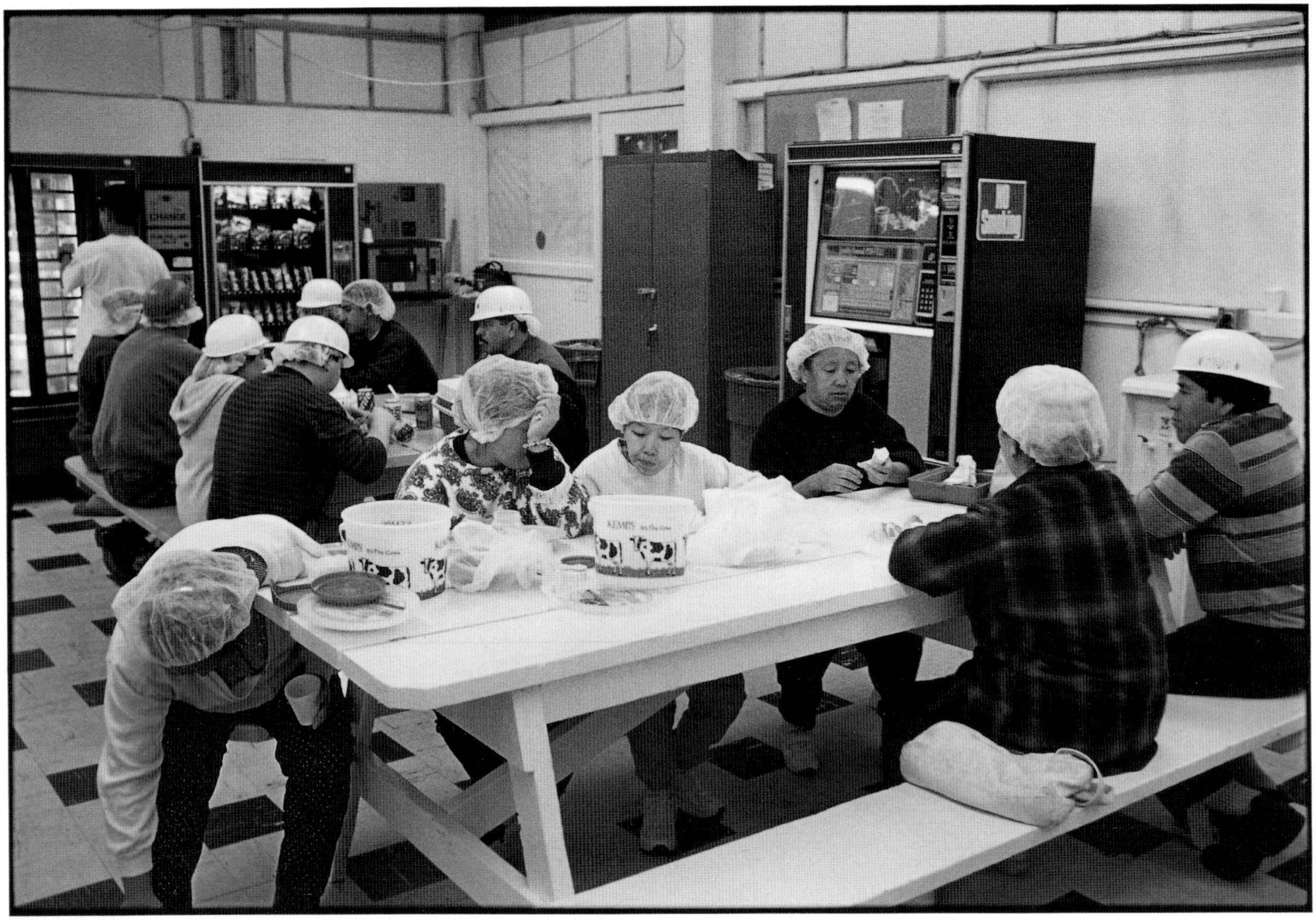

Lunch break
GFI America

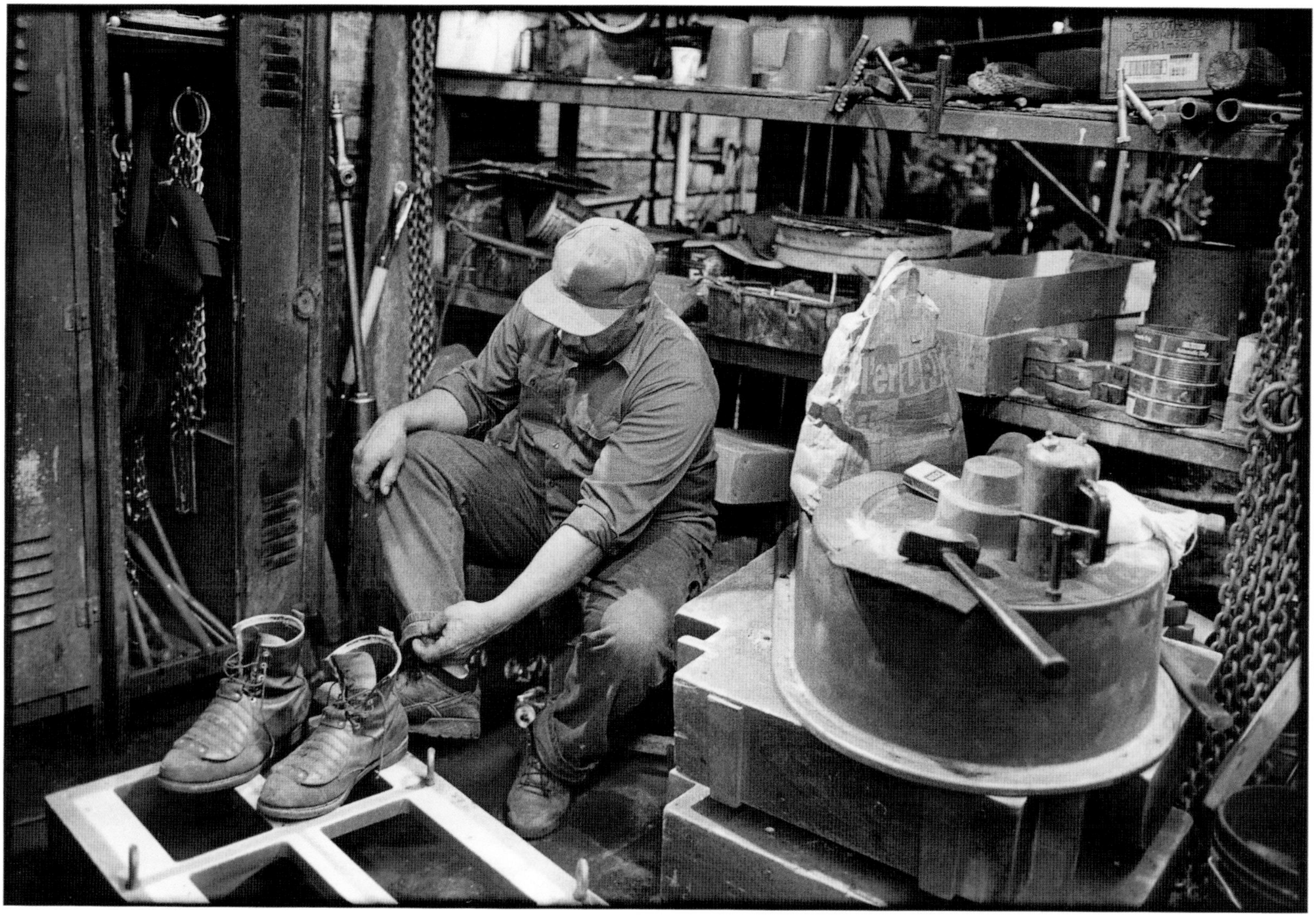

Changing at end of day
Smith Foundry

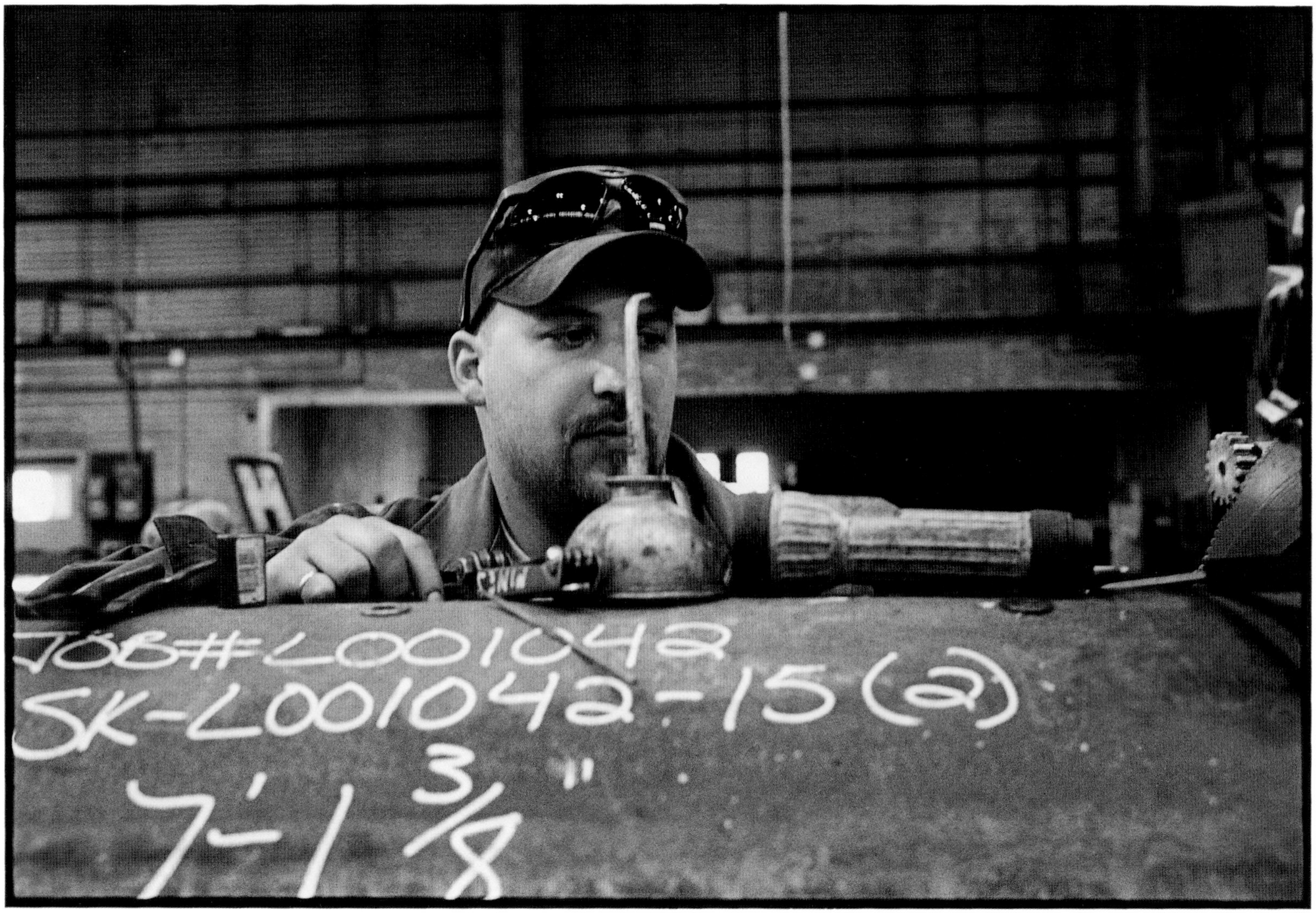

Pipe assembly
BendTec

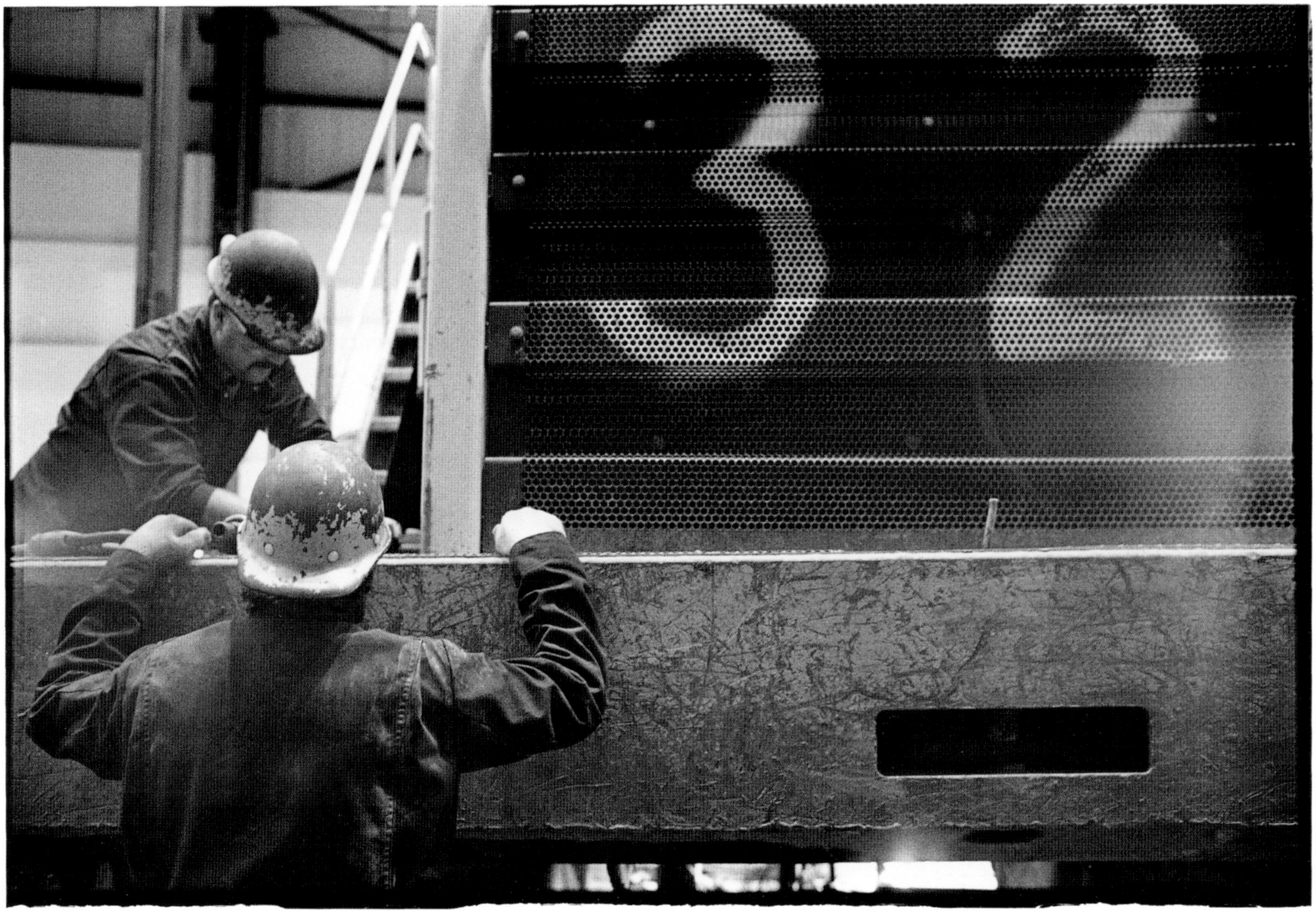

Machine maintenance
Ispat Inland Mining

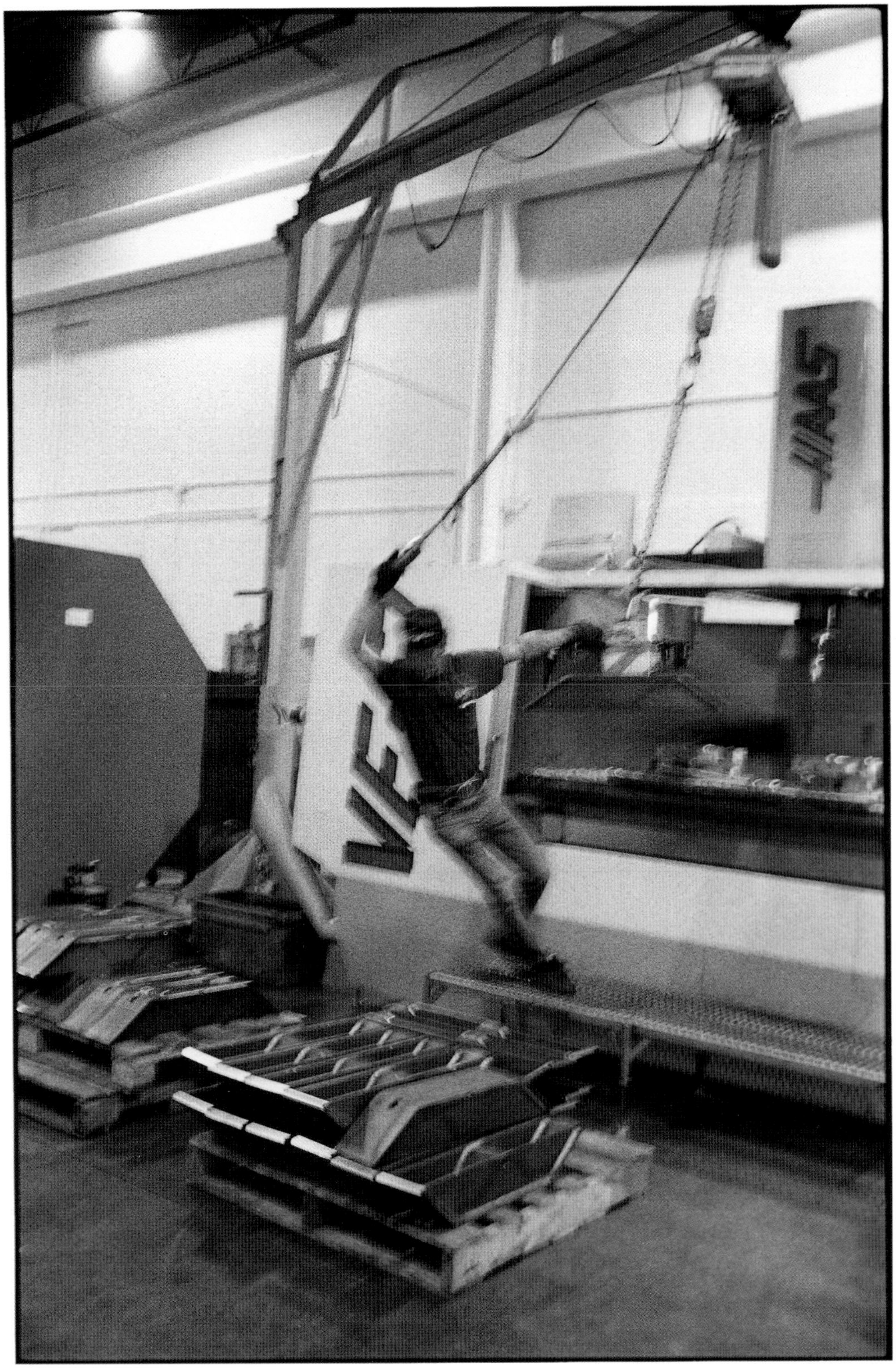

Machine assembly
Lull International

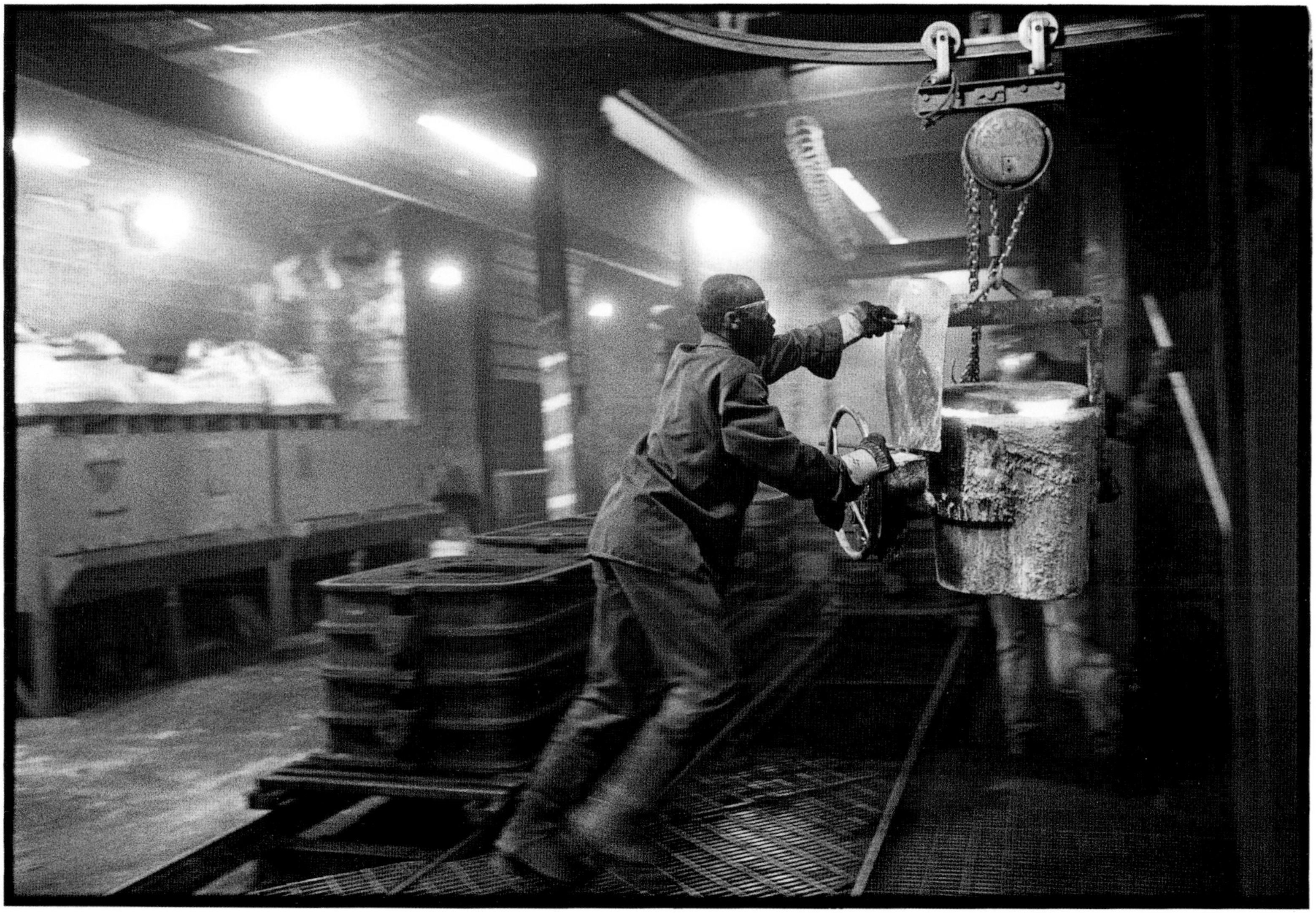

Moving cauldron of molten steel
Smith Foundry

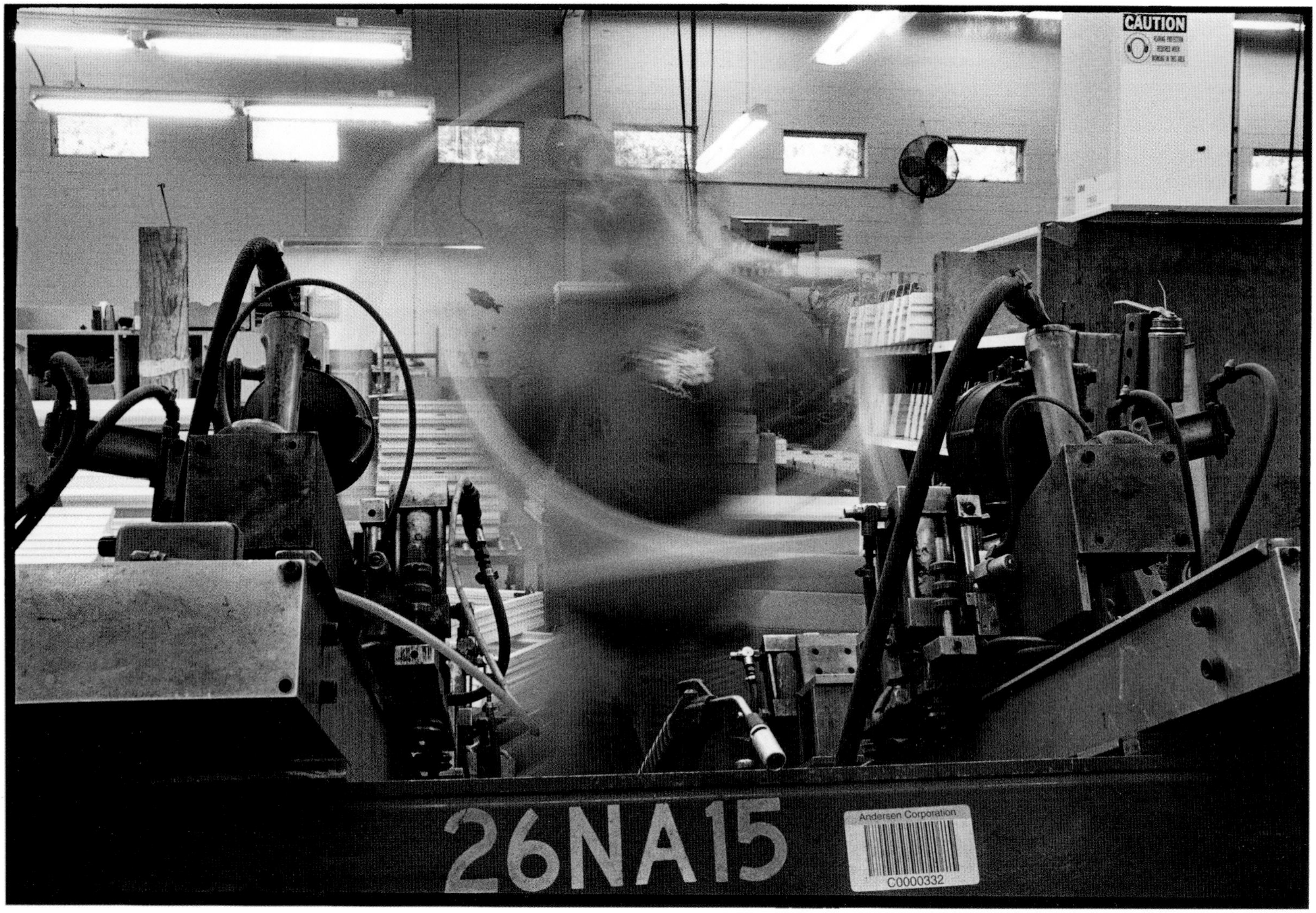

Frame assembly
Andersen Window

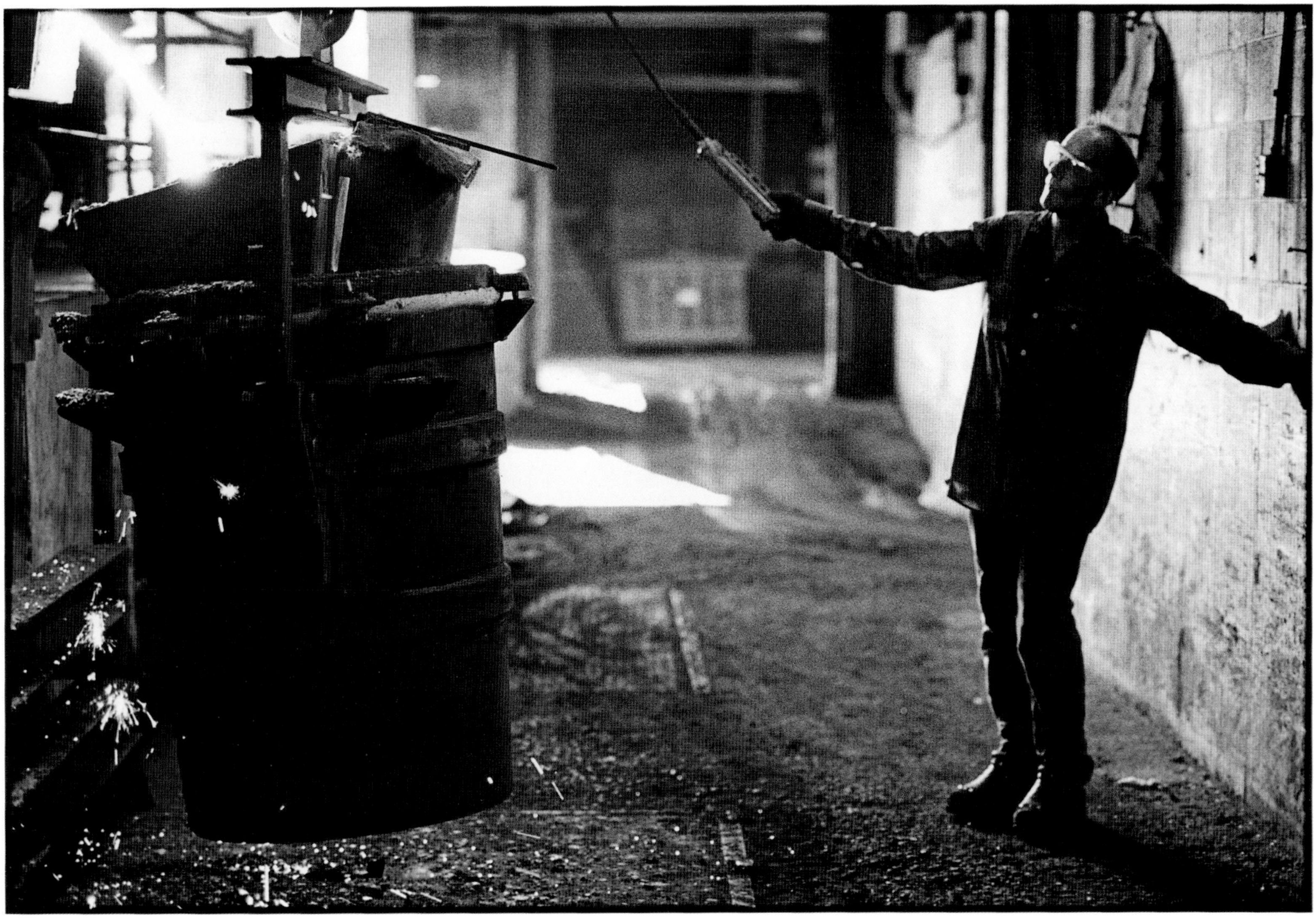

Emptying ladle of steel
Smith Foundry

"We were always together. You'd stop after work—as a crew you'd stop after work—and have a few beers or whatever. It wasn't just by yourself. Or if you had car trouble out in the parking lot at eleven o'clock at night there'd be people pulling up finding out what's wrong. They'd be in there, tearing into the engine if they had to, to get you going so you could go home that night."

ROBERT OSWALD
POTLATCH

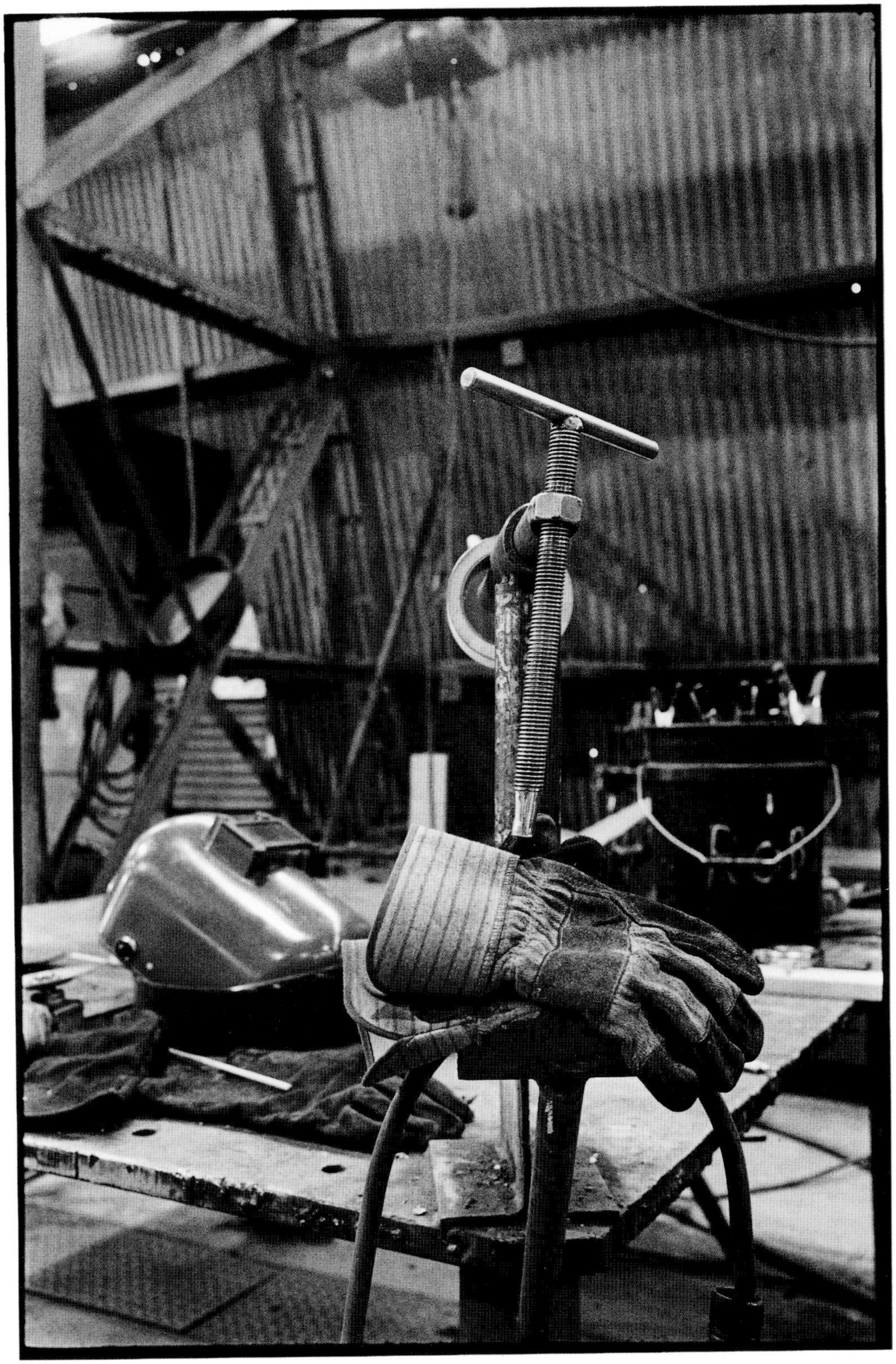

Glove

BendTec

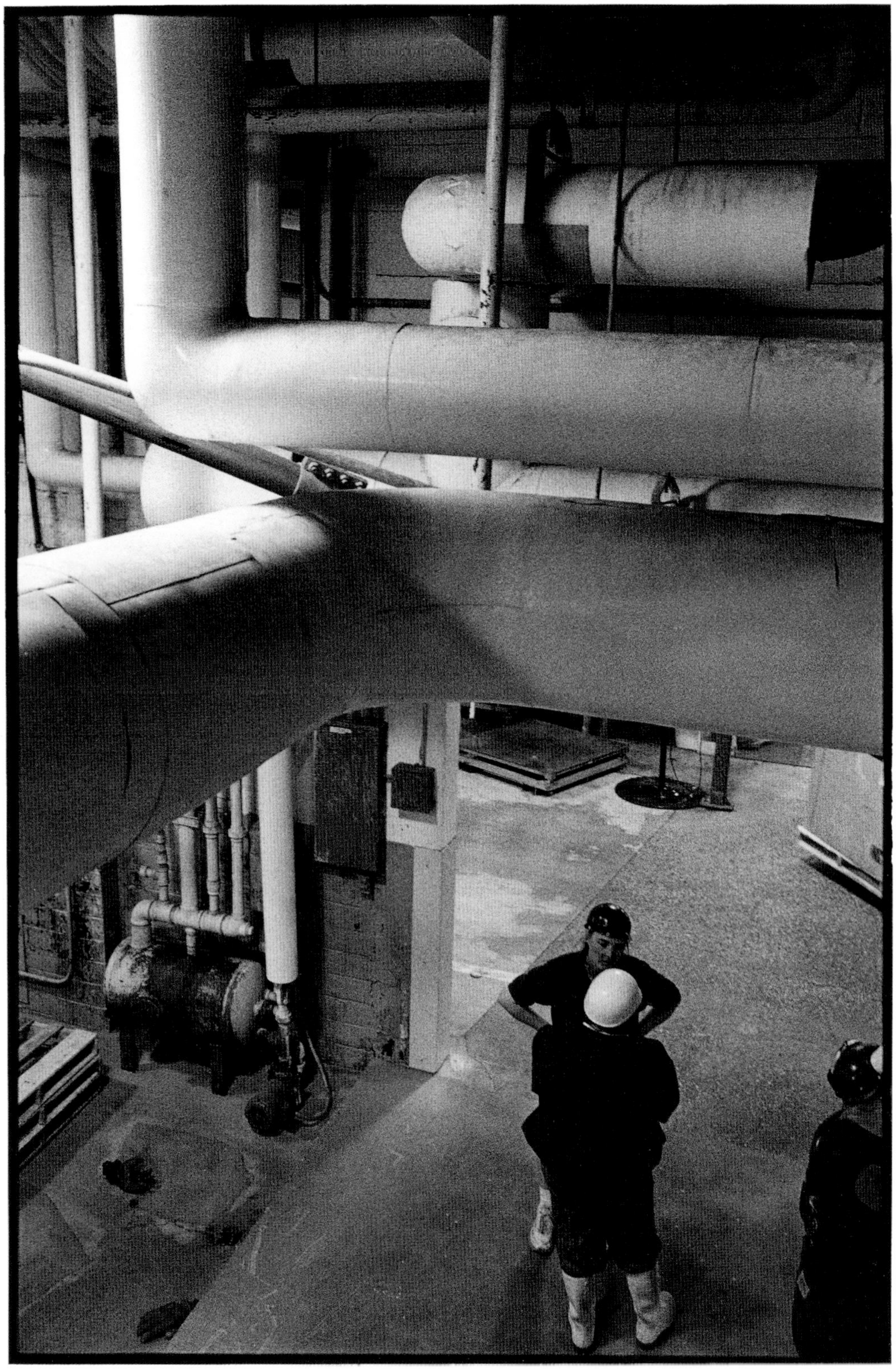

Workers
Agrilink

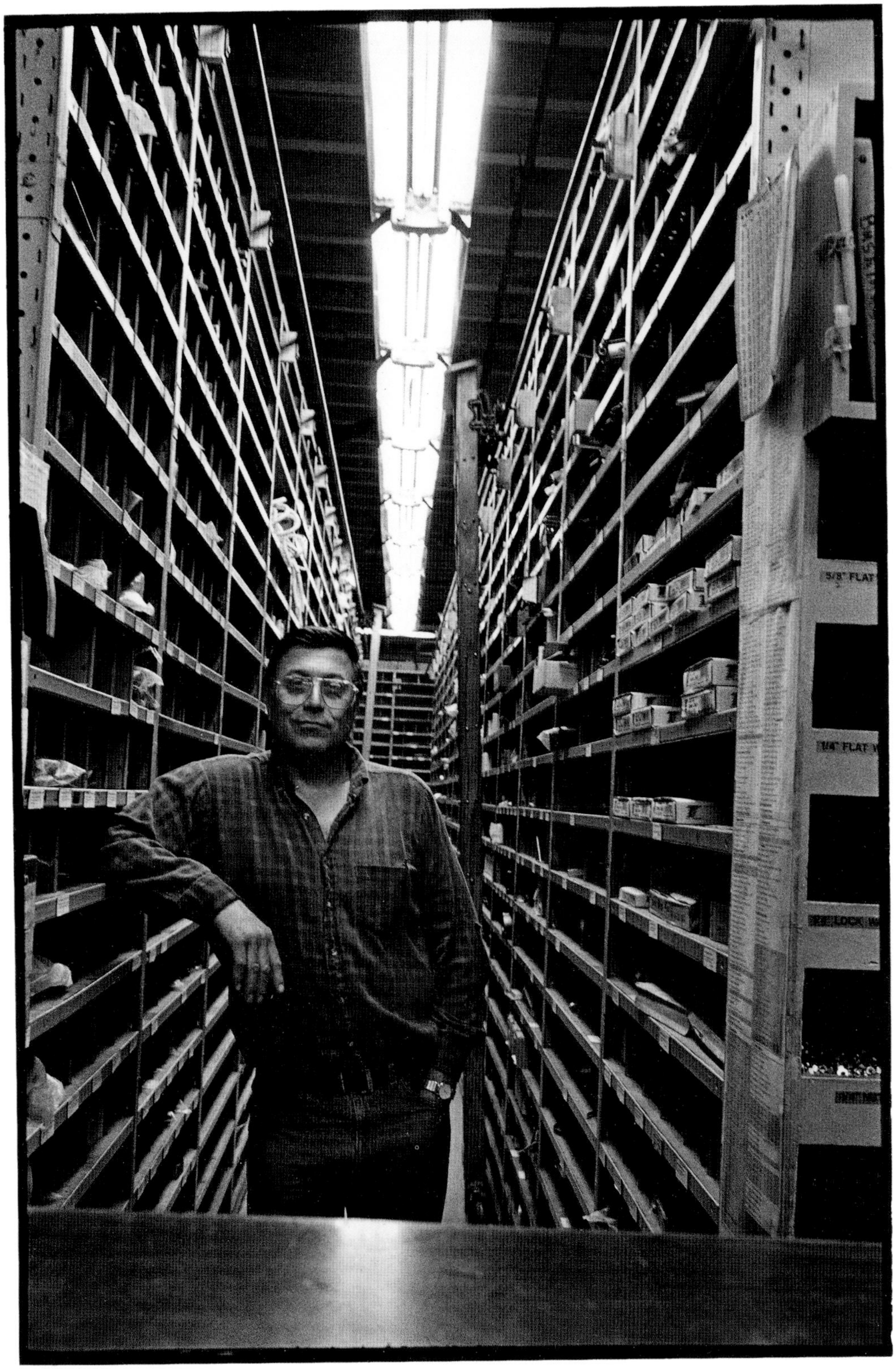

Parts room

Andersen Window

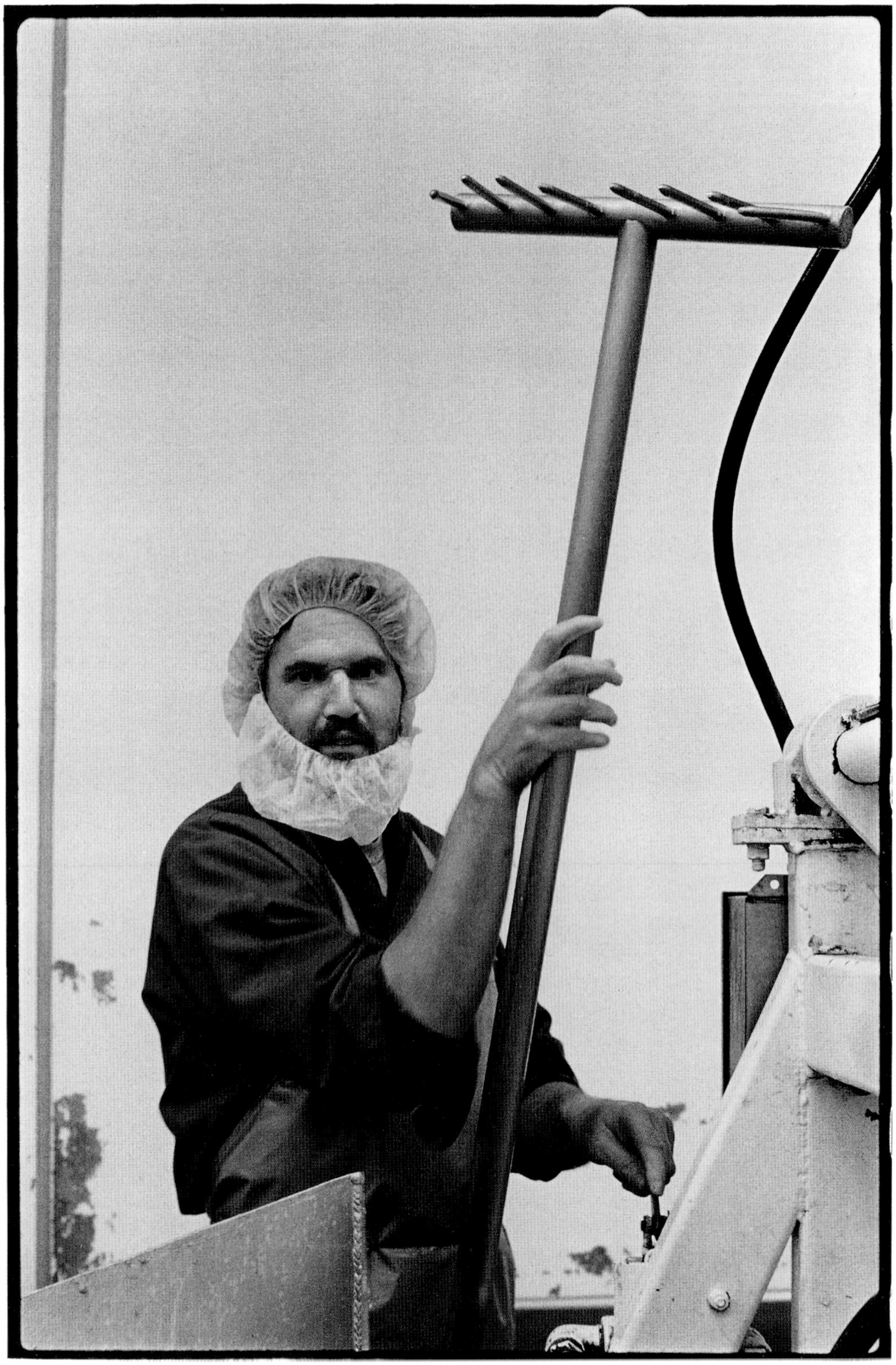

Raking fish
Morey's Seafood

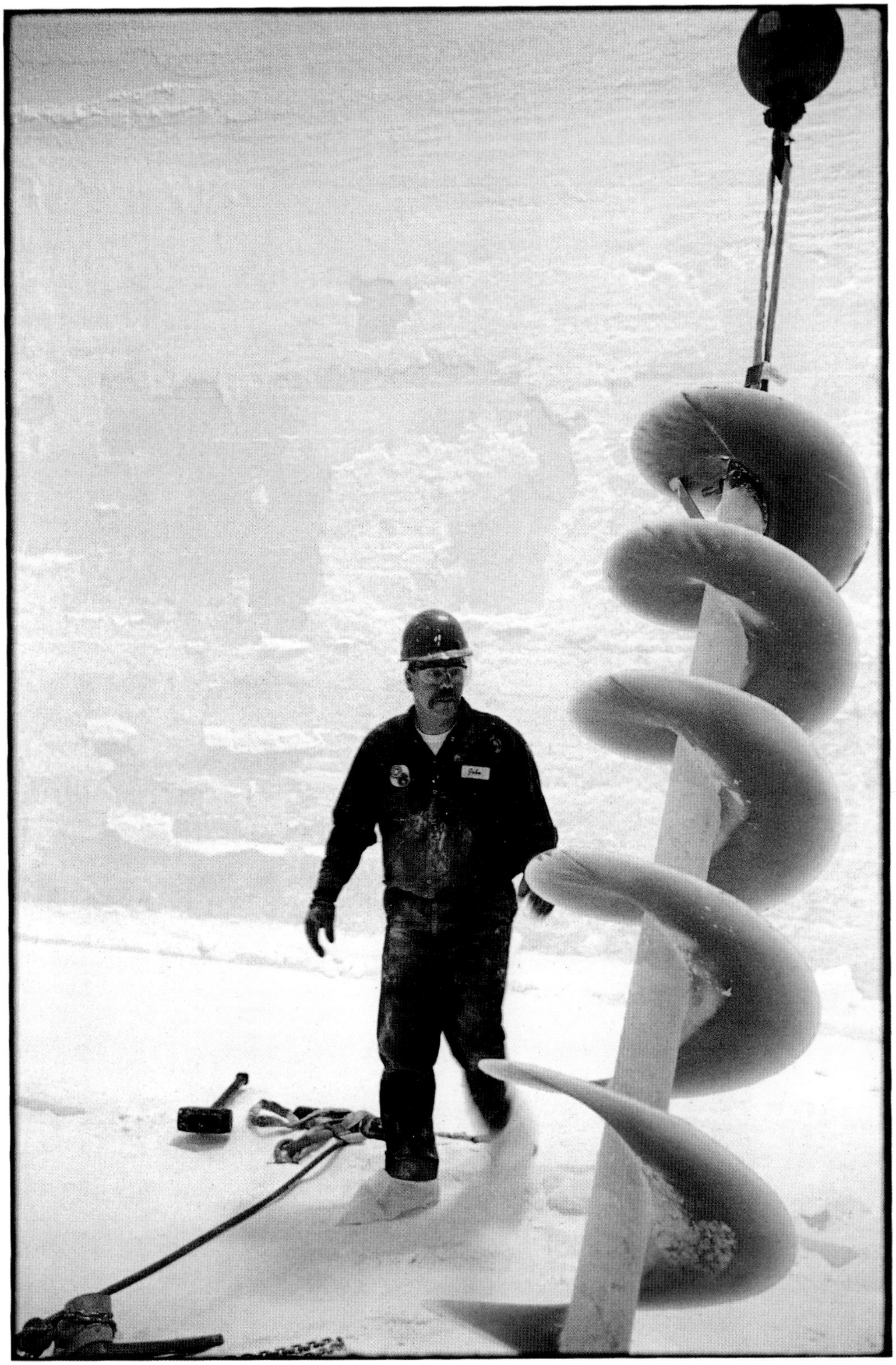

Fixing sugar auger
American Crystal Sugar

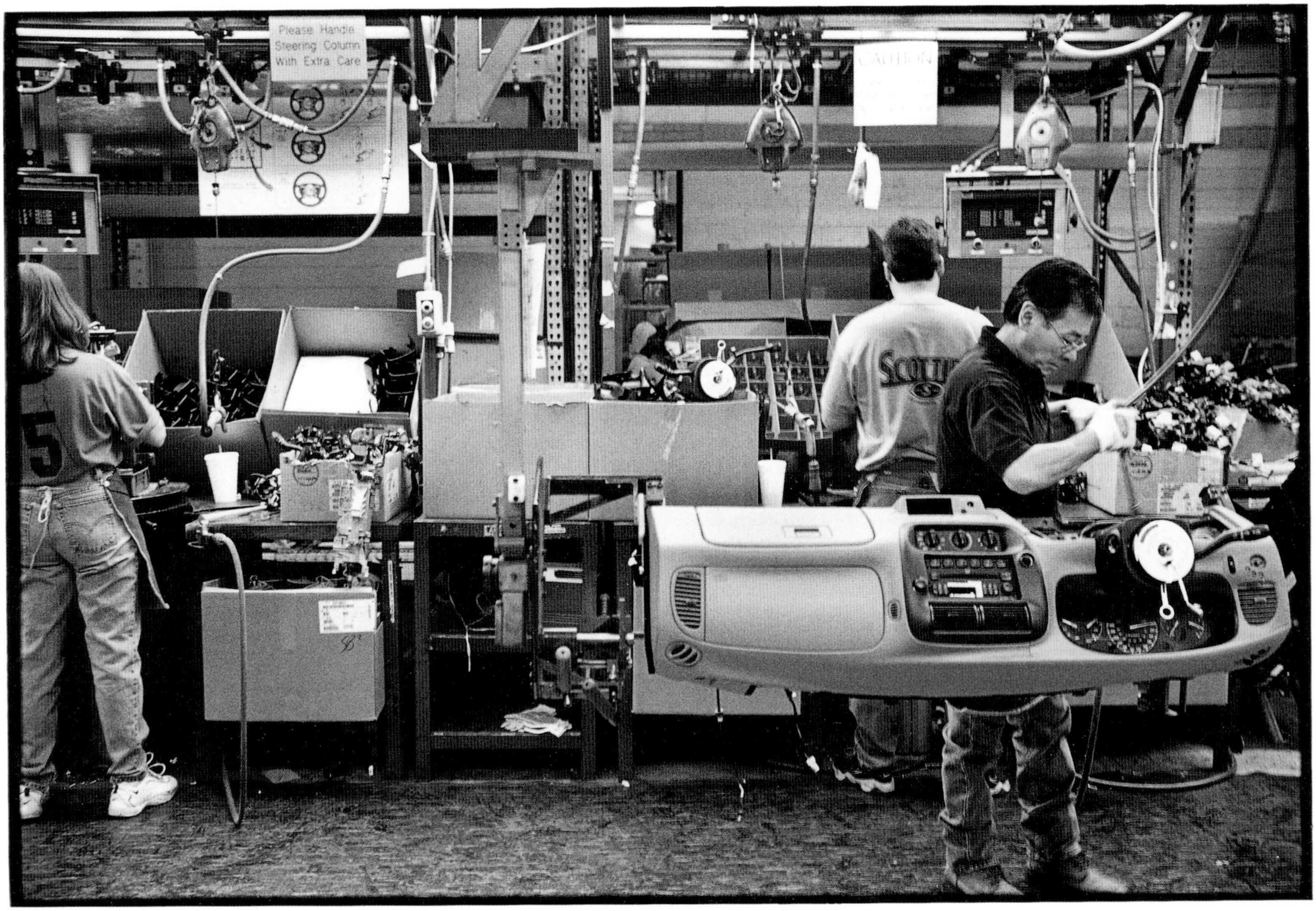

Assembly workers
Ford Motor Company

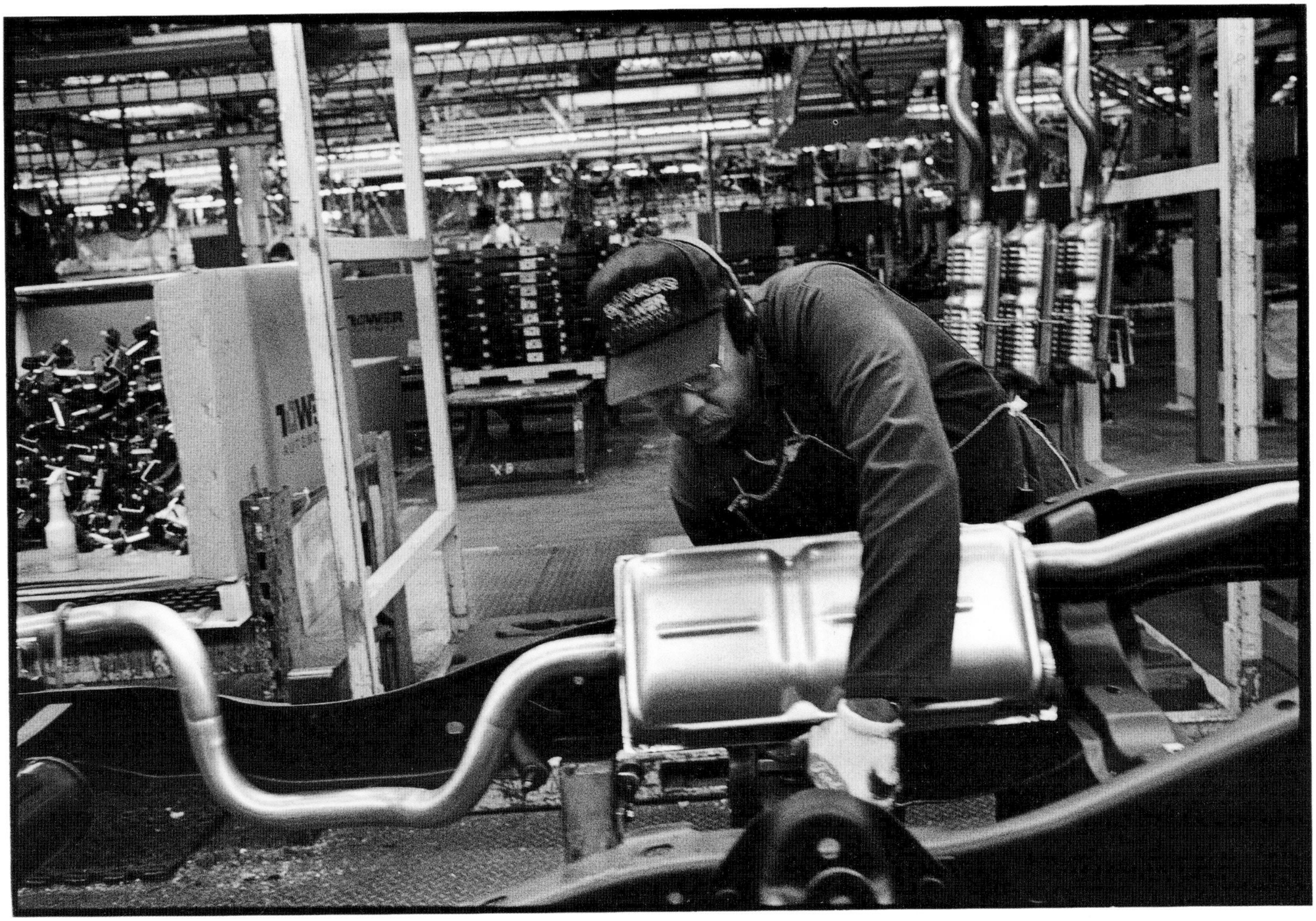

Muffler assembly
Ford Motor Company

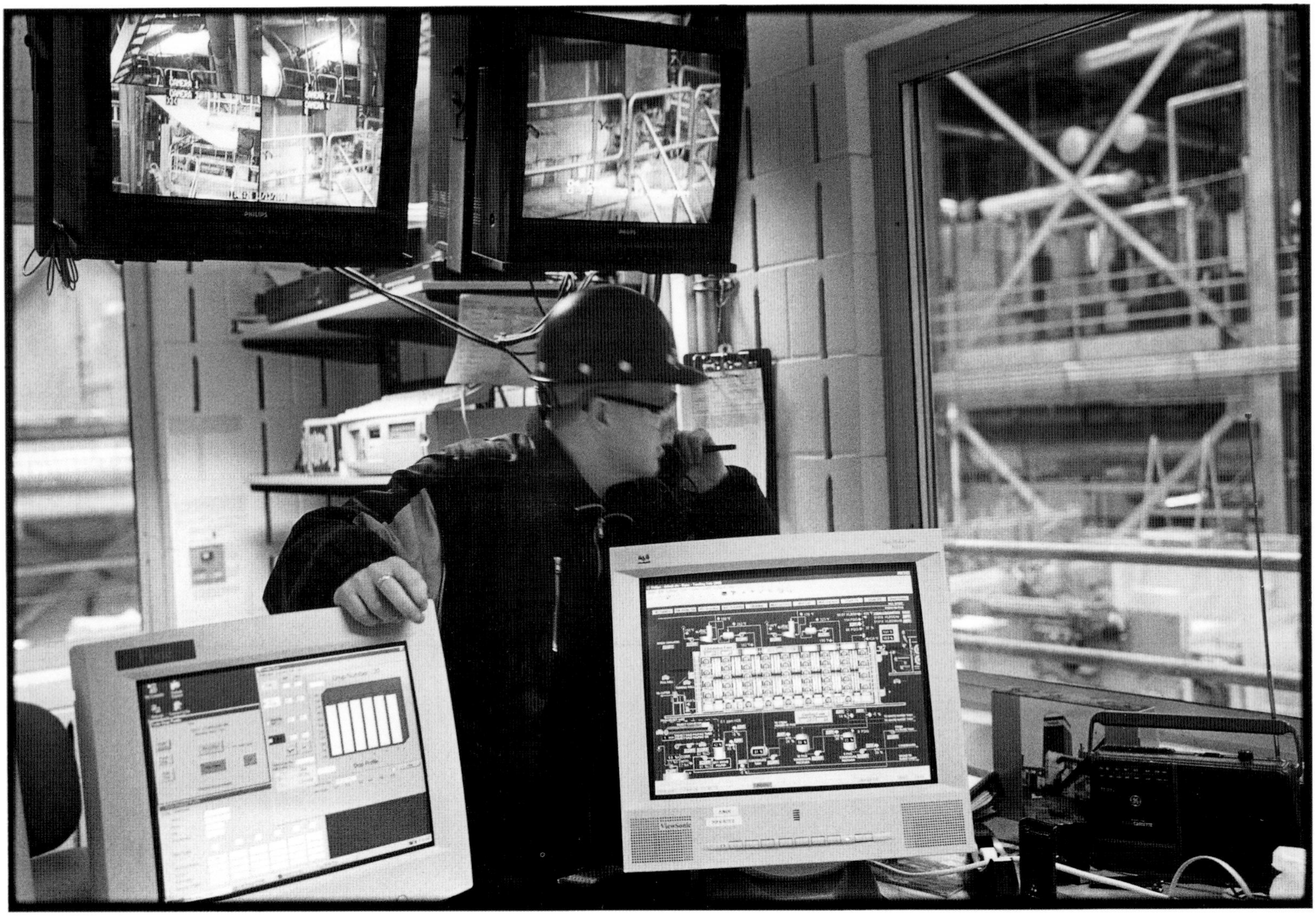

Machine operator
Potlatch

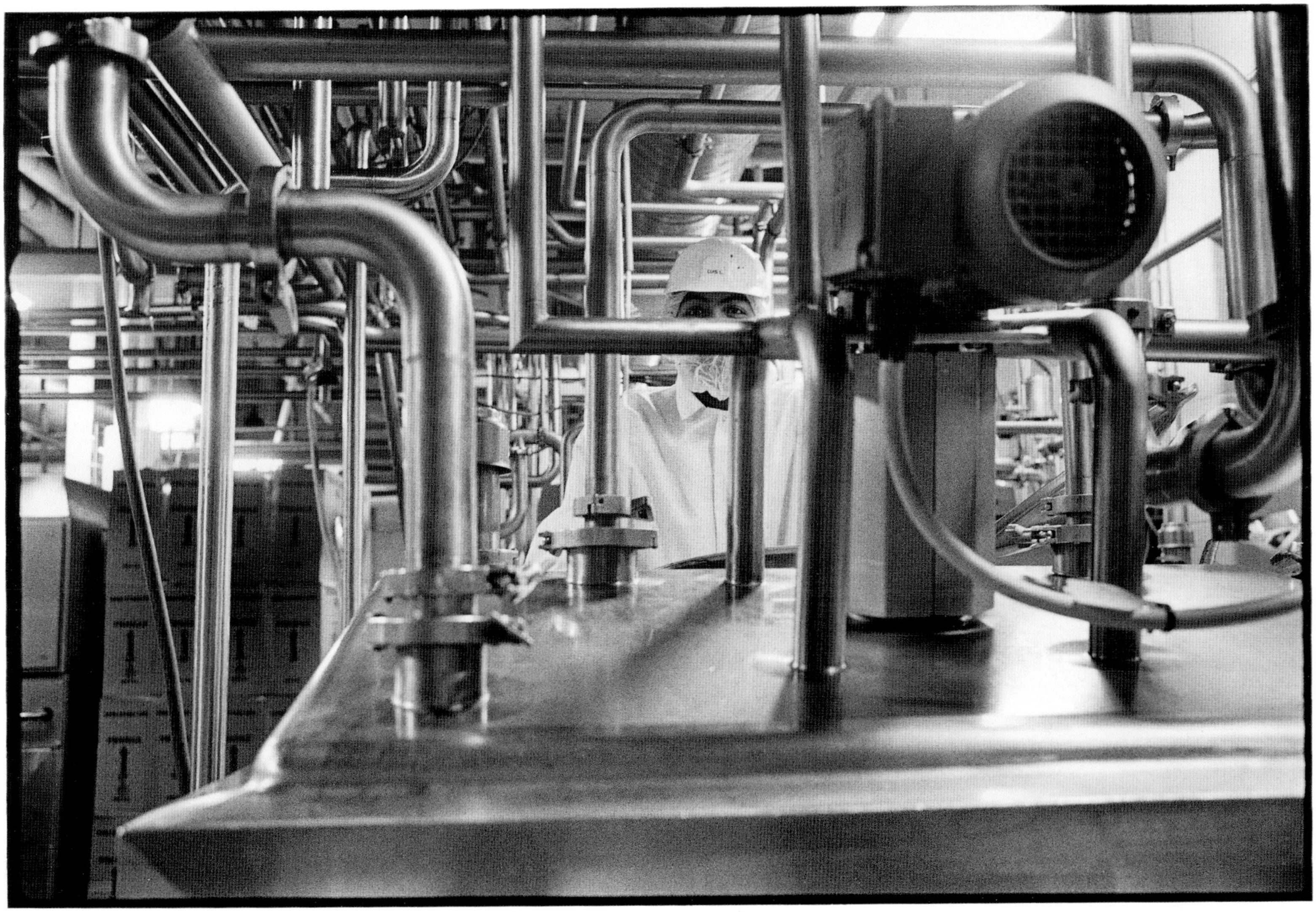

Ice cream room
Schwan's

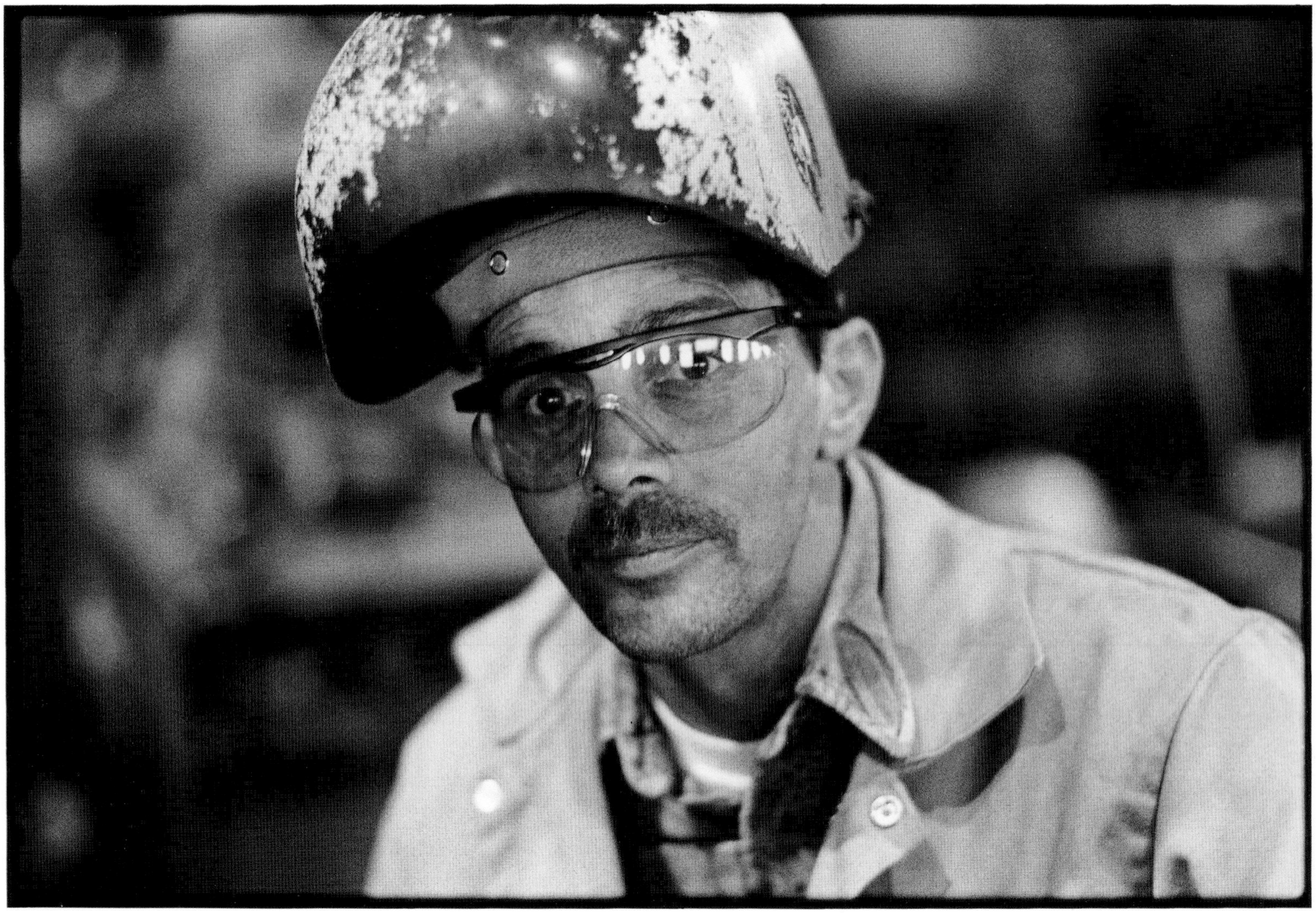

Worker
BendTec

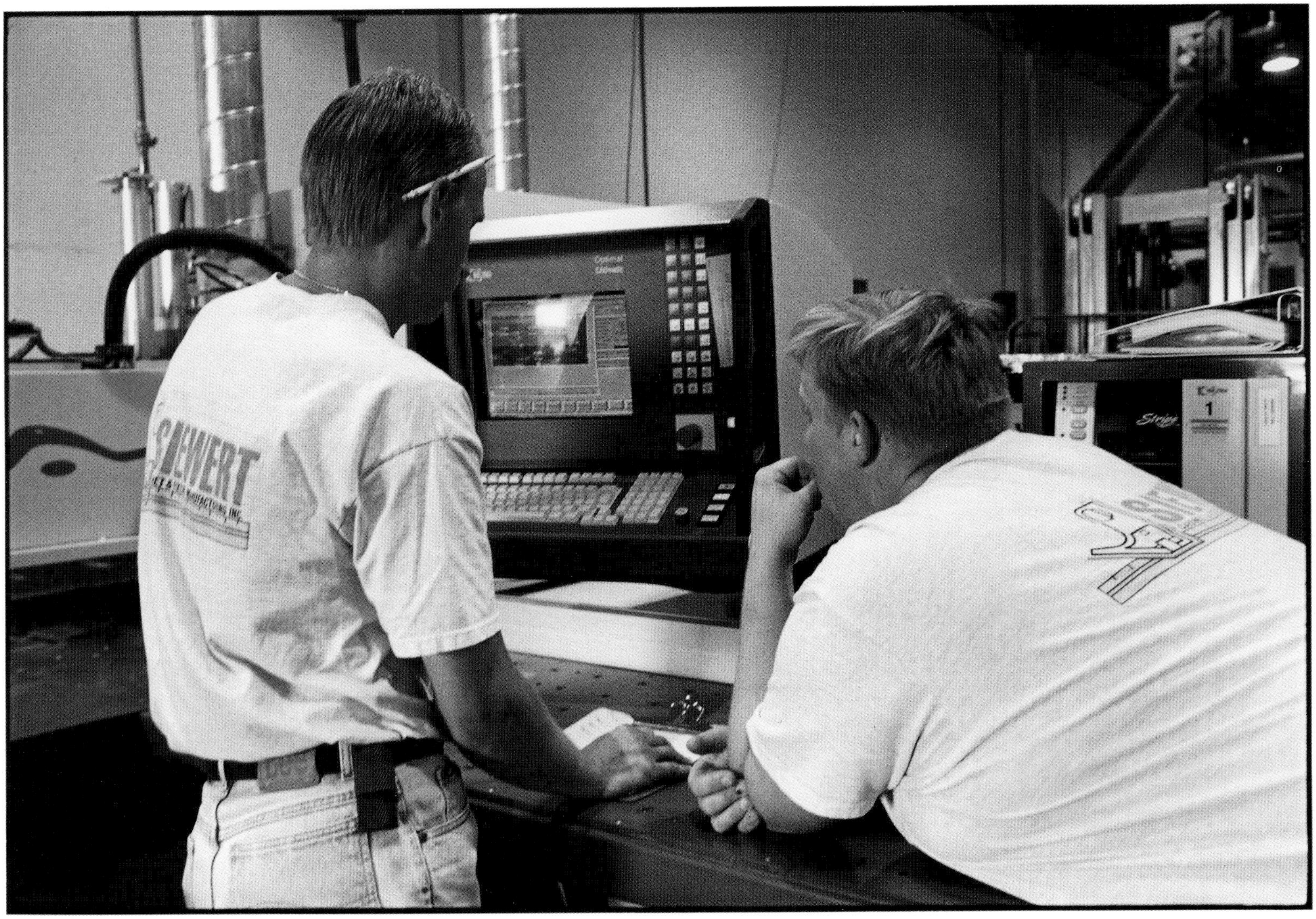

CNC operator
Siewert Cabinet

"But I think everybody sometimes wonders, Do I make a difference as far as my job, making my union better? Doing my job as efficiently as I can? Particularly someone like myself who hits mid-life and you kinda wonder. . . . But I do know that I work with a better group of people—brothers and sisters here in the union at American Crystal Sugar. They're the best people in the world. They make me real proud."

MARK FROEMKE
AMERICAN CRYSTAL SUGAR

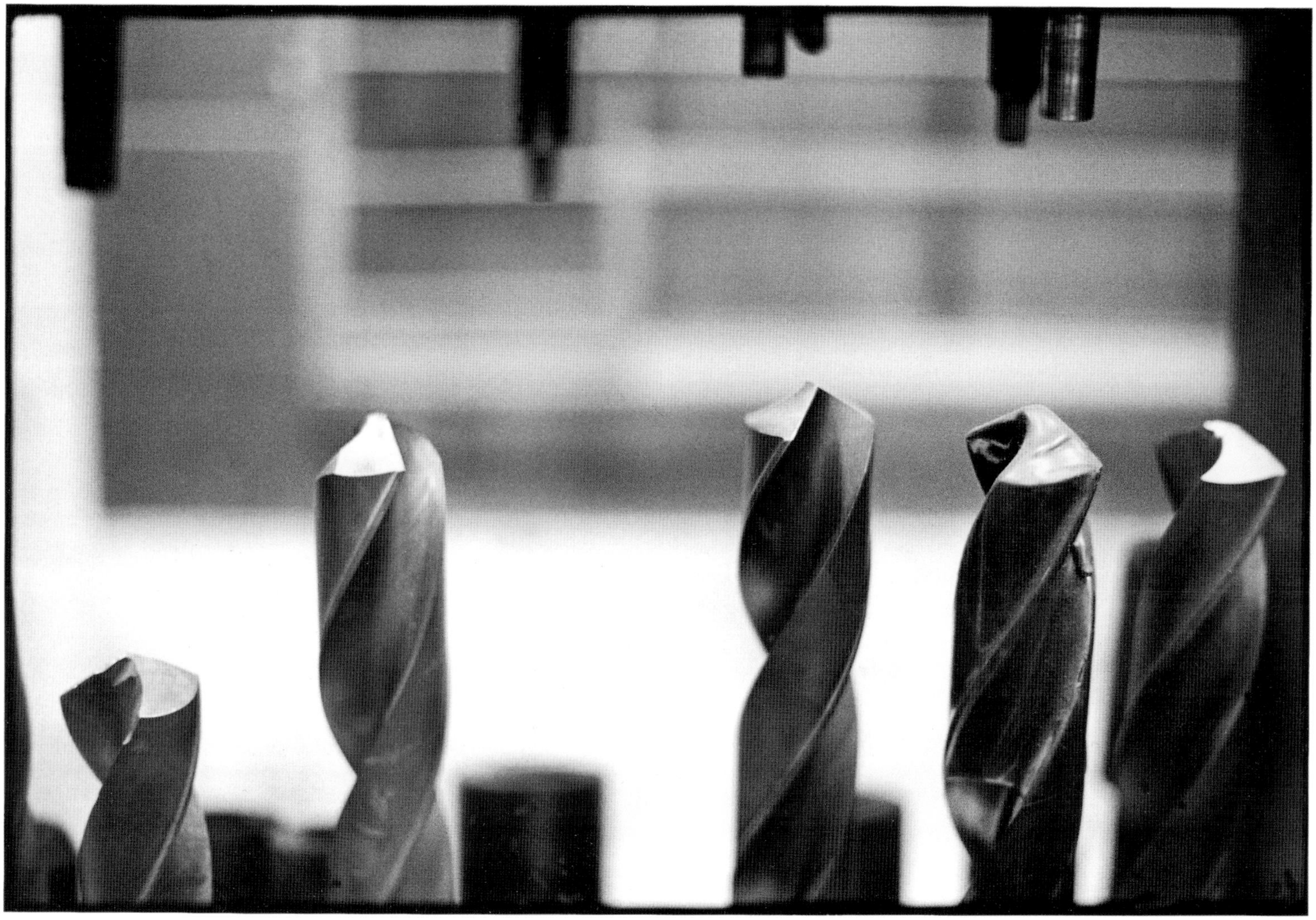

Drill bits

BendTec

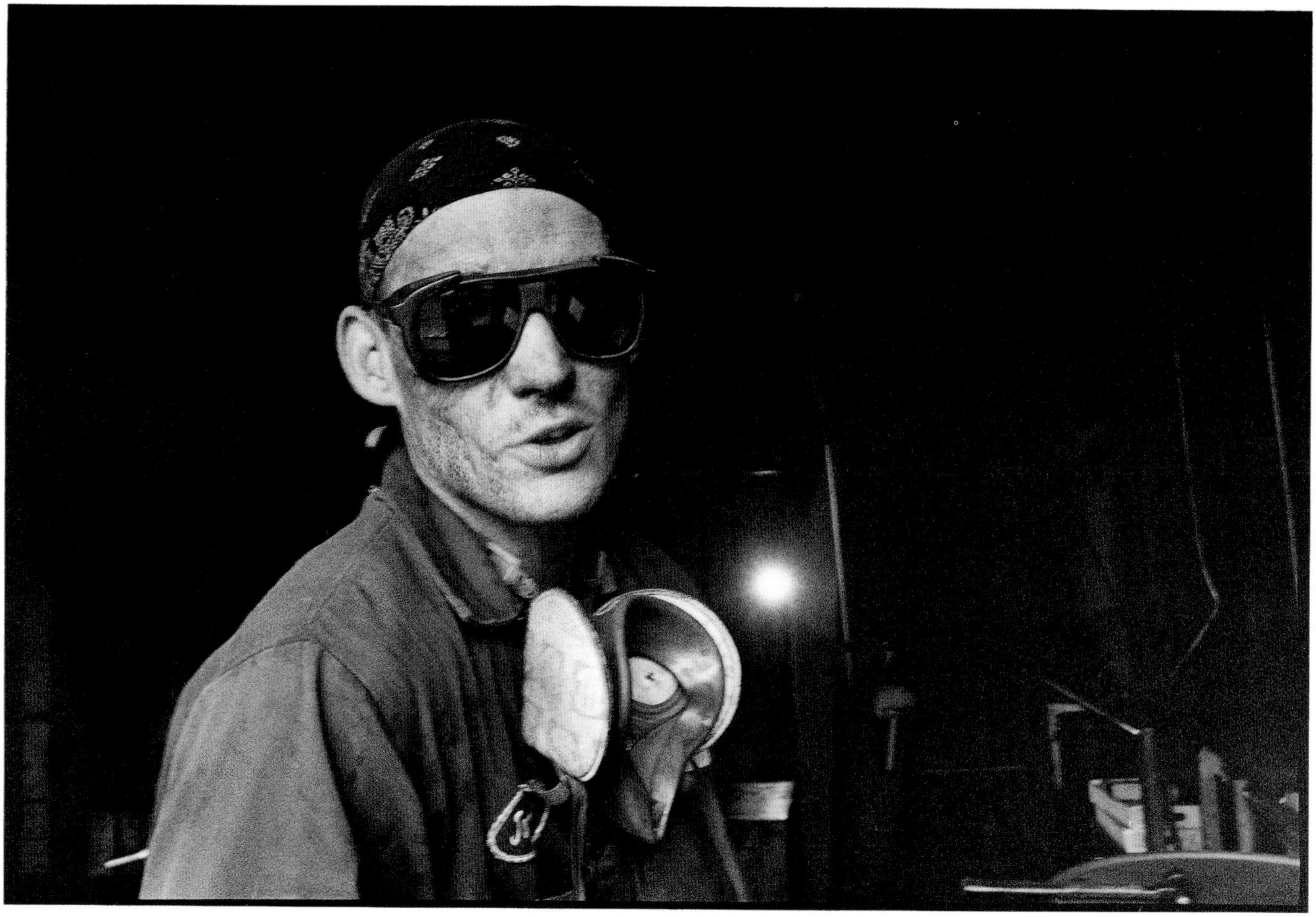

Laborer
Smith Foundry

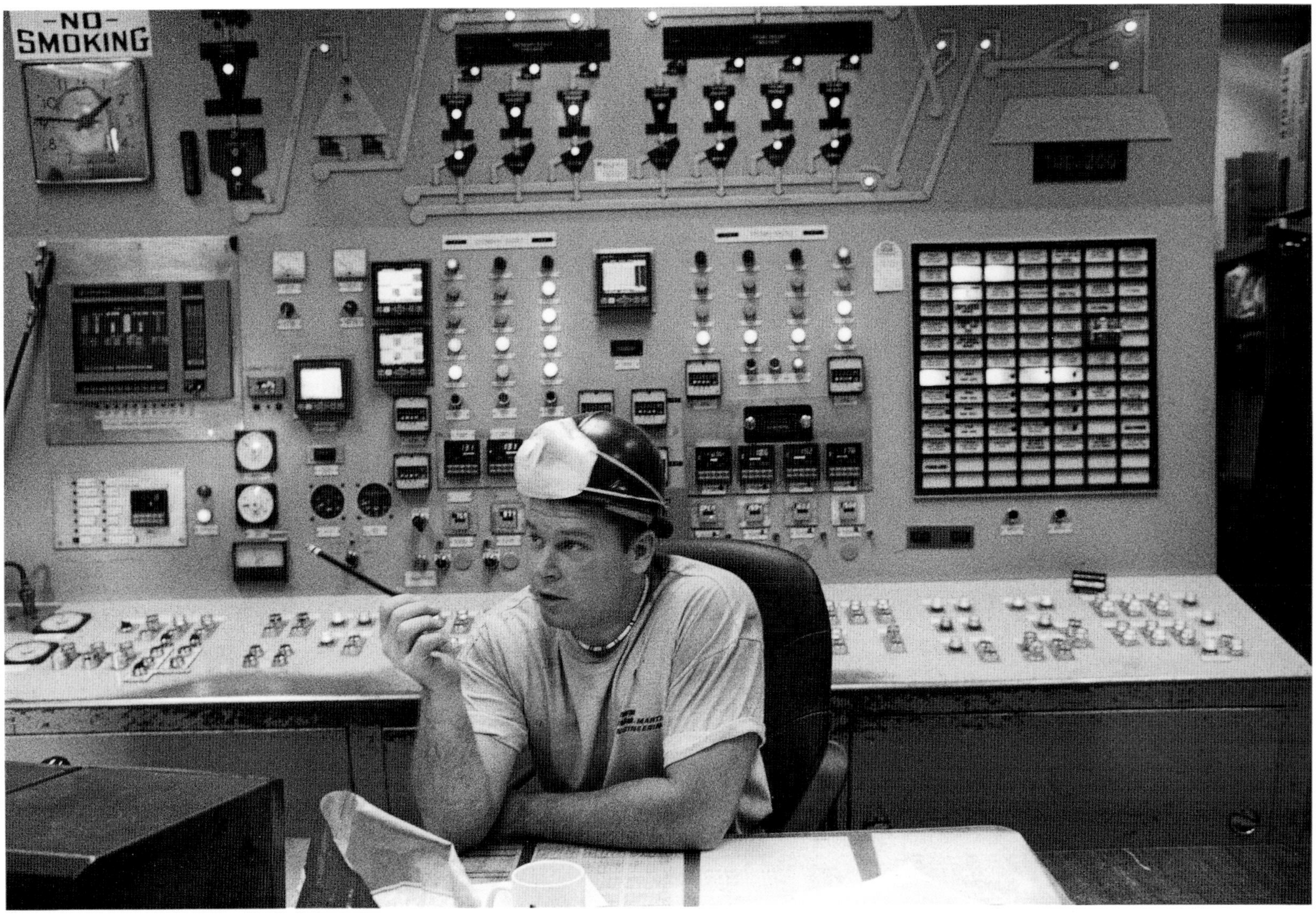

Machine operator
Ispat Inland Mining

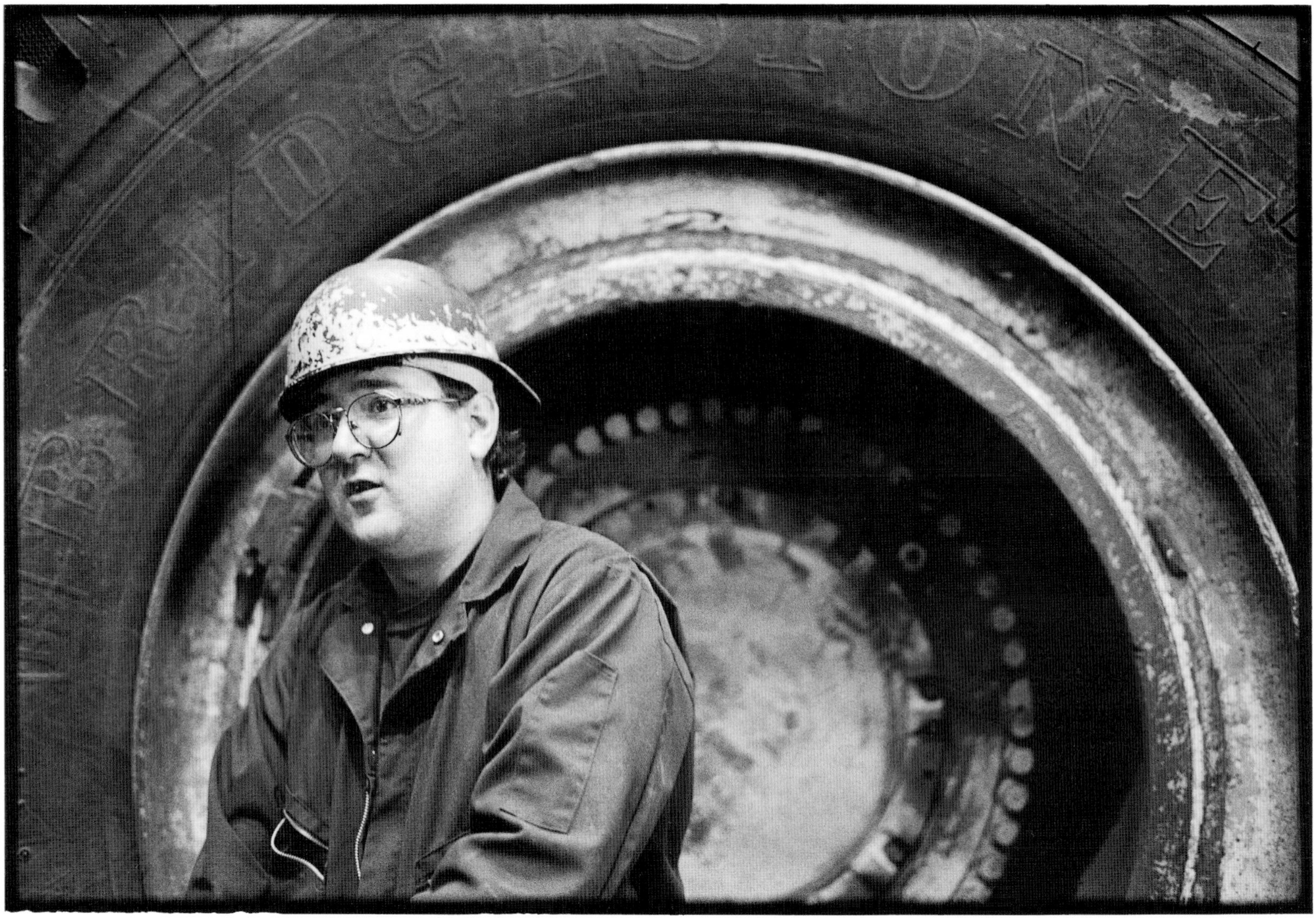

Truck maintenance worker
Ispat Inland Mining

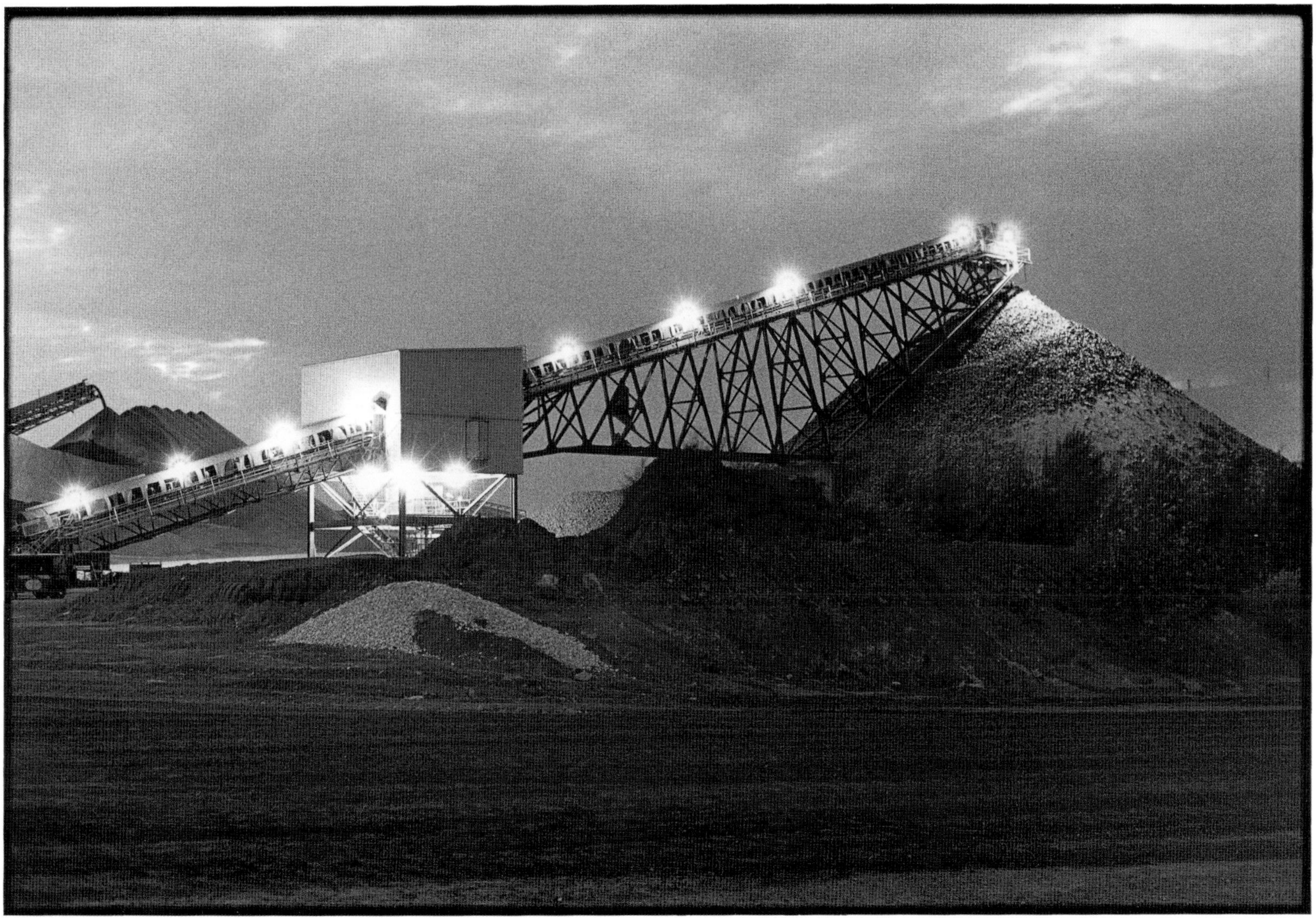

Taconite piles
Ispat Inland Mining

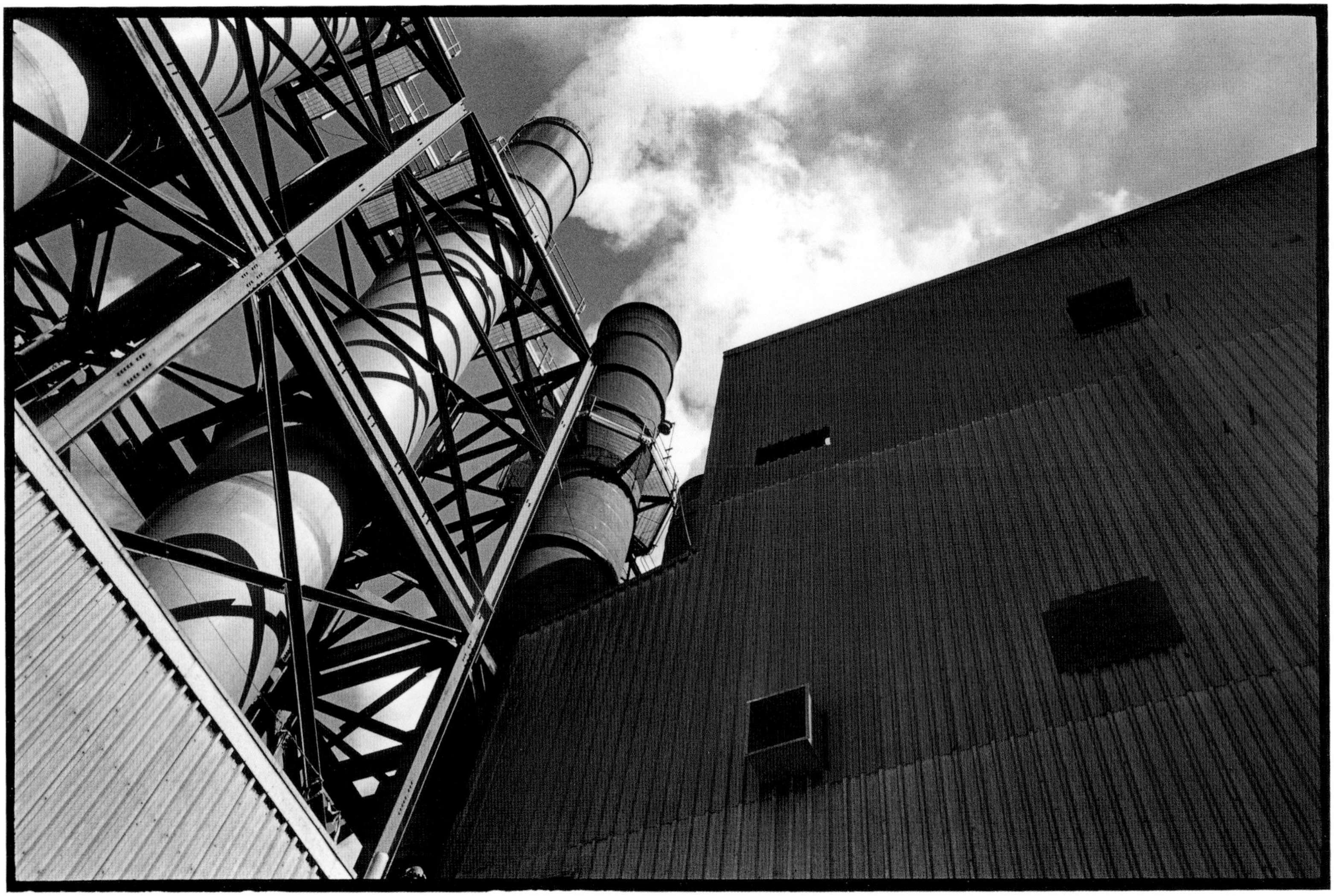

Outside the factory
Ispat Inland Mining

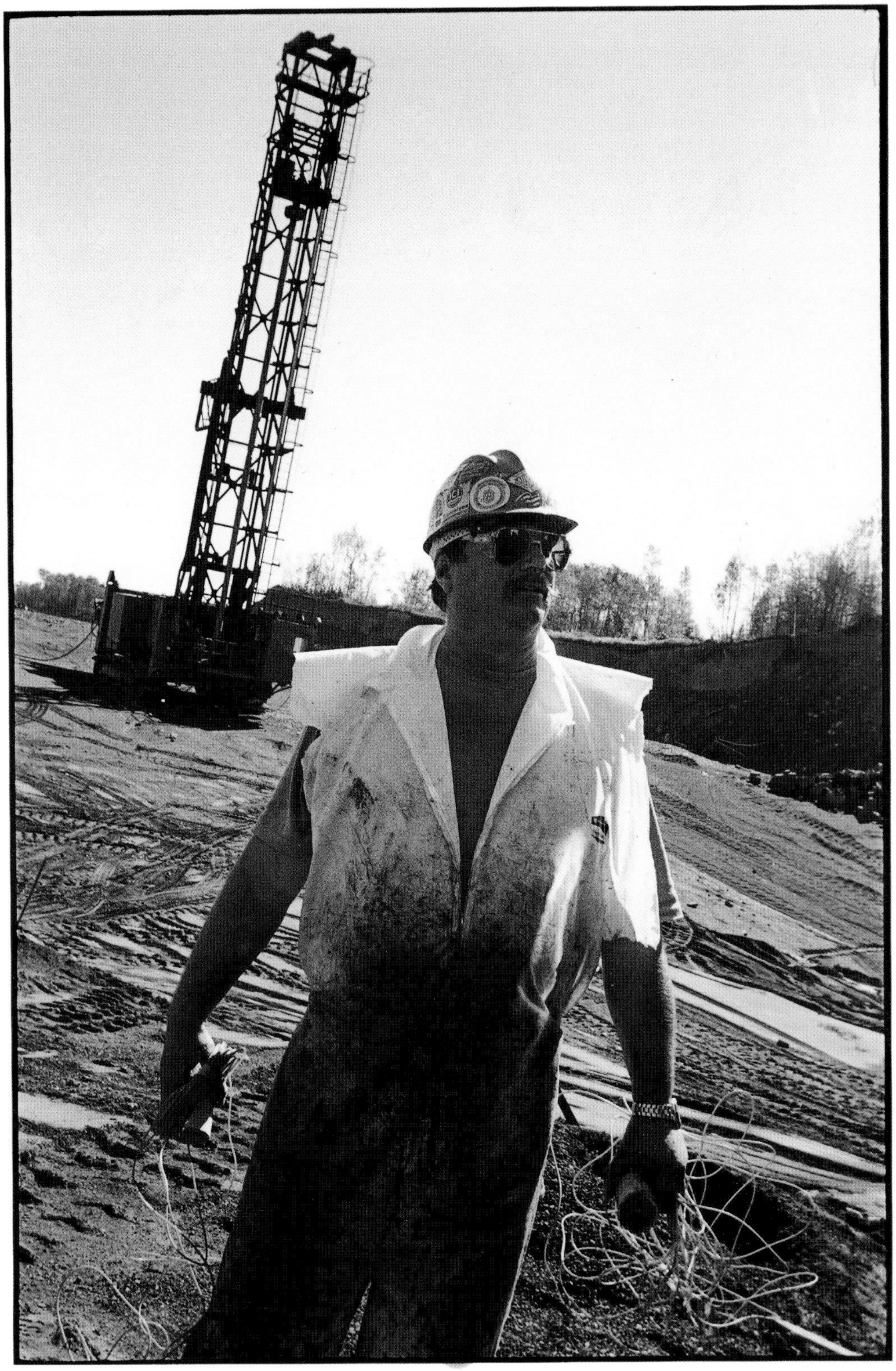

Explosives worker
Ispat Inland Mining

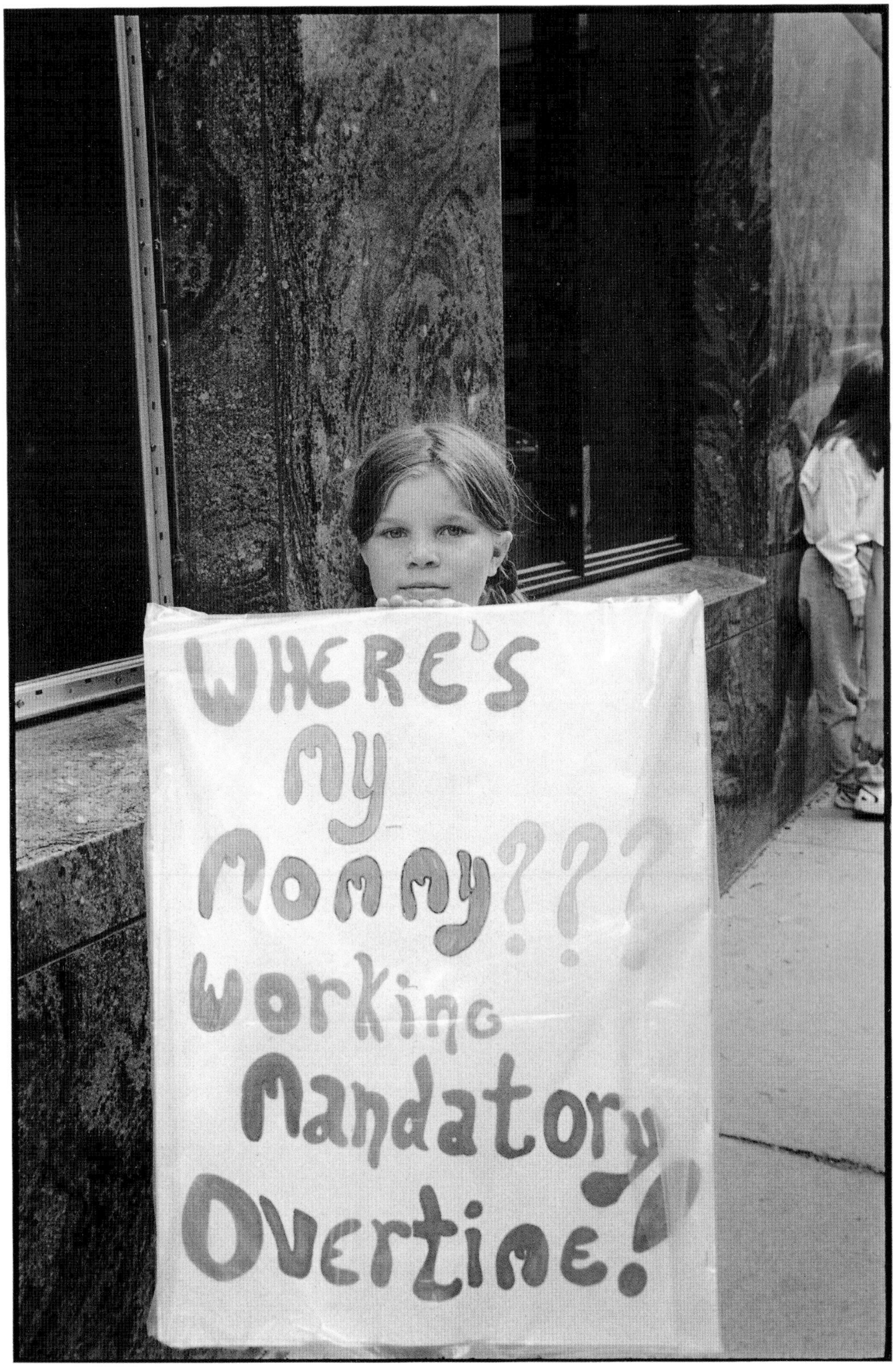

Strike line
US West

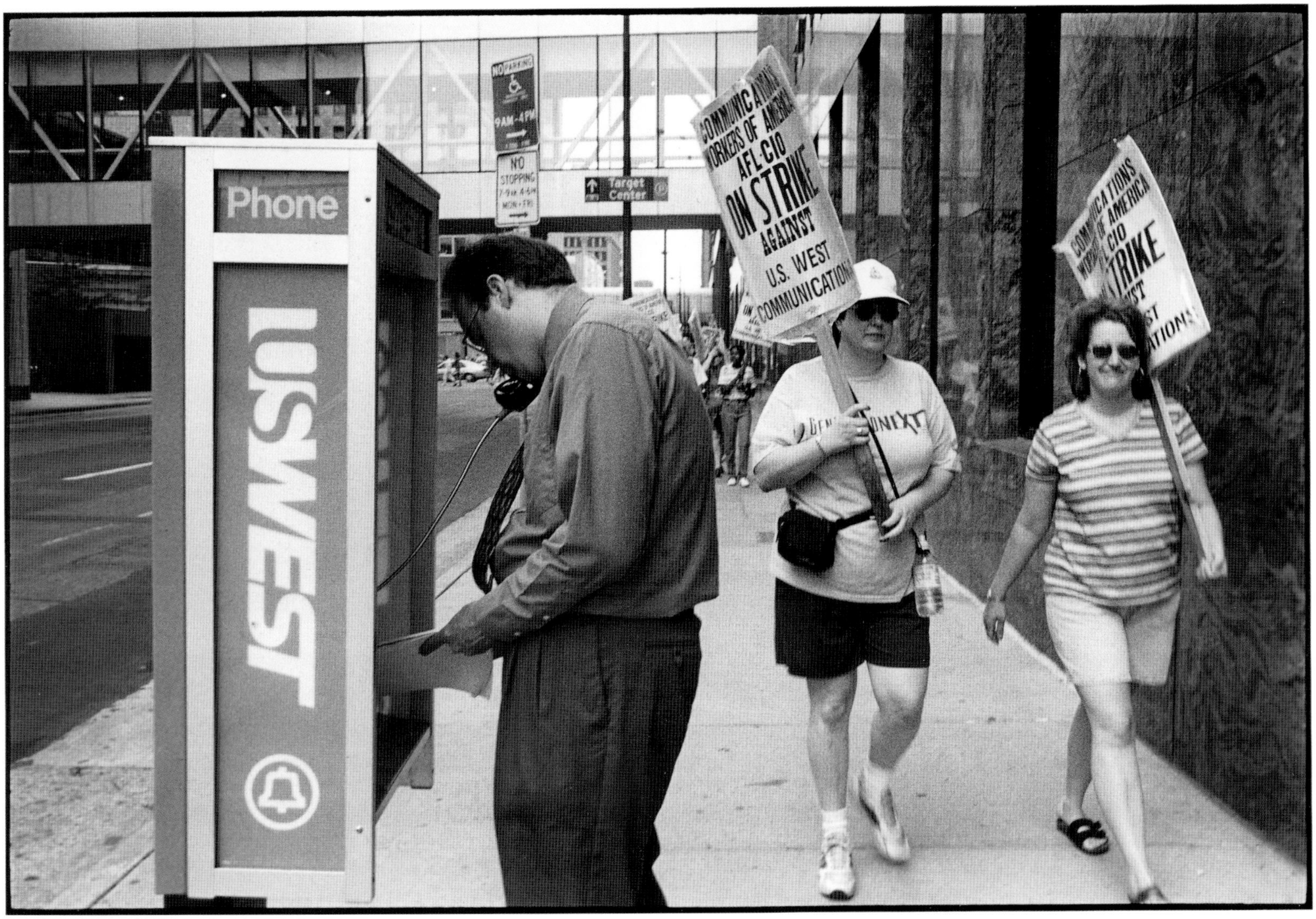

Strike line
US West

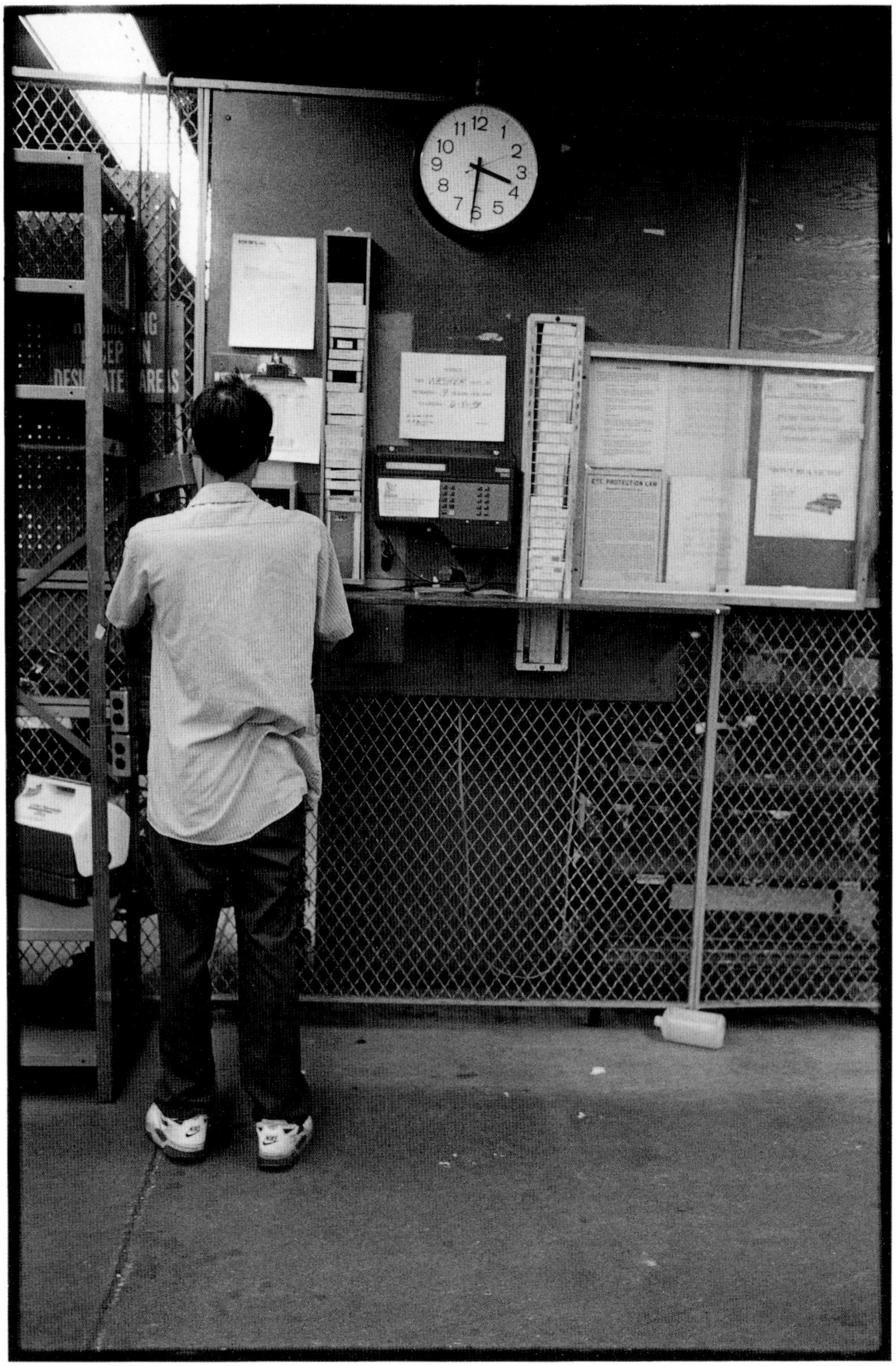

Punching out

Boker's

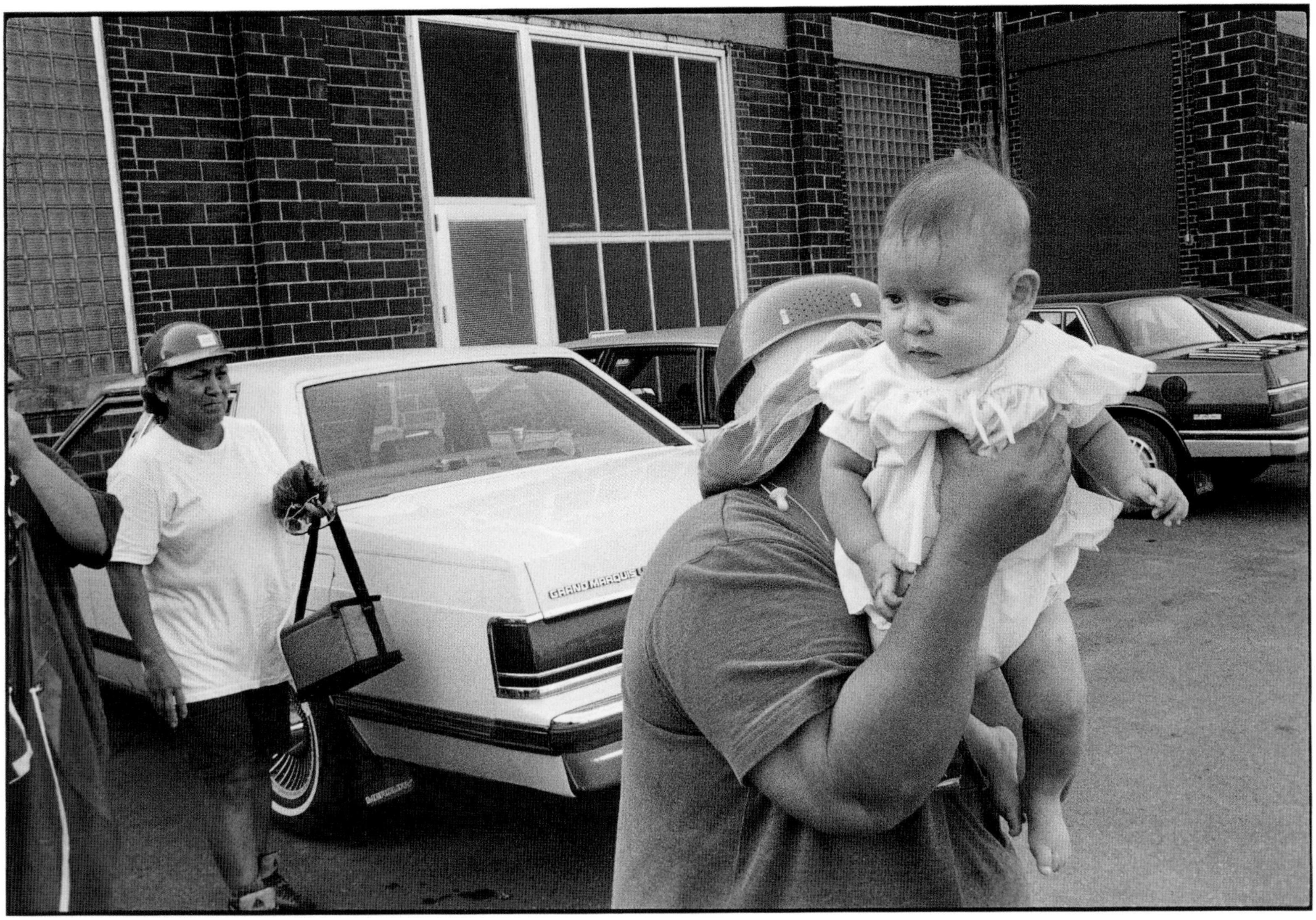

End of work day

Agrilink

“Factory work is factory work whether it deals with sewing machines, whether it deals with wood, or whatever it is, it’s an assembly line that basically does not change, what changes is maybe the types of machines that you use. . . . We’re kind of dreamers but we try to make our dreams come true.”

JANE QUADE
RED WING SHOE

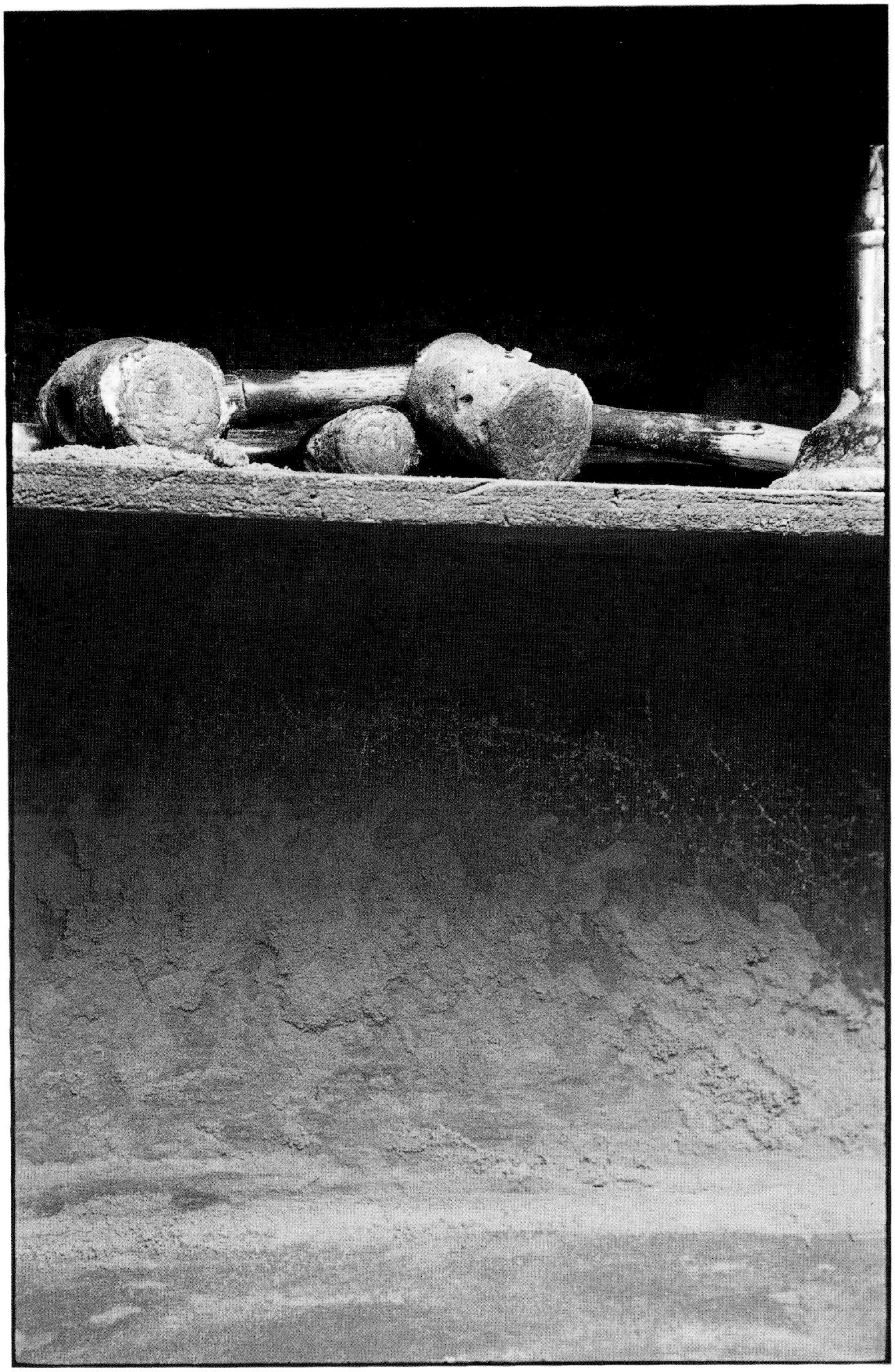

Pattern-maker tools

Smith Foundry

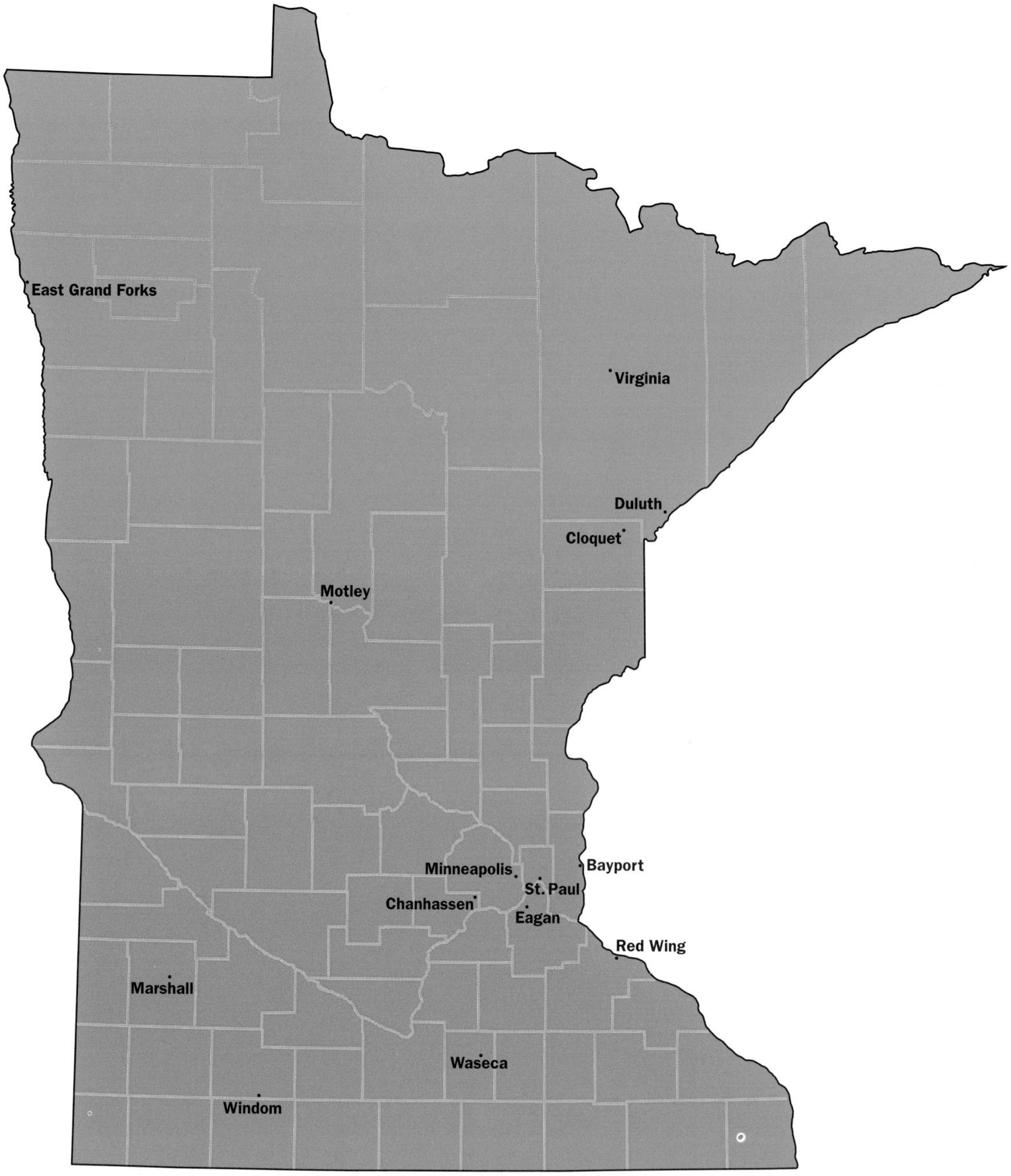

BAYPORT
Andersen Window

CHANHASSEN
Rosemount, Inc.

CLOQUET
Potlatch Corporation

DULUTH
BendTec, Inc.

EAGAN
Lull International
(OmniQuip International)

EAST GRAND FORKS
American Crystal Sugar

MARSHALL
Schwan's

MINNEAPOLIS
Acme Foundry Company
Boker's, Inc.
GFI America, Inc.
Nico Products, Inc.
Siewert Cabinet
Smith Foundry Company

MOTLEY
Morey's Seafood, LLC

RED WING
Red Wing Shoe Company, Inc.

ST. PAUL
Ford Motor Company
North Star Steel

VIRGINIA
Ispat Inland Mining Company,
Minorca Mine

WASECA
Agrilink

WINDOM
Toro Company

NOTES ON THE FACTORIES

Many of the processes with which we are familiar, such as processing corn or creating a metal casting, use complex and expensive technologies. Short of a textbook on industrial processes, it is not possible to provide readers with a complete understanding of the process by which many of these products are made; however, it is possible to demonstrate both the magnitude of production and the ingenuity that is needed to produce even the most common products.

Acme Foundry Company
Minneapolis

Acme Foundry Company was started in 1913 in northeast Minneapolis. It moved to its current location in south Minneapolis in 1931. During the late forties, Acme employed almost 50 workers; the business has contracted over the past decade, and it now employs between ten and twelve workers. The foundry makes castings using pig iron (raw iron ingots) imported from Brazil. The iron is heated to between 2,500 and 2,600 degrees and then poured from large ladles into molds. Acme Foundry pours approximately 1,000 tons of iron each year. The cost of energy to produce this quantity of iron accounts for 8–10 percent of the operating budget.

Each year the foundry industry in the U. S. produces an estimated 14 million tons of castings. These castings have a market value of about 25 billion dollars. Markets for castings include automobiles, trucks, pipes and pipe fittings, heavy equipment, railroad parts, and any number of thousands of complex metal parts.

Agrilink
Waseca

Agrilink is an agricultural marketing cooperative, formerly called Pro-Pac Cooperative, which consists of 600 growers located across the country. The company is based in Rochester, N. Y., with a processing plant in Waseca. These grower/owners supply the raw commodities, which are then processed and marketed by Agrilink Foods, a wholly owned subsidiary of the co-op. Agrilink is now the nation's largest frozen vegetable processor.

In Minnesota, Agrilink processes food from 250–300 growers within a 45-mile radius around the plant. During peak season, the plant processes 72 tons of corn per hour, 21 hours per day, and employs about 180 workers. Each year the facility produces 38 million cobs of frozen corn and 22 million pounds of corn kernels. Each kernel of corn is individually frozen and optically scanned at the rate of 20,000 pounds per hour. Corn kernels that are rejected are removed by a puff of air coming from one of 64 small air jets located under the conveyor belt.

Corn and other vegetables processed in the plant are sold under the Birds Eye brand name.

American Crystal Sugar
East Grand Forks

In the early part of the twentieth century, farmers of the Red River Valley were suffering from falling wheat prices, and the North Dakota legislature authorized tests to see how well sugar beets would grow in Red River Valley soil. In 1918, Carl Wigand, a farmer in Crookston, Minn., grew five acres of sugar beets. Encouraged by his success, others soon followed. By the mid-1920s, farmers were growing more than 7,000 acres of sugar beets in the Red River Valley. In 1926, American Beet built a factory in East Grand Forks to process sugar beets. In 1934, American Beet changed its name to American Crystal Sugar.

In 1973, at the suggestion of the secretary of the Red River Valley Sugar Beet Growers Association, approximately 1,300 growers purchased American Crystal Sugar for $86 million. Within a few years, sugar beet cultivation nearly doubled to 300,000 acres and by 1999 sugar beet production had increased to almost 450,000 acres per year. Today, the American Crystal Sugar plant in East Grand Forks processes 2 million tons of sugar beets with a sugar production of 5 million (cwt). A single sugar beet weighs approximately 2 pounds and yields 30 teaspoons of sugar.

Each year, the Red River Valley produces approximately 10 percent of the sugar consumed in the U. S. This vast production of sugar beets is a sharp contrast with the early days of the sugar beet industry. Early growers used one-row, horse-drawn planters. "Field workers walked the rows of beets, stooping to chop out excess plants with short-handled hoes. At harvest time, human hands touched every beet at least twice, first to top the beets with a knife and then to load them into wagons with a pitchfork. The job was so exhausting that the pitchfork became known as the widowmaker. It often took more than a month to harvest less than 10 acres of beets."

Andersen Window
Bayport

Hans Andersen and his sons Fred and Herbert founded the Andersen Lumber Company in 1903. In 1905, the company was making 120 window frames per day at a cost of 50 cents each. The idea was simple: "make standardized horizontal and vertical frame pieces, available in several sizes. Pieces are quickly assembled—in as little as 10 minutes—without cutting or trimming." The mass production of window and door frames began nine years ahead of Henry Ford's assembly line for automobiles.

By the end of the decade, annual frame sales exceeded 100,000 per year. In 1932, Andersen produced the first completely assembled window unit including sash, frame, and hardware. By 1999, Andersen employed more than 6,000 workers nationwide. The manufacturing facility in Bayport, Minn., covers 65 acres. Each year the company uses 108 million square feet of glass, 25 million pounds of vinyl resin, and 22,000 miles of lumber.

BendTec, Inc.
Duluth

Modern Plumbing and Heating was founded in 1906 by Rubin Meierhoff. The company was primarily involved in converting heating systems from oil to coal. Shortly after World War II, the company changed its name to Modern Constructors and began building pipes for oil terminals and constructing piping systems for ice rinks. Starting in 1947, the company built piping for pumping stations, tank farms, and terminals for the U. S. portion of the Interprovincial Pipeline. This pipeline was designed to carry oil from western Canada to markets in eastern Canada.

In 1972, a second company, Pipe Benders, was formed to design and market machines to bend large diameter pipes using induction furnaces. This process was unique in the western hemisphere until 1980. BendTec was formed in 1989 when Modern Constructors and Pipe Benders merged.

Today, BendTec is a metal fabrication company that specializes in the production of pipe bends for pipelines and steam electric power generating plants. BendTec is known internationally for its ability to bend large diameter pipes. In addition to bending pipes, BendTec provides other fabrication services such as metal machining, heat treating metals, and adding ceramic and epoxy linings to pipes. BendTec employs approximately 100 workers. Because of its location near the Duluth harbor, BendTec is able to ship to and receive goods from throughout the world.

Boker's, Inc.
Minneapolis

Boker's was founded in 1919 by Vitus Boker and his son John. The original manufacturing facility was in the basement of their Minneapolis home. The first products were an envelope folding machine and a small "hand check protector," a tool used to emboss checks for the amount payable in order to prevent alterations. In 1939, after several moves, the company established a manufacturing facility at the current site of its corporate offices on Snelling Avenue in Minneapolis. Vitus Boker retired in 1942, and his four sons operated the facility until 1968 when it was sold to four employees.

Today, Boker's is a nationally known producer of special metal stamping products and custom washers. Parts are made when sheet stock is pressed through a hardened tool or die. Boker's manufactures parts from more than 2,000 different materials ranging from stainless steel to Teflon. The company provides parts to more than 9,000 manufacturing companies across the U. S. and employs about 135 workers.

Ford Motor Company
St. Paul

The Ford Motor Company finished construction of its St. Paul assembly plant in 1925. The original plant was built to assemble Model T cars and later Model A cars. The plant has always produced the equivalent of small trucks. The plant was built along the banks of the Mississippi for navigation, power, and proximity to available workers. At the time of its construction, it was felt that proximity to water would lessen the dependence of Ford on rail for transportation. The Ford site also offered proximity to silica, which was used to manufacture glass. The Ford plant stopped making glass during the mid-1950s. Each year the facility assembles approximately 225,000 trucks. The plant employs 2,000 hourly and 150 salaried workers and has a total payroll of $139 million per year.

GFI America, Inc.
Minneapolis

In 1974, Bob and Howard Goldberger founded GFI America, Inc. Both were former executives at King Foods, a leading beef processor in the sixties that was started by their father, beef industry pioneer, Sam Goldberger. Like their father, the Goldbergers dedicated themselves to advancing the beef industry. Today GFI America, Inc., remains family owned and operated and a major processor of portion-controlled beef products. Through sustained growth and the purchase of several independent beef companies, GFI America, Inc., has evolved into a beef industry leader.

For a quarter of a century GFI America has built its foundation on innovation, quality, consistency, and food safety. GFI Premium Foods is committed to providing food service operators and consumers nationwide with the finest quality beef products available. GFI distributes to more than 400 food service providers around the nation. Products are eaten by millions of people each week throughout the United States.

Ispat Inland Mining Company, Minorca Mine
Virginia

Ispat Inland Mining Company, formerly Inland Steel Mining Company, produces taconite pellets at its Minorca Mine for use in Ispat Inland Inc.'s blast furnaces located in East Chicago, Indiana. The Minorca taconite processing plant shipped its first pellets in June 1997. Since then, it has produced more than 57 million gross tons (2,240 lbs.) of pellets, enough to make 40 million tons of steel.

Located on 15,000 acres in the heart of Minnesota's Mesabi Iron Range, Minorca provides high paying jobs for more than 350 employees. The mine processes 8.2 million tons of ore in order to produce 2.8 million tons of taconite pellets each year. Taconite ore is 24.5 percent magnetic iron, and the final taconite pellet is 63 percent iron. Each load (dump truck) of ore weighs between 175 and 195 tons. Trucks carrying the ore to the crushing facility get approximately two miles per gallon of fuel.

Lull International (OmniQuip International)
Eagan

Lull International was founded in 1956 and was privately owned until 1996. The company went into bankruptcy in about 1991 and was subsequently reorganized. In August 1996, the Harbour Group purchased Lull Industries. The Lull product line includes 11 machines with lift capacities ranging from 6,000 to 10,000 pounds and lift heights of 26 to 62 feet. Lifts produced by Lull allow the operator to move a load horizontally for placement without moving the machine position. This is advantageous to the users who need to lift and unload objects at the same height and to maneuver machines in tight areas. The manufacturing facility where these photographs were taken was closed in April 2001, and manufacturing was moved to Port Washington, Wisconsin.

Morey's Seafood, LLC
Motley

In1937, Ed Morey was driving though Motley when he saw a broken-down pickup truck loaded with fish. He traded the owner of the truck a load of sweet corn for the load of fish. This started his business of smoking and processing fish. Today the facility processes hundreds of products. The plant in Motley is the only manufacturing facility in the company. However, there are seven distribution locations throughout the U. S. responsible for shipping products to 38 states.

The Motley plant smokes and processes fish to make products such as Marinated Atlantic or Pacific Salmon, portion-controlled fish (e.g., 8 ounce salmon steaks), breaded fish such as pollack, and fish spreads. Fish is smoked using hardwoods, such as birch, beech wood, and maple. Smoked salmon is made from wild Alaskan salmon, and the company's marinated salmon is raised on farms and imported from Chile. Each year the company processes about 2 million pounds of salmon to produce about 1.5 million pounds of finished salmon products. In addition, Morey's produces an estimated 3.5 million pounds of other fish products each year from approximately 4 to 4.5 million pounds of fish. The company employs 125 people from a 35-mile radius.

Nico Products, Inc.
Minneapolis

Nico is a job shop metal finisher primarily performing electroplating. In 1971 the first parts were processed out of 55-gallon drums in the basement of a barbershop in south Minneapolis. In 1973, the operation was moved to 2929 Stevens Ave. S. occupying the old Sunshine Creamery building. As business grew, an adjoining building was purchased from the National Expert Bait Company, and the first piece of automated plating equipment was installed. In 1978, a 35,000 square foot building was built at the company's current location on Lake Street. Today the company employs about 85 people.

Electroplating takes place when an electric current is passed through a solution containing ions from a dissolved metal, and the object to be coated serves as a cathode (i.e., attracts the metal). The object then attracts metal ions from the solution. At Nico, objects may be coated with a variety of metals such as zinc, copper, nickel, chrome, tin, brass and cadmium. Each year the company plates several million parts.

North Star Steel
St. Paul

North Star Steel was founded in 1966 in St. Paul. Cargill acquired the company in 1975. The St. Paul facility is the oldest of North Star's seven mini-mills. The St. Paul facility of North Star Steel produces carbon and alloy steel rebar for the construction industry as well as lawn and garden equipment.

The process begins with processed and unprocessed scrap and

crushed automobiles. On average, 274 rail cars and 800 trucks per month bring scrap steel and appliances to the plant. Scrap automobiles are shredded at a rate of one car per minute; maximum production is one car shredded every 30 seconds. Molten steel is produced at the rate of 90 tons every 55 minutes. Rebar is produced at speeds of up to 2,200 feet per minute. The company ships an average of 800 trucks and 90 rail cars of rebar each month. The mill has the capacity to produce 327,000 tons of steel in each year.

A continuous casting machine produces steel for four markets: quality steel for a variety of forging markets, reinforced bar for highway and building construction, grinding balls for the mining industry, and heat-treated structural steel. Electric bills for the plant average $1 million per month at the St. Paul facility, approximately as much electricity as used by the entire city of St. Paul.

Potlatch Corporation
Cloquet

Potlatch Corporation was founded in 1903 in Potlatch, Idaho. Today Potlatch is a diversified forest products company with 1.5 million acres of land in Arkansas, Idaho, and Minnesota. The company manages 337,000 acres of aspen and pine timberland in Minnesota. The company produces lumber, panel products, bleached wood pulp, paperboard, consumer tissue, and printing papers. The current pulp and paper mill in Cloquet was started in 2000 and has a capacity of 425,000 tons of pulp per year. Each ton of pulp makes approximately one ton of paper. The Cloquet mill produces about 230,000 tons of paper. Excess pulp is sold for paper production elsewhere.

The paper production facility in Cloquet began production in 1898 and was purchased by Potlatch in 1964. Total employment in Minnesota is approximately 3,500 with 770 employed in Cloquet. The Minnesota Pulp and Paper Division of Potlatch produces a broad line of printing papers. The Cloquet facility was recently sold to the Sappi paper Company. Sappi will be eliminating 200 jobs from the Cloquet plant as well as negotiating a new labor contract.

Red Wing Shoe Company, Inc.
Red Wing

The Red Wing Shoe Company was founded in 1905 in Red Wing, Minn. By 1919 production exceeded 200,000 pairs of shoes per year. The company underwent continuous expansion until it was hit by the Depression following the stock market crash in 1929. During the years that followed, workers were forced to burn scrap leather in the factory in order to stay warm. Today, Red Wing Shoe Company produces more than three million pairs of shoes per year in more than 180 styles. Slightly less than half of these shoes are made in Red Wing. A typical shoe requires about 3.5 hours of labor and between 150 and 225 different operations. Over 90 percent of every shoe is handmade. Red Wing Shoe Company employs about 1,200 workers in four manufacturing facilities. Two of these facilities are in Red Wing, one in Missouri, and one in Kentucky.

Rosemount, Inc.
Chanhassen

Rosemount, Inc., was founded in 1956 with an initial focus on aerospace products. With the growth and success that resulted, Rosemount adopted a unique diversification strategy in the process-control instrumentation industry. As the company's growth continued, Rosemount gained the attention of Emerson Electric and was acquired by Emerson in 1976.

In 1986 Emerson formally brought together its instrument companies to form an organization that could provide customers with more solutions than any other instrumentation and control system company in the world. This company became a billion-dollar company in 1989. In 1993 Emerson finalized the acquisition of Fisher Controls Instrumentation, Inc., and the subsequent creation of Fisher-Rosemount.

Recently the Fisher-Rosemount group has been renamed Emerson Process Management. The company is a world leader in the design and manufacturing of process instrumentation, including a complete line of pressure, temperature, flow, and level products. Rosemount made detectors used in high altitude flights by pilots such as Chuck Yeager as well as the oxygen, pressure, and temperature sensors on Neil Armstrong's backpack when he became the first man to set foot on the moon. The company has approximately 2,000 employees and $620 million in sales.

Schwan's
Marshall

The late Marvin Schwan founded Schwan's in 1952. The small dairy run by Marvin and his parents, Paul and Alma, was struggling under a government price freeze on milk. When Marvin learned that ice cream was bringing higher prices north of their Marshall dairy, he acted on the opportunity. On March 18, 1952, the 23-year-old entrepreneur loaded up 14 gallons of homemade ice cream in a 1946 Dodge panel van and set out. That same day he sold all of the ice cream and proved the concept that would become the Schwan's Home Service system. Today, Schwan's daily production uses the buttermilk from 140,000 cows and produces 14.5 million gallons of ice cream each year excluding specialty items. The plant also produces 1.5 million ice cream sandwiches each week.

Schwan's is an international company with manufacturing facilities in the U. S., England, France and Germany, and has more than 22,000 employees. The privately held company distributes its products through home delivery, retail grocery, and food-service channels under well-known brand names that include Tony's, Red Baron, and Freschetta pizzas, Minh egg rolls, and Smash Hit Subs.

Siewert Cabinet
Minneapolis

Siewert Cabinet is a commercial store fixture and architectural millwork manufacturer. Wayne Siewert founded the company in 1965 in his south Minneapolis home. In 1975 the company moved to its first manufacturing facility and hired its first two employees. One of these individuals still works for the company as the shop foreman. The company has remained within one mile of its original location since it was founded. Siewert has become a national leader in the manufacturing of store fixtures and architectural woodwork.

Smith Foundry Company
Minneapolis

R. W. Manuel, M. H. Manuel, and Leo C. Smith founded the Smith Heating Company, predecessor of the Smith Foundry Company in 1905. The business was started in order to manufacture space heaters for rural schools, town halls, and churches. In 1923 Smith purchased a gray iron (a type of iron) foundry to produce castings required for use in its heating units. The business continued through the Depression and the early 1940s with only modest changes. Ultimately the market for space heaters disappeared as one-room schoolhouses consolidated and town halls gave way to larger city and county administrative buildings.

During World War II, the entire production of the foundry was dedicated to producing castings to support the war effort. After the war ended, the heating business and the foundry were split, and each developed its own market and products.

Today Smith Foundry is a leading producer of cast-iron parts for a wide variety of customers including 3M, Toro, Tennant, Advance Machine, and Dow Chemical. Each year the foundry pours 5,000 tons of iron and produces 2,500 tons of finished products. The primary products are valves, metal housings, and pumps. Smith Foundry is the second largest consumer of electrical power in Minneapolis and draws 2,000 kilowatts per hour at full power.

Toro Company
Windom

The Toro Company was founded in 1914 as Toro Motor Company, an engine supplier for Bull Tractor Company, and survived the tumultuous years of World War I by building steam engines to support the war effort. In 1920 the name was changed to Toro Manufacturing Company, and the company refocused its efforts on manufacturing farm equipment. In 1921 Toro created the first mechanical golf course maintenance equipment by mounting five lawn mowers behind a Toro tractor to mow the fairways at the Minikahda Country Club in Minneapolis.

Toro entered the international marketplace in 1928, shipping golf course and grounds maintenance products worldwide. Throughout the 1900s, Toro developed innovative products to serve homeowners and professionals alike, a growth that continues in the new millennium. In 1935, Toro produced the first power mower for homeowners.

Toro's manufacturing facility in Windom produces gas-powered lawn mowers and snow blowers. Each year the facility produces 100,000 snow removal units, 50,000 home riders and tractors, and 600,000 walking power mowers. The facility welds approximately one million parts per year and casts 2.6 million pounds of aluminum parts each year. In order to maintain their extensive parts inventory, it is necessary to make 75,000 calls to suppliers. An assembly line for riding mowers has 35 people who construct 70 mowers per day. The facility employs about 720 hourly and salaried workers. A simple push-style power lawn mower contains about 150 parts while there may be up to 1,000 parts in a 20-horsepower riding mower.

U. S. West
Minneapolis

In August 1998 approximately 34,000 U. S. West workers from 13 western states went on strike for less mandatory overtime and to counter company demands for health benefits concessions. Workers were frequently forced to put in 60 or more hours per week and meet rigid, unrealistic performance measures. The negotiated contract gave workers an 11 percent pay increase, a 21 percent rise in pensions, a voluntary pay-for-performance bonus plan and a reduction in overtime hours to no more than 8 hours per week by 2001.

By These Hands was designed and set in type by Will Powers at the Minnesota Historical Society Press. Printed in Hong Kong by Kings Time Printing Press Ltd.